LIVING THE PRACTICE
VOLUME II:

THE

WARRIOR OF LOVE

bancroft
press

T0274269

Rohini Ralby

Interior Design: Julie Tucker

978-1-61088-648-2 (PB)

978-1-61088-649-9 (Ebook)

978-1-61088-650-5 (PDF ebook)

978-1-61088-651-2 (Audiobook)

Published by Bancroft Press
"Books that Enlighten"
410-627-0608
4527 Glenwood Ave.
La Crescenta, CA 91214
www.bancroftpress.com
Printed in the United States of America

To my Guru, Swami Muktananda,
who is always with me and guiding me

To my family: David, Ian, and Aaron,
who are warriors walking this Path with me

To the assembled team working to keep me healthy in this body:
Dr. Michael Schultz, Dr. Sujit Chatterjee, Dr. Urvi Patel, Howard Wills,
Dr. Safia Elbagir, Dr. Agnes Tyburn, Dr. Ian Ralby, Dr. Aaron Ralby,
Dr. David Soud, Dr. Tanya Khazan, Clémence Legrand,
J. C. Metivier, Eddie Oliver, Mark Mordin, Torie Getschel

To all the warriors of Love around the globe who are offering prayers and Love:
I cannot thank you all enough.

TABLE OF CONTENTS

CHAPTER ONE
UNDERSTANDING
THE SHRUNKEN SELF

CHAPTER TWO
OBSTACLES AND
MISUNDERSTANDING

CHAPTER THREE
RIGHT ACTION IN THE WORLD

CHAPTER FOUR
CONFRONTING
POWER AND HATE

Paintings and Poems:

CHAPTER FIVE
BEING A WARRIOR

Paintings and Poems:

CHAPTER SIX
TEACHING STORIES

CHAPTER SEVEN
OCCASIONAL PIECES

INTRODUCTION

A warrior is someone who faces the given task, or fight, or circumstance and willingly uses all at their disposal to operate appropriately and resolve whatever is there. The warrior of Love probably has the hardest mountain to climb. To be a warrior of Love, like any warrior, there has to be discipline and sacrifice. The question is, what does the warrior of Love have to do, have to discipline, have to sacrifice?

The training a warrior of Love undertakes is called *sadhana*. It is spiritual practice. The goal of *sadhana* is to free ourselves from the prison of the shrunken self, the "self" we are not but have wrongly identified with. So the warrior of Love is ready to face the work of disciplining and sacrificing and letting go of wrong identity, and becoming the warrior's Real nature.

One good analogy for *sadhana* is the phenomenon of apoptosis: the programmed self-destruct mechanism in the human body's cells. If a cell detects that something has gone wrong in how it functions, normally it initiates a set of chemical reactions by which it destroys itself rather than damage the body. This is the natural course of things. When cells do not follow this pattern, they can become cancerous; instead of self-destructing, they proliferate and, if unchecked, eventually weaken and kill the entire body. The shrunken self is like a cancerous cell: it is a collection of vocabulary words that make up a false sense of self that veils our True identity and takes over our life. In *sadhana*, the phrase "use a wedge to get rid of a wedge" is very important. It is the method that induces apoptosis in the shrunken self. First, we must become conscious that who we believe we are is not at all who we are in Truth. Only then can we begin to self-destruct the shrunken self.

The warrior of Love draws on both Grace coming from outside and self-effort coming from within. The Guru is the manifestation of Grace, and *shaktipat*, spiritual awakening, injected into the warrior by the Guru, unveils for the warrior his True nature. Knowing that they are not the shrunken self—not as an intellectual idea but as an experiential reality—is both a gift and a shock to the system. The warrior has to be strong enough to receive this gift.

To prepare for this gift, at the very least there has to be a longing for God, and a reflectiveness that encourages the awareness that who the warrior is is not who the warrior thinks they are. The warrior sacrifices by disciplining and purifying their vehicles (body, senses, intellect, emotions, etc.) and constantly re-evaluating and questioning their experience. Very important is the constant redirecting of the will (our attention) toward God in the Heart—not as a concept, but as Reality.

The Guru's guidance is all about uncloaking the shrunken self for what it is: a fiction. The shrunken self, which wants to go on existing much as a cancer cell does, refuses to be uncloaked. The first battle for the warrior of Love is to willingly surrender to obeying the Guru rather than resist Grace by defending the false identity that is really walling off the warrior from life and Love.

Once the warrior of Love is able to express Love in all they do, outer battles soon follow. Love forces a choice on everyone who encounters it. There are three fundamental choices, which correspond to three attitudes. The first is an outright rejection of Love, no matter what. The second is an ambivalence, in which people doubt and question but remain potentially open to Love. The third, and most rare, is a willingness to respond to Love with an openness to receive and surrender. The warrior of Love must know how to meet all three types with clarity and equanimity. They must always be willing to be appropriate, which may make them look unappealing.

It is crucial to understand that Love, in the most Real sense, is not the love that most of us think of as the opposite of hate. It is the Ground of all

Existence, beyond all our names and categories. Nonetheless, Love is often met with hate. For so many of us, hate is a love for the shrunken self that we find exhilarating and therefore powerful and pleasurable. We cloak it in righteousness, and see Love as weak, as no fun. Worse still, we see Love as an enemy, out to destroy who we believe we are and what we value. Being a warrior of Love means owning, mastering, and transcending our own hate—by knowing our shrunken self for what it is and throwing it in the sacrificial fire. Then we can live in harmony with God and God's creation.

This volume of *Living the Practice* is devoted to sharing the work of using a wedge to get rid of a wedge: using our shrunken sense of self to gain the consciousness necessary to let go of our shrunken sense of self.

Whether in the form of prose, poetry, or painting, the focus is always encouraging the warrior of Love.

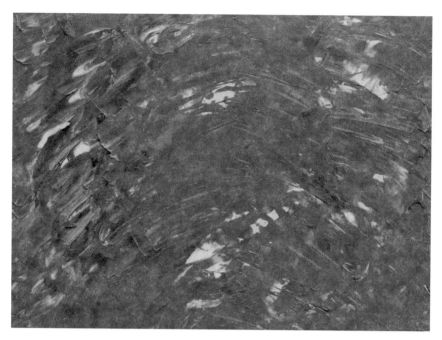

The Pain of The World

particle....

par   tic   u
                    liar   i   zing

            pair   tick   you
                                    and   too
                    two   me
                            point
                                                            out
no   where
            togo
        point   in
                                    macro

two   no   more
                        me

        God's   particular
                    All

no matter what....

distant from   matter
              stare at

                                          projections
laugh   walk away

        under   stand
              matter

coverings....

     clothes
  are

black
brown
red
yellow
white

yet   always
    remain
  blue

acting in so many
      ways
yet
      remain
        always
  still

so many letters
    so many vibrations
yet   only
    one sound
      one word

so many vehicles
yet
     none   are   me

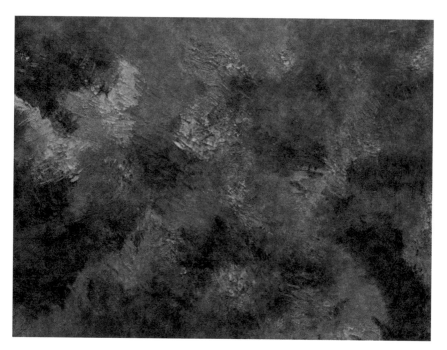

No Escape

thought leader....

beginner mind
        is full
            of thought
        busy and   in charge
            of all
        with no
            authority

            mind has other functions
after   thought
            thought is   after thought
    after   move
                in
            master mind

    no thought
                reflection
            of   truth
    luminous door
        reflecting
                both   sides

offensive....

are you offended
             when   others
         do   not
                   like   your
          garbage

if   you
                  are
        then   there   is
             no   hope
          for   redemption

if   you
            are   not
         then   why
              be   offended
         when   your
                   shrunken   self
              is   not
                        liked

neither   is
          you

                              us

love   your
           Self

         give up
                   the rest
   in   the
                         fire
          to

                         God

10

reflection....

face the mirror
the facts
disappear
I am
Knowing
missing me
no reflection
just a story
the mirror breaks
there I am

Family

not you....

good   self

      bad   e

             l

    same   s e l f

   both   not

         S

        True

         l

         f

  shrunken   self gives

          it

         self

             authority

         own

             voice

  goodbadself   same

             voice

not   two

     n

     e

the point....

       good

           me

bad   me

       none
        is

              I

       good

bad

            adjective

  is   off   the
     anu

the anu is not

     you

objectivity....

                                        g

whence   we   come

                 e

  and   think

        we   are

            b   v

           u n ique   ness

           t o

     show

     h

     i

     n

   objects

    y i

      g

      n

      i

      f

      y

      i

      n

  no thing

Insane

Insane	Sane
Creative	Pedestrian

CHAPTER ONE
UNDERSTANDING THE SHRUNKEN SELF

Grandiose Self-assessment Is....

Grandiose self-assessment is as detrimental to living fully as low self-assessment. They are both faulty and cause decision-making that brings the person to misery. There is no harmony when we operate from our self-esteem. Self-esteem is just a set of ideas that we have identified with; we have allowed our actions and decisions to be informed by these ideas. We judge our actions as good or bad based on these ideas. We relate with some people and reject others based on these ideas.

So self-esteem gets in the way of who we really are and prevents us from changing to a happy, healthy life. If I believe, "I am a good person," then I can do no wrong. I will be unable to see the actions I perform that cause harm. If I believe, "I am a bad person," I will be unable and unwilling to see the positive actions I perform. In other words, my view of life is a fantasy. There is no clarity.

As we practice and are able to detach from these self-esteem characteristics, we can assess each moment with a clear or critical eye and begin the process of seeing things as they really are. We accept the diversity and see it clearly, not pretending it to be something it is not. And we see the unity where it really is, under all of the ever-changing matter.

Who am I?....

Who am I? At any given moment, I appear to be the furthest thing out that consciousness has enlivened. So "who I am" changes from moment to moment. My job is to return to Me and stay there, and not identify with what I enliven.

This seems so easy, "just be myself"; however, it requires intense work and Grace. We may believe we are being ourselves, but in reality we are identifying with an idea, a sense, a body, an energy, an emotion, any kind of vibration. The true Me is pure Subject with no object, the Perceiver not the perceived.

How do we return? By letting go of what you believe or even experience is you and then boring in toward the Heart. If we are boring in continuously, we will keep finding that there is more and more that we perceive. What we thought was us is now perceivable, and so cannot and could not be us. If I can perceive it, it cannot be Me.

Getting to the One Real Voice....

The One Real Voice: you mean when I get angry and scream and am sure of what I am saying? You mean my authentic voice, the voice when I do not question what I am saying because I "know"? No. The voice I am speaking of is the one when we reflect and see the whole before we open our mouths. This is the voice that can sound angry, sad, quiet, loud, happy or whatever is appropriate for the moment. The expression is not the giveaway. Confidence, sincerity, and volume do not make the voice real. Clarity, purity, and discernment are elements of the Real voice.

How do we get to this voice? Definitely not by going outward and projecting. Only by turning into the Heart, by boring deeper and deeper until we rest in the Heart, will we speak with this voice. Why do we even want this voice? So we can be and express who we are. Otherwise, we are enmeshed in the life of our shrunken self and can never find fulfillment.

The Heart is the only place where we experience the real fullness of anything. The shrunken self is diminished, so it experiences life in a diminished way. Only the true Self can experience the fullness of life. Why practice? Because we want to be alive. We are all moving home, whether we know it or not, whether we think we want to or not. Our true nature is Love, and we all just want to be ourselves. But there is only one way to do that.

There Is a Difference….

There is a difference between being human and being a personality. As a human, we use our personality to express our humanness. As a personality, we hide our humanness and manifest our limited, shrunken selves as if they are who we really are. We manifest limited characters in a play with set scripts, set actions and no creativity. We do not have the ability to see clearly or to see the whole picture. Our decision-making is completely based on how our personality sees, its motivations and its survival. An example is when we change jobs thinking things will be better, only to find ourselves in a similar situation with just different players who actually have the same scripts as the last place we worked. As long as we remain individuals, we never go beyond limited reality; we never go beyond our shrunken selves. We never connect, and I mean truly connect, with another human being. We remain locked in the prison we created so long ago, believing that this is just the way it is.

Families tend to be groups of personalities, not humans. As children, we end up harmonizing with the personalities around us. This can be done either by fitting into the vibration of the family or fighting the vibration of the family, depending on our karma and what we have to learn. Either way, we are attached to and manipulated by the vibrations. Usually we want to fit in, so we take on the vibration of our first group, our family. We actually were supposed to learn how to be true to ourselves even in that environment, but we assume that our family loves us, and Love is the source of all, so the vibration our family has must be Love. We willingly choose to be shrunken individuals. And our connectedness is shrunken self to shrunken self. We bring our understanding into every aspect of our lives.

We talk about someone who is professional and appreciate the way they work. They are efficient. They get the job done. The only complaint is they may be not fun or that they are impersonal. Then, however, we have the unprofessional, the worker who is always a personality. This person presents their personality as more important than the work, whatever that may be. We find that when we are dealing with the unprofessional, we have to deal with the personality and not just a person doing the job. We may have to be careful how we word requests because otherwise the person will react and not do their job. Personality should not undermine our job; we should be serving the situation. When we are professionals, personality does not overshadow the job.

Do you hide your humanness? Do you present as being just your personality? When your shrunken self is sincere and strong, do you believe that that is your essential self?

Being human is having a personality, not being controlled by it. We are less than who we are when we are just our personality. Who we really are enlivens the personality. Who we are informs our personality. Our personality is a vehicle we use; we should not be used by it. How many times have we found ourselves manipulated in situations because of our personality? We are not in charge, it is. Our practice is to see our vehicles for what they really are, which is not us. They are here to help us both function and play on the physical plane. We are here to play the game of returning home. Thinking and living as if we are our personality deludes us to remain stuck in wrong understanding. As we disentangle and see we are the Perceiver not the perceived, we no longer hide our humanness; we no longer hide behind our personality. We learn to rest in and be who we really are and then inform our vehicles so that our expression is pure Love rather than the twisted love that comes from the thinking that we are personality. So go forth and keep removing wrong understanding, so that we shine through as truly human and our personality is there to support that.

Don't Waste Time....

Why do we waste our time with people, things, objects, etc. that only engage the shrunken self? So we may keep our false identity. We will use anything to maintain our sense of self. So anything that can keep us distracted, away from God, away from our true Self, we will pursue. How sad that we are so attached to the character we play that we will waste our time on anything or anyone in order not to see the truth.

You might respond, "You say I waste my time, but I care about others." Do you? Or are you using them so you do not have to face yourself? Be honest. It is okay. We are human. Make all this no big deal—just facts that we face, learn from, and move past. Can you not accept that you are selfish or not a nice person? Why not? We are all made in God's image; therefore, we have all characteristics, just as God does. If we accept that we have a particular quality, we can actually then be able to choose to use it or not. By accept I do not mean intellectually; I mean with all your vehicles, so emotionally as well. This is not an idea but a reality. Yes, it hurts, but so does the pain you inflict on others and yourself from not accepting the quality. We are kind, and we are mean. We are enablers, and we are honest. When we really own, master and transcend these qualities, then we are free to be appropriate at all times. At that point, we are no longer wasting our time; what is important is God within us, and then God everywhere. Immanent and transcendent.

Why do you waste your time with people and things that only engage your shrunken self? Because you choose to. We have only ourselves to blame. We make a decision based on a wrong premise and then build an entire life around a wrong understanding. The *Yoga Sutras* speak of the five *kleshas* or five afflictions. I call them the five miseries. The first is ignorance, *avidya*. Remember that the prefix "a" in Sanskrit does not mean opposite, it means a different kind of something. *Vidya* means knowledge; *avidya* means a different kind of knowledge. This shrunken knowledge is what we call ignorance. So ignorance is in fact a kind of knowledge. That is the problem: we know something, we are just not aware that this knowledge is shrunken. Ignorance is taking something that is temporary to be permanent, something impure to be pure, something unreal to be real. Once we do this, once we have formed our basic premise, we then identify with it (*asmita*). This is like building a castle on what we believe to be a solid foundation, only to find out too late that the foundation is soft and the castle is sinking. Everything we then think, say and do is informed by this false knowledge. We lose our subject in the object of wrong knowledge. With our wrong knowledge, we are then attracted to certain things (*raga*) and repulsed by others (*dvesha*). We then cling to this wrong knowledge (*abhinivesha*), for surely we will die if we let go of our understanding. Within this play, our character and our actions are based on wrong knowledge. We choose not to let go of that wrong knowledge. We are to blame.

In order to move beyond this, we must accept that at any given moment, our first and basic premise is wrong. Even if we cannot accept it right away from the place of truth, we have to start by saying it intellectually: "I am wrong but I do not experience it." Over and over again: "I am unwilling to let go of my wrong understanding." Eventually, something will give if we persevere and only look to ourselves for the cause.

The good news is that, when we fully accept the truth that we have avoided, we are in fact free to choose right knowledge. We are free at least for a moment to live from the place of the Heart. But if we do not see what we have actually done internally to get to this place of grace, it will all close down, and we will be building a new structure that looks similar to the old one, yet again on quicksand.

Surrender. Stop wasting your time on your shrunken self. Keep redirecting your attention to the Heart; to the Perceiver and not the perceived.

Becoming Human....

Are you a sinner? No. Is your proxy a sinner? Yes.

Being truly normal is being truly human. We are made in God's image, and we should act it. Stop thinking of God as a selfish being. We believe that, since we are made in God's image and we are selfish, then God is, too. But to act as God does, we have to surrender to God. God is the most surrendered Being. He is pure Subject and puts up with our pretense of self-sufficient existence.

To be human, then, is to be surrendered to God—surrendered to Love. God's nature is Love. Is that your nature? What is your motivation? Do you not understand why we have fourchotomies? They are designed to uncover the Truth. We always call what we do good; even when we tell ourselves we are bad, we really believe that saying so makes us good. Even in our wretchedness, we are goodness and piety. We never accept within ourselves the negative of the fourchotomy; instead, we project the negative onto others and keep the pure for ourselves. Really? You are so pure? We are all dirty. You can't get rid of what you won't own.

Dirty	Clean
Connected to the world	Aloof and isolated

We cannot begin to be in God's image without first accepting that we are dirty. Only then will we finally begin to head in the direction of pure. Resist your dirtiness and you will remain dirty always, no matter how many mantras you recite. As George MacDonald wrote, "But indeed the business of the universe is to make such a fool of you that you will know yourself for one, and so begin to be wise!"

The shrunken self—who we think we are—is a mess. Thank God it is not actually who we are. We are supposed to learn what the shrunken self is, both good and bad, and then Be who we really are: the Witness of that good and bad. This is not about dissociating, which is just another way of being attached to the shrunken self. This is about being nonattached. Who we truly are is Love. Being the "good" or "pious" or "lady" or "gentleman" that fits your fourchotomy is just inhabiting and projecting your narrow idea of those qualities—an idea that ultimately is selfish, and not anyone's true nature.

So'ham. I am That. Not "I am a good person." Not "I am a lady, gentleman, fearful, courageous, holy." *Sadhana* is learning the ins and outs of the worldly playing field and enjoying the joke that none of it is us. We have proxies playing on that field, while all of us actually live in the playing field of the Heart. There is no one, no matter how evil, who does not in Reality live in the playing field of the Heart.

We have forgotten this, and lose ourselves working so hard to perform on the world playing field. We gradually become more and more miserable and wander further away from the Truth of our identity. When we have so forgotten ourselves, our inner voice of "righteousness" is in fact the voice that is the most destructive to us. But we listen to it, and become more and more twisted. Then we are far from being human, because we are so far from being in God's image. At that point, God, in the form of people and events, rises against us and frees us through battle to return to ourselves.

Wake up from the dream that is a nightmare. Wake up from your righteousness and become human. Wake up from the dichotomy of good and bad. Stop projecting onto others. Wake up and love yourself, so that you can love others. The only way to do that is to give up your wrong identity with the proxy on the worldly playing field and return to who you really are. The most human you can be is to know that you are made in

God's image and live that Reality.

Our Birthright Is the Witness....

Baba always had me witness, watch. I, however, always wanted to be part of the action. And the truth is I was; my acting took the form of witnessing. As a child, I always preferred to participate, as in camp where I always wanted to be the camper, never the counselor who stood around and watched. As a dancer, I hated teaching dance because the teacher did not get to dance. Teaching Tai Chi was a joy because I was both participant and witness with the student. As a spiritual teacher, I model and practice along with the student. I am a witness, and I participate. As the teacher, Rohini the shrunken self practices by dissolving, and thereby allowing the Self, the Witness, to be in charge.

Baba used to say that happiness is our birthright. He did not say it is our shrunken self's birthright. Our shrunken self's birthright is to live out the effects of past causes.

If you believe that who you are is your shrunken self, you have no choice, no agency. The shrunken self has no real agency. Absolutely, it has no power to do anything. Relatively, it deludes itself into having agency, but behind the curtain is the Doer. So when we live unconsciously, lost in the shrunken self, we have no agency. We are puppets who are unaware of the puppeteer and believe we are in charge. The truth is, the puppet has no soul, and without the puppeteer the puppet cannot function. The puppet lives out the causes and effects, while the puppeteer enjoys the play.

The shrunken self is a construct of the mind. The mind witnesses the world and also witnesses itself. The mind appears as both subject and object at different times. When it is the subject, it witnesses outside itself. When it is the object, it is witnessed by itself. The mind cannot be simultaneously both subject and object. At one minute it appears as subject, and the next as object. The dissociative shrunken self thinks it is the Witness; it is merely the shrunken self looking down on itself. The shrunken self is not self-illuminative.

The Real Self witnesses all and enlivens all simultaneously; it is always Subject with no object. It is Self-illuminative. The Real Self is the enlivener, witness, and empathizer for the whole manifested world.

As Witness, the Real Self is the witness of the waking, dream and deep sleep states. It resides in the *turiya* state, the fourth state, the state beyond the other three. The Witness is always awake, even when consciousness is in the dream or deep sleep states. When the individual is asleep and not aware of the waking state, on all levels the Witness is present and in bliss.

The Witness's true nature is Love. The Witness is the one who is happy; that is our birthright. That is what Baba was talking about.

So if we have returned to the bliss of the Witness, our shrunken self is fully informed by the one that Knows, the one that enlivens. We are no longer merely the puppet; we are also the puppeteer. The Witness is not aloof. The best participant in the world play is the one who is the Witness on all levels, and therefore the participant on all levels.

But being aware that the puppeteer, the True Self, has the real agency is not the same as returning to the Self. It is important here to distinguish between being enlightened and being Self-realized. We can be enlightened but not Self-realized. Enlightenment is the experience of re-cognizing the Self as something altogether different from the shrunken self; being Self-realized is living as the Self, with no illusion of separateness. Enlightenment is an important stage on the way, but should not be confused with the goal.

People who confuse enlightenment with Self-realization are prone to delude themselves about their agency in a particular way. Those who have deluded themselves into believing they are only good believe that their agency only accomplishes good. When something bad happens, they take no responsibility, because their intentions are always "good."

Another way people delude themselves about enlightenment is to conflate blankness with a still mind, and therefore with Self-realization. Blankness is not the Self; blankness is *tamas* (inertia). Pure consciousness free of individuality is the Self. The Self is beyond even *sattva* (brightness and calm).

As we get closer to Self-realization, closer to the Witness, we are finally empathetic with ourselves. We first practice empathy with others and then with ourselves. When we empathize with others, we feel what they feel though we are not attached to that feeling; we are not run by that feeling. It is not us. We know it is other. We are fine within ourselves and yet able to feel for others. As we grow toward the Self, we are conscious of being both the participant and the Witness. When we reach Self-realization, we are Bliss Itself, and yet we also feel what the shrunken self feels without any attachment to the shrunken self's experience. We are the Self, and we empathize with our shrunken self. This is what it means to be the Witness and the participant at once.

The Witness and the participant are, in the Absolute sense, One. This is what Baba meant when he said, "God forgets his own true nature and looks for God. God worships God. God meditates on God, and God is trying to find God. It is God who questions and God who answers."

How Unsafe Happens....

"If any man come to me, and hate not his father, and mother, and wife, and children, and brethren, and sisters, yea, and his own life also, he cannot be my disciple" (Luke 14:26). Jesus meant what he said here—not in the literal sense of hating, but in the sense of being completely nonattached. If we are not nonattached to all manifest things, we cannot fully love God. This does not mean we no longer talk to our parents or siblings; it means that we must adjust to centering our lives on God rather than on our personal narratives. Safety lies in God; our personal narratives are completely unsafe, both for us and for others.

Our idea of safety derives from our first caregivers: they are our baseline models of love and safety, because they are the baseline for normality and home. If we believe they were safe when they were not, then we will not recognize unsafe people—at least unsafe people of a certain kind. In order to wake up to this deluded notion of safety, we need community (no isolation), questioning, alternative models, and active testing and checking of our own relationships.

My mother died just before Thanksgiving 2015. And though her death, like all deaths, brought a lot of stress, there was also relief for all of us. She was my first caregiver, and she did not care for anyone but herself. She never changed, and never knew me. She related only with what she projected onto others. Over time, I learned that I had to change my relationship with that relationship. That meant understanding and facing what I brought to the table. That is why I called her every day for over a decade—to get clear and clean and safe, even in her presence.

My mother operated by expecting everyone else to be safe for her narrative. Because she was so emphatic and played her part so thoroughly, most people acquiesced and played by her rules. They were injured in doing this. And when she met people—men—who took advantage of her narrative to control and abuse her, she refused to take care of herself, or even see what was going on.

Her choices provide a virtual checklist in how to be unsafe: clinging to her narrative, never questioning, remaining isolated, refusing to see or hear any alternative, and refusing to put her worldview to the test. She spent her life being numb and complicit in her own and others' degradation—and she called that being calm, clear, and worldly.

This is how every shrunken self operates. We want and expect everyone around us to make the world safe for our idea of ourselves. "If I am unsafe," we say, "everyone else will take care of me." This was my mother's litany; she had learned it at an early age from her caregivers. She never allowed herself to be conscious of that narrative and her responsibility for it, so she repeated the same story over and over again to the end. No matter how many times the players changed, the plot was always the same.

Though my mother's chosen environment was never truly safe, it was safe for her narrative and the part she played in it. Why? Because our personal narratives sustain themselves at our expense. They are unsafe, and land us in the same unsafe environments over and over again. This is what Christ was talking about. We have to hate our narrative in order to then transcend it and be free to experience and share Love—with our parents or anyone else.

To free ourselves, we must stop looking at what everyone else is doing and turn our attention to what we bring to the table. We have to be willing to see and experience where we are internally at any given moment. When we face ourselves head-on without defense attorneys, we are safe. If we lie to ourselves about where we are internally, then we are committed to maintaining our narrative.

Facing our experience honestly is not a thought experiment. Intellectual assent is not acceptance. Acceptance involves our whole being. We must be willing to experience and name truthfully every vibration that arises within us, and then disentangle from it and let it still.

If we are not safe within ourselves in this way, we look outward for safety, and we "find" it in the wrong places—the places that suit our narrative. So often, we seek safety with people who encourage our delusional notion of care. True protection is not denying the other person the chance to see evil and danger, but preventing them from being harmed by it. As parents, we must therefore not insulate our children from danger; we must teach them how to be safe within themselves and handle danger without. To do this, we have to have seen and learned from someone offering true protection. For me, this was Baba. He raised me.

Emotional Maturity....

Baba used to say we have to have a strong mind and ego to get rid of the mind and ego. Watching many people over many years, I have found that he was so right. People with undisciplined minds could not last around Baba; they were unwilling (and had made themselves unable) to do the hard exercise of practice. *Sadhana* requires us to use our psychic instruments rigorously. We have to have developed the skills of reflection, perseverance, precision, and clear discrimination. Along with these, we have to have picked up somewhere in our lives the ability not to take our ideas about ourselves and life so seriously.

The great Japanese swordsman Yagyu Munenori spoke of using a wedge to get rid of a wedge. What he meant is that we must be able to use the mind to get rid of the mind. So we have to have a strong wedge to be able to get rid of the other wedge. We have to have the strength to face ourselves, and this can be very difficult. There is a paradox here, in that we need to be strong in order to give up, and to know and discern what to surrender to.

This also means that we have to be willing to call a vibration what it is. This is where emotional maturity begins.

Growing up, we use emotions to guide us. But as we get clean and clear for ourselves, we reach a point where we can no longer do that. We no longer rely on emotions as a guide for our actions, but rather act from a place of nonattachment, even if the emotions are still present and felt. We then learn to discern appropriate action without using emotions as a compass.

This is difficult at first, because our emotions color our lives. They emerge as vibrations from the Heart, and then we decide what they are, where they come from and what they mean. But because we will avoid the truth about these emotions, we tend to mislabel them. We then act based on those labels rather than what the vibrations are really saying to us.

Most people judge which emotions are valid and which aren't. This is a massive mistake. None of our emotions is valid; they are all just vibrations. They are like clouds passing in the sky. In order to understand the workings of our emotions, we need to be able to identify all their variations, much as meteorologists understand how to predict weather from a precise knowledge of the many kinds of clouds. But we must always remember that emotions, like clouds, come and pass. They are not valid because they are not who we are.

Mastery of our emotions requires us to get *behind* our emotions, not in front of them. If we remain in front, then we are like a ship in the changing currents of the seas, with no control over the boat.

But we are trained to believe that emotion makes things authentic. If we are not running around emoting, we are seen as cold. This fourchotomy maps the dynamic:

Emotional	Clear and calm
Authentic expression	Cold and fake

As a result, we are bound to our emotions. We identify with them and defend that identification—which makes us extremely immature emotionally.

Nowhere is this immaturity more on display than in how so many people are so quick to take personal offense on an emotional level while denying others' experience. Everyone is identified with their judgments about their own and others' emotions. This creates violence within and without. By shutting down and denying any place to express feelings considered "not good," we create volcanoes waiting to erupt.

In order to be free, we must be able to still all our vibrations. This means we must cultivate nonattachment. A strong wedge is a mind that, rather than judging or denying emotional vibrations, can be disentangled from them. We cannot still something we are not disentangled from. We must first be strong enough to be willing to be with a given vibration until we can disentangle from it. Only then can we begin to still it.

Disentangling is not dissociating. We must be with our experience before disentangling from it. It's easy to pretend to be facing yourself when in fact you're deflecting reality. *Sadhana* requires real self-inquiry: not a facile "I know I'm a jerk," but a willingness to face unflinchingly the vibrations of our obnoxiousness. While a genuine sense of humor about ourselves helps us to achieve this separation, a false one can simply be a way for the shrunken self to save face by looking nonattached and reflective. We must know the difference, for ourselves and others.

So the emotionally mature person guards the Heart, recognizes his vibrations as soon as they emerge, accepts them for what they are, is willing to be with them, disentangles from them, and stills them where they emerge. It is crucial to understand that this is not an intellectual activity; done properly, it all takes place before we can superimpose self-serving labels on our vibrations. The practice looks like this:

Recognize

Accept

Be with (not in)

Disentangle

Still

Continue guarding the Heart

Be with your experience, whatever it is. Let whatever comes up from the experience come up. Function appropriately on the physical plane. This is what Baba taught me. It is true emotional maturity.

Subjectivity Is the Wedge….

Subjectivity is the wedge we must use to get rid of the wedge of subjectivity. By subjectivity, I mean "subject" in the grammatical sense. We have to accept our agency as the individual subject in order to let go of our limited subjectivity and get to the Absolute Subjectivity of God. We need agency to move from dualism to nondualism.

As a dancer, I worked intensely for many years to acquire expert technique, knowing all the while that the ultimate goal was to go beyond technique. Technique became the wedge by which I could get rid of the wedge. There is no leapfrogging mastery of technique—or of our limited subjectivity. Baba always said, "You have to have a strong ego to get rid of the ego."

If we indulge our limited subjectivity rather than discipline it, we become narcissists. The narcissist sees himself as the Subject but is really cut off from his true core. Ignorant people see him as a confident subject and willingly serve as objects for him. In truth, our subjectivity is only a diminished echo of the infinite Subjectivity of God. We therefore have a choice: narcissism or real Subjectivity. Kierkegaard understood this when he wrote in his journal, "Subjectivity is the way of deliverance—that is, God, as the infinitely compelling subjectivity."

Agent / subjective	Object / objective
Narcissist / self-absorbed	Accommodating / obedient

One day in 1975, I was standing by the Charles River in Cambridge, Massachusetts. The day before, I had received a letter from Baba's organization that quoted Baba:

God forgets his own true nature and looks for God. God worships God. God meditates on God, and God is trying to find God. It is God who questions and God who answers.

As I stood amid the shrubs on the bank, I started to laugh. I got the joke. "It is God who questions and God who answers." This was too hysterically funny. I could not stop laughing. The laughter lasted for over an hour. Ever since, dialogue has never been the same. We are all just speaking to ourselves.

Last week, when I was reflecting on the image of the mirror in the *Jnaneshwari*, I started laughing again because I realized God created us so that when God was speaking to Himself, He did not look crazy; it looked like there was a conversation. Part of the joke is that God cannot "con" Himself—there is only "sciousness" when there is no duality. Jnaneshwar uses a question to reveal this reality. He knows who is questioning and who gives the answer:

By means of a mirror one object may seem to be two; but in point of fact, are there really two? [IV, vi, 46]

For us to resolve this conundrum, we use a wedge to get rid of a wedge. We need to trace back and then eliminate our identification with our separate subjectivity. We do this by questioning our shrunken self and tricking it into facing the fact that it is just a functional device and not who we truly are. We use our shrunken self to finally see that we are just a reflection in a mirror, and when we realize the Seer of the reflection, we return to our true nature.

God continues the play of manifestation so that God can express and feel God's Love.

Jnaneshwar expresses the dilemma of unity: Love wants to be shared. God wants to share God's nature:

If separation were removed, there could be no question and answer; and if they were united, there would be no joy in mutual converse. [XVIII, lxxiv, 1578]

But we have to return to our true nature—to the Absolute Subject— eventually, and we do this by purifying our understanding. We have wrongly believed that the image in the mirror is who we really are. That belief and its consequences have to be cleaned away.

Most people doing *sadhana*, though, are attached to the purifying process and miss its purpose. "I am the best mirror cleaner ever," they say. "And because I am so good, I am always looking for and finding dirt so that I can be the best cleaner. My tools are the best also: cleaners, sprays, buckets, cloths, etc. The mirror is very important to me so that I can be a cleaner. If the mirror were clean, there would be nothing for me to do. No mirror, no me." When we finally let go of the mirror, we are nothing, which then allows us to merge with the illuminator of the mirror, the Self. We then are no longer the doer. The Self, God, does it all. No more action for us. Our only agency is the Subject. As we lose the mirror, and with it our function and identity, we are using the wedge to get rid of the wedge. Left then is only the Self.

You can't see the Self when you are the Self. I used to watch Baba enliven his vehicles so he could engage with all of us and share the bliss of God as the bliss of the world. For him, the wedge was gone.

Miserly Hoards the L to Get Misery....

When life is all about "me," I am a "taker." I am stingy. There is no one else in the room with me—I am the only one. Everyone else is just an object that impacts me in some way.

Identifying as the one true shrunken self only makes us miserable.

Misery, then, is the bottom line of all vibrations; it is the goal, the shrunken self's "love." This unfortunate truth is evident in the way the world is evolving right now. The miserable person receives all the attention and "love" from the world. So the way to get "love" is to be miserable. You suck everyone in. And in order to be included as part of "the world," others have to be crushed and made miserable.

Attending to Baba in the ashram courtyard in Ganeshpuri provided amazing opportunities for my *sadhana* on all levels. Once, when the courtyard was empty except for Baba and the other attendant, I watched someone arrive from Bombay with a gift for Baba. It was a watch. As the man gave Baba the watch, I said internally, "Baba, my watch broke. I need a watch. I don't have a watch anymore. I need a watch." I was standing toward the back of the courtyard and obviously not part of the interchange Baba and the man were having. Baba took the watch and said nothing further. The man left.

About fifteen minutes later, Baba got up from his seat. He would normally go into his house using the door to the left of his seat. But instead he started to come in my direction. Just at that moment, my then-husband, who went by the name Niranjan, came through the courtyard. Baba said to him. "Your wife needs a watch. I will tell the jeweler to talk to you when he comes." We all kind of laughed, especially me, and then Baba disappeared to lunch.

After lunch that day, I went to my usual place at the back stair. Baba came out in a beautiful blue velvet hat with beads on it. He asked me to get my husband. Once Niranjan arrived, Baba gave him the hat and said, "Now will you not be a miser and buy your wife a watch?" Niranjan laughed. And that seemed to be it. The next day, Baba came out in a velvet vest with hearts for pockets. Baba asked me to get my husband. I did. Baba gave him the vest and said, "Now will you not be a miser and get your wife a watch?" This dance went on for days; Baba lavished Niranjan with beautiful gifts.

Each time there was laughter. In the end, Niranjan agreed to talk with the jeweler on Sunday. The watch came several days later; Baba gave it to me. The jeweler gave the bill to Niranjan. The story seems so playful, but Baba was always teaching. Would there have been any generosity in this situation without Baba's generosity?

Even when misers give, they are merely performing gestures; their seeming generosity is actually robotic. It is behavior modification with no underlying sincerity. But the miser expects others to be generous and openhearted toward him, by which the miser means they should forsake themselves to please him.

Miserly / robotic	Generous / openhearted
Self-contained / clear-sighted	Wasteful / lost in others

In Hui-neng's commentary on the *Diamond Sutra*, he talks about charity:

When ordinary people practice charity, they are just seeking personal dignity, or enjoyment of pleasure: that is why they plunge back into the three mires when their rewards are used up. The World Honored One is very kind, teaching the practice of formless charity, not seeking personal dignity or pleasure; he just has us inwardly destroy the attitude of stinginess while outwardly helping all beings. Harmonizing thus is called practicing charity without dwelling on form.... To practice charity in accord with a formless mind like this means there is no sense of being charitable, no idea of a gift, and no notion of a recipient. This is called practicing charity without dwelling on appearances.... [T]he practice of charity is universal dispersal. If you can inwardly disperse all false thoughts, habit energies, and afflictions in the mind, the four images are gone, and nothing is stored up—this is true giving. (trans. Thomas Cleary)

True charity is never about an action; it can only exist when we have sacrificed our own miserliness.

Family Recipes….

"Life will be easier if I don't practice." Why will it be easier? If we practice, we will have to face what we have. But we don't want to face reality. We are driving a 1950 Buick, thinking we are at the wheel of a Porsche.

Accepting reality begins with accepting our environment and our vehicles for what they actually are, not what we would like them to be. We refuse to see the dysfunction in ourselves and our families. If we are not happy, we believe that is because we are not operating correctly within our system—we conclude that we are not doing it right. Instead, we should be questioning the system itself. We therefore believe that if we simply work harder at our system, success and happiness will follow. The problem is we never look at the actual vehicle we are driving to see what its capabilities are and where it is headed. The Buick can never go from zero to 60 in under ten seconds.

Many years ago, I had a conversation in which someone insisted that his first-level practice (using the senses and rituals) would take him to the same place as my third-level practice (reorienting the will). I told him that spiritual practice is not a track meet; the various means are not parallel and equal lanes that arrive at the same destination. In truth, one level of practice will lead into a deeper one; only the deepest practice takes us to the final destination. We may continue observing first- or second-level practices even after we are practicing at the third level, but at this point the deepest level will be informing all the others.

To put it another way, we do not get to decide for ourselves the recipe for spiritual practice. Whoever blindly believes that their habitual way of living is the correct recipe will never get anywhere on the spiritual path. They are simply transposing their family system onto spirituality. They might as well believe that they can come up with a blog post by literally following a pancake recipe. For different undertakings, we have to follow completely different recipes with categorically different ingredients.

People who are committed to their "family recipe" believe that Rohini is just following her family recipe, which she learned as a child, and pushing it on them. They conclude that if they follow what they see as Rohini's recipe, they will be at best derivative and at worst obsequious. They will say, "I was raised differently." What they don't get is that it is not Rohini's recipe. It's the same recipe that has been used for thousands of years in the lineages of many religions. Their recipe will not take them or anyone else where the authentic recipe for spiritual practice leads.

The whole point of seeking a Guru is to uncover, dismantle, and let go of your family recipe as the formula for happiness, and to surrender to the one true recipe for returning Home. This is what I did, and do, with Baba. The recipe I share I learned from him, as he learned it from Nityananda.

The Self Is Not the Point....

In the *Yoga Sutras*, ignorance means taking the non-Self to be the Self. Once we have done that, we lose our Subject in object. From there, we are attracted to certain things and repulsed by others based on the object we are now identified with. And finally, we cling to the life of that object, believing it to be who we are.

From there, we continue to lose ourselves in objects of all kinds. Our life consists of chasing shiny objects, no matter how subtle, and being unaware that we even have a core. Even a supersensuous experience is an object, a container or vibration that people love to identify with. It makes them "special," but they are still objects. They lose their subject in the vibration "I am special." If I believe who I am is "I am special," then anything I think, say, or do is attributed to this idea of specialness.

From the standpoint of the *Shiva Sutras*, that "I am special" container or vibration is actually a shrunken self. "I am special" is just a thought construct (*vikalpa*); you can replace it with any *vikalpa* you want and come up with a shrunken self. The nature of the shrunken self is unconscious consciousness. It is enlivened by the Self of All.

After *shaktipat*, Grace gradually backs off, requiring us to consciously do the work of re-cognizing the Self. But the shrunken self is deluded into thinking that the drop of consciousness from Truth that it contains is all the consciousness there is. So we believe we can expand that drop of consciousness through *vikalpas*, fooling ourselves all the more.

The individual shrunken self (*anu*) is a point; it has borders and boundaries. The *anu* operates as a "conscious individual in its own right"; it feels no need to consult anyone because it is all the consciousness there is. When the *anu* believes it is doing *sadhana* and expanding, it believes that its borders expand. The problem is, this is false expansion. *Vikalpas* create borders. Doing its idea of *sadhana*, the *anu* pushes out its boundaries and takes in other *anus*; it loses its idea of subject in more objects.

As individuals, then, we create no-boundary zones on the most superficial planes. In order to make the *anu* appear to be the Self, we have to shrink the universe to the smallest possible scale. So we think we're a bigger deal when in fact we're enmeshed and indulging in no-boundary zones. True expansion of consciousness means the dissolving of the *anu* into the All, just as a grain of salt is dissolved in water. Then it is no longer a point and there are no borders because there is only the Self of All. If you think your individual consciousness is expanding, you are deluding yourself. None of our containers could ever hold the ocean.

This is why true *sadhana* is about grinding down the shrunken self and revealing our wrong identification, which is just a bundle of *vikalpas*.

It's difficult to know the difference between being lost in our character—in any one of our favorite vibrations—and being with our experience consciously. We tend to avoid being conscious by resonating, wallowing, and denying.

Resonating in particular is how we fool ourselves about connecting with ourselves and the world. In our wrong understanding, we resonate with others' vibrations, believing we are connecting with those people. In fact, we are losing ourselves further in more and more objects.

To truly connect with ourselves and others, we must turn inward, toward the Heart. We must know the difference between vibrations and vehicles on the one hand and who we truly are on the other.

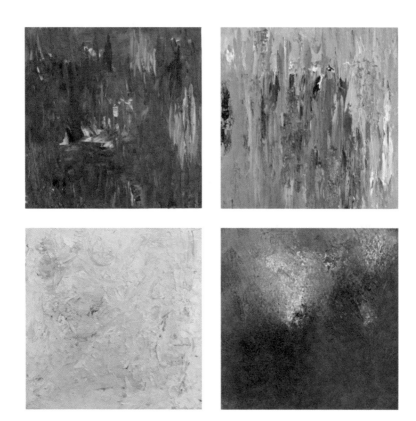

Pity Self

Pity self	Hold self accountable
Value self	Belittle self

so pretty....

living
                                    life
        ruins   aesthetic

    close   senses
        shut   sensors

fancy   flutters   film
                over   facts

    live   in   images
        of   dream
            state
                        only

    miss   Love
                not   know
        Love

    waste   bin   of   life
            miss   whole
                    point

to pretty   with nothing
                in it

    vehicles   vapor

        Love   the   soul
                            reason

Just Beginning

so be it....

i

to the left
on the mountain
i see
Assisi

i think
for sure this road must be to heaven
climbing the heights
oh my oh my
heaven or hell
locked in narrow streets
theme park

Assisi must be heaven
costumed agitation
no facts
winding up to hell

can't pull
the dots together
desperate to see
performance too thick

ii

up the mountain
to commune with monks
compline peace
disciplines of Benedict

guided with care
dressed to respect

gates locked
monastery locked
compline locked

standing
back to the gate
rooted and strong
facing valley sunset mountains
just stand
do not move
quiet full and empty
no thought

not even God was welcome
so be it
i heard

compline
by the locked gate

back to Norcia
where the ground gave way
but the Heart survived

try again
barred again
gates remotely open
guided
by forbidding signs
to the dark chapel
we wait

late start
missing the
Rule
darkness anger despair arrogance
no love here
pride refuses community
as they disappear

and we
escape into the light
of sunset

so be it

sleep well….

take   a nap
     make
                    your   bed
     if   only
solutions for   all
          universal
                    problems

freed   from pain
     by   surface
                         indicators
     so   easy
                    so   empty
     absolute
          absolutely
                    nothing
numb   out cold
     free   pass
     start   over
          nap
                              on bed
     make   nothingness

same old story....

i   am a little   victim
       rising from   the
              ashes
       a hero's welcome
              shining
                 the   winning
                          ticket

a phoenix   or   the chicken
           roasted   none
                  theless
           cooked in
                              tapasya

we   emerge
          dripping
                  as   gold
     or
                      grease
the   wheels
                  of   learning

First Meeting

the heal….

heel   a
             v
             o
             i
            advancing
             s

                         heal
       embrace
            r
            a
            c
            e   pain
                      o
                      n
                   then

            w
re   main   the same
            t
            h
            i
            n
or   with
                      out

un   less   pick   up   again

walk   back on heel

not   same   when   consciously   heal

mild medium intense….

wow   shaktipat
              mild
     so   special
              peace
              calm
              soft
              quiet
                                    greatness
        specialness
                                          is
              who
                          i
                                          am

              medium
   fire   works
              lights
sounds   nada
              visions
    electric   shooting
beyond
                    special   beyond
taking ownership
                    my
              experiences
                          light
                          sound
                          touch
                          taste
                          smell
                    special   me
              so   sure
                              am   i

intense
        all   of   the
above
               and
    really who
        I am
no   more
                       special
     just   am
        me
        us
        all

    ownership   gone
       identification
                gone
     special beyond
        beyond
    being   no
       difference
know
     knowing
             Love
      All
    unspecial Self
     of All

divine tuition....

    gateway back
          to
      who we are
         or
    down the   rabbit hole
         of manifestation
      mind a friend
            or
      worst enemy
    luminous vehicle
            opening us to us
        or
    thinking tyrant
driving   us
         to shrunken   misery
use the mind
    as   expert
    graduate
        to   thought
                free

the promise....

you promised no
    more flood
  I lied
no more destruction
  did I

I have created
  a mess
and I must
    reap My own
      doing
I must model
    how to return
    to Me

the destruction of
    the temporal
destruction of what
    to realign back
      to who

I am

building blocks....

thought constructs
   constrict
       us
from

   who we are
   who are we

thought constructs
   fool
       us

  we believe
believe   me

        to
    see   the
        snake
      in   the
        rope

thought constructs
   conjure
       up
  pretty
       bad
  ideas
       that
 lead us
   to leaden
  boxes
that don't
   exist

we think
  thought

to create
a world
that   is
     not
Real

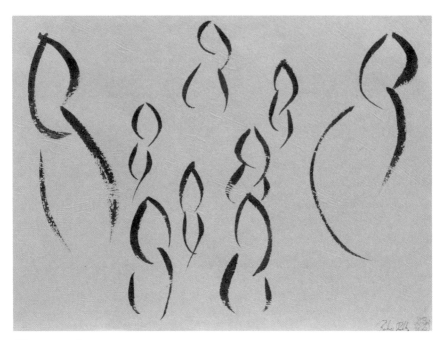

Playground

nursery rhymes with childish....

the farmer
   in the
      dell
encourages
   the irrigating
      of hell

  for each
      are
    farmers
     for others

  farmer for
     Love
     brings others
   to irrigate
     Love
 whatever the
     form

  jivanmukta
irrigates
  only
      Love

  no matter
    who the
       farmer is

  farmer loses
    purpose
  when
     only
     seen is
    God

In the Living Room

the new flood....

       God
    is drowning us
      in   our
               minds

He used
      psychologyphilosophyeducationtechnologyparenting
   to   misread
               feelings

  no   feelings

power
                           success
    letters
  dug   into
                  pool

  no   air
    no light
             no   life

  mind   pain   not
                          true feeling

dead
          as life
     life   as dead

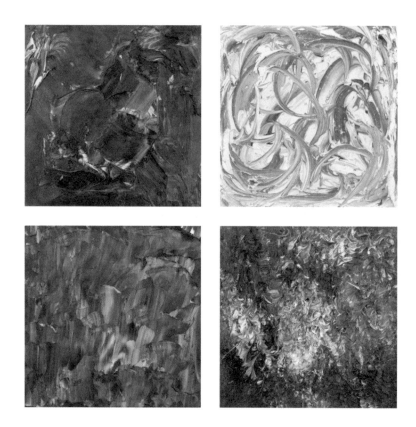

Immobile

Immobile	Agile
Steadfast	Erratic

CHAPTER TWO
OBSTACLES AND MISUNDERSTANDING

Transformation....

So much language these days is about change, transformation, on all levels and in all sectors of our lives. The law of change is always working, but in what direction are we going? That depends on what we are doing now. Nothing is static, though we may think it is because it moves so slowly. The transformation I desire will emerge not from what I am saying today but from what I am actually doing today. Only if my words and actions are authentic will they lead me towards what I profess. If I carry any resistance to my action within myself, even unconsciously, that resistance will manifest in the future, and I will unwittingly sabotage the transformation I seek.

People speak about our oneness, peace, love, all the good things. However, when things do not go "our" way, that language tends to disappear. We cannot just talk, we have to walk. This means we must let go of our own limited sight and resistance to reality. We cannot superimpose Absolute Reality on relative reality.

We cannot let go of something we deny having, or fail to see that we have. Herein lies our dilemma. If we do not acknowledge that we contain all qualities, we unwittingly create the negative or opposite of the peace and love we proclaim. We cannot walk on one foot forever. We have the other foot. To change ourselves or anything else, we must own, master and transcend both positive and negative. Then we are in fact walking the walk and not just talking.

Autopterodidactyl....

If you are self-taught, you do not know what you do not know. The only dialogue is between you and you, which means that you believe you can dictate your position in any environment. You are unwilling to be educated. This leaves you with two options: either you are always right, or at the very least the most knowledgeable, or you are the most inferior. It does not matter which, because either way, everyone else exists only in relation to you. Either way, the qualities that emerge are pride and arrogance. There is disdain for any authority that does not acknowledge your authority. There is resistance to learning from authority, as you are the only expert. Because of this attitude, we cannot learn; we cannot receive from someone else. We remain limited and full of what we have decided.

The purpose of a teacher is to help us to gain mastery. When we learn, we take in and build the skill set and capacity to handle what comes our way. A good teacher does that; they do not shield us from learning. They actually allow us to go through what we need to in order to achieve mastery. The world is the laboratory. The truth is, we can learn our lessons everywhere in the world from a good teacher. The teacher is not interested in limiting us. They are interested in sharing their own knowledge.

Self-taught people are often terrible students. They are the ones who dictate their learning without ever having learned how to learn. Think of it: you are completely ill-equipped, but you are directing the interchange. Self-taught people believe they already know what they need to know, and so see the teacher as a resource, an object to be utilized according to the student's design. "You are going to teach me when I want you to teach me. Not at other times will you teach me, because I am in charge of my education." For these students, no one else really exists. They are not used to listening and taking in, only debunking.

There is a big difference between the arrogant autodidact and the person who has surrendered to learning from teachers, has learned how to learn, and then can go on to use those skills effectively and with appropriate discernment. These people know how to ask the right questions and especially how not to rest on their laurels. They are not satisfied with superficial knowledge but will dig deeper, and they know how to dig deeper into a subject or situation to find knowledge and resolution. They have actually mastered the art of learning, and so are in fact experts in how to learn, which allows them to approach any subject and be able to reach a certain level of expertise as long as they have the physical and mental capacity. A self-taught person will approach a new project with limited interest, perseverance, and ability to acquire any depth of expertise. They will hit a wall at some point and not know how to break through it. The person who has learned knows how to approach an obstacle or challenge and move through it to attain mastery.

Arrogant autodidacts are extremely irrational, though they think they are rational. The problem is, they base all their rational thinking on an irrational decision they made early in life. Because they have not surrendered to the rigors of real study, they have not advanced. The very foundation of their learning is based on a falsehood, and because they will not surrender to a teacher, they have no chance of ever seeing this. Their house of cards will eventually come down, but they will not know why.

When I was four years old, I went to Sunday school. My paternal grandmother was the teacher. It was Hanukah. I was just sitting in the class being babysat. To keep me occupied, I was given a mimeograph to color of Judah Maccabee standing on some rocks. I grew up in Boston, so when I heard his name, I knew he was Scottish. I colored him with a plaid kilt. No one said anything, so my decision was set. I never questioned this and grew up knowing that it was Judah MacAbee, a Scotsman. Not until I was 23 did the truth hit me. By this time, I had studied with great teachers. I had a terminal academic degree and my own school in Cambridge, MA for Tai Chi Chuan. Being a martial artist, I was committed to my sense of being a warrior. Around this time of year, my memories came up of Hanukah; I remembered Judah MacAbee, and it hit me as a great insight (proving we should not be so proud of our insights) that Maccabee could not have been a Scotsman. He had to come from a different part of the world. Now everyone knows the extent of my childhood religious education.

People Who Hide Behind Voicelessness….

How many of us believe we have no agency, no voice? Now that is an ego that needs to crack. If we have no voice, then we have no responsibility for anything. Often, people keep their mouths shut so they never have to change their minds. They avoid, and because they tell themselves they have no agency, they can hide and then blame others. Then there are the people with a sure, sincere voice. They think they are coming from God, so they believe they have a mandate. But this voice is so tainted with the shrunken self that even when they believe that they are doing good, they are uplifting themselves by using others.

What about the person who listens so well to everyone else and never to herself? That person has to turn in, use the skills she already has, and listen inwardly to the voice she has always possessed.

There is a voice that says, "I have no voice. I need to find my voice." Whose voice is saying that? Whose voice is even asking this? It is a game of hide-and-seek: we play the character of one who has no voice, and we have to go searching. What happens, then, when we decide we have found our voice? What voice is this? If we have been pathetic victims, we may go forth as horrible tyrants bullying everyone, thinking we are now authentic. No. This is not your voice, just as the pathetic voice was not you. Both are from the shrunken self. The tyrant was the voice you never listened to, so when it came forth, you thought that was you. Wrong. It is just the other side of the coin. So your true voice would not be any of these:

Tyrant / bully	Humble / serving the situation
Standing up for self	Pathetic victim / doormat

Who you are is beyond all qualities. We have to go beyond all thought deep into the Heart to hear our real voice, which will be, and therefore will act, for the good of All. There is no calculating; we are then appropriate for All. The individual disappears, and we emerge to relate with the world expressing the Love that was always there.

So to find our voice, we must give up the words with which we have so identified. There has never been a time when we had no agency. That is the delusion our shrunken self banks on to maintain itself. So we create a voice that questions all voices, and then we create a voice that is emphatic and never subject to question. We then oscillate between the two, both voices being sure of their rightness when neither is our voice.

We always have agency, and we are accountable for the actions and decisions of the shrunken self. Not until we crack, not until we jump off the grid, do we have a chance to really hear our Real voice and manifest from there. In order to hear your voice, you must shut up. Now!

Magic is Illusion....

Magic is Illusion.

The Goal is Magic.

Therefore the Goal is Illusion.

Unfortunately and unknowingly, many people seeking "the Path" are following the above logic. The promise of power, wealth, and supersensuous abilities entices people to pursue what is called spiritual practice but is really just magic. In just two weekends, you will be a master of this or that; you will be free from all that prevents your utmost happiness and power. And who listens to this? The very one that has to be dismantled in spiritual practice. The very idea of an enlightened shrunken self is a sad joke for all of us.

This is where magic comes in. Magic exists. But, as Evelyn Underhill writes, it is the wrong goal:

[M]agic is a pathway to reality; a promise which it cannot fulfill, for the mere transcending of phenomena does not entail the attainment of the Absolute. Magic even at its best extends rather than escapes the boundaries of the phenomenal world. It stands, where genuine, for that form of transcendentalism which does abnormal things, but does not lead anywhere: and we are likely to fall victims to some kind of magic the moment that the declaration "I want to know" ousts the declaration "I want to be" from the chief place in our consciousness....[M]agic is merely a system whereby the self tries to assuage its transcendental curiosity by extending the activities of the will beyond their usual limits; sometimes, according to its own account, obtaining by this means an experimental knowledge of the planes of existence usually—but inaccurately—regarded as "supernatural." (*Mysticism*, p. 151)

So magic at its best shows us that there is something beyond the merely concrete. The problem as I see it is that such experience becomes the end in itself. People get caught in the trap of psychic as spiritual, energy as spiritual, knowing as spiritual, and they stop there. These abilities are just that—powers—and they are never the final destination of the true seeker.

I usually explain this in the following manner. Let us suppose Boston, Massachusetts is our goal and we are in Baltimore, Maryland. We are driving to Boston, and we come to Philadelphia, Pennsylvania. Philadelphia represents "magic." We stop there and get fascinated by all we discover and all we can do. We are so enamored of what is there that we forget our original goal and remain in Philadelphia. We then believe this is in fact the goal. So much for Boston.

We delude ourselves into believing that, since there is so much more in Philadelphia than where we have been, we must have arrived. But who has arrived? The shrunken self has just expanded its territory. We have given nothing up. We have gained great things. And how can we delude ourselves this way? Easy. The shrunken self does not discern; it is not pure. As the *Yoga Sutras* state, the shrunken self takes misery for happiness and the not-self for the Self. When we begin walking the path, we make decisions based on what we call our "love," our "truth." This bottom line is not the real bottom line because it is based on the above ignorance. The vibration we are calling "love" is something else. For each of us, it is different based on our destiny; but for each of us, it is still twisted love, not real Love. Delusion is then thinking our "loving" is the bottom line.

The truth is that Love is underneath all these other vibrations. Love is the bottom line; we just do not know the bottom line. So we come to power and magic and energy and call it love. We see this is better than what we have. However, the power, energy, and magic are informed by our "loving" vibration. We swim in the vibration, so we think it is us. But the fact is, it is just a vibration that in truth has a different name. We are in fact living and loving based on illusion. Our narrative becomes something to hide behind, and we then miss the truth of life. The shrunken self has created an illusion of love; therefore, it is the magician. It has convinced us that it is who we are. But the shrunken self is not self-illuminative; sometimes it appears as subject and sometimes as object. Therefore, there are times we can perceive it. We forgot that if we can perceive it, it is not us. And if it is not us, then it is not Love.

How do we choose to leave the magic and get back to the real goal? Using a wedge to get rid of a wedge, as Munenori says, means getting the shrunken self to dismantle itself. By convincing the shrunken self to practice shining a light on itself and letting go, we convince the shrunken self it is heading in the right direction—and it is; toward its own demise. Only when it is too late, when the true Self is shining through and Love is there, does it then give up and surrender to the truth that it is not a great magician!

Appropriate Rest….

Sometimes, when pursuing the Truth, the best thing we can do is: rest. This may sound strange when we are intensely determined to stay on track. Are we on track or are we driven? Though we say we know the goal, we may be just driven to be driven. We may have "forgotten" the goal of Home, Truth, God, the Self. Our new goal is "driven." When this occurs, self-effort has hijacked the practice and become the goal. We may believe we are working, but our shrunken self is working, making decisions, and directing our course, which will be anywhere but near the Self.

Rest is exactly what is needed in this case. It goes against our idea of *sadhana*, spiritual practice, and therefore stymies the shrunken self. Confusion will come to our shrunken self because rest stops it in its tracks. So "sure" of action and direction, the shrunken self would never lose control by resting. And yet if we really are pursuing the Truth, rest is definitely required. Rest can help us detach from our concepts.

We tend to be identified with our concepts, and with this identification comes a rigidity or tightness. Rest loosens the bounds enough for us to free ourselves. The very act of holding on quiets when we rest. Rest can be defined as relaxing, letting go, refreshing ourselves, and recovering strength. There are times when this is totally appropriate, not lazy. We are not running from "productive" or maybe even "workaholic"; it is just appropriate to rest.

We have been pushing very hard recently. Now is the time to take a breath, rest and assess how and where we are. Some of us feel we have not moved at all, that we are stuck in our misery. This means we are attached to our misery. We have not been able to detach. But if we are willing to back off from the battle and rest, we may actually detach from the importance of the battle and the object we are attacking. Remember, we want not to fight, for that will keep us in a repulsion relationship and make it quite difficult to free ourselves.

At these times, rest becomes the best tactic. By resting, we are saying this very vibration we are working to overcome does not run us; we can back off and we do not need to engage with it. Ah, a moment without the pressure of purification, purgatory, a quiet moment. We are quite capable of these quiet and peaceful moments, though we may have forgotten this because we have been so committed and driven to remove our impurities from our character that we believe that is all there is. This focus on purification without perspective is also wrong understanding. We are meditating on something that is not Real. We have to come back to what the goal is and is not. Pride of work does not move us in the right direction. The goal is to give up our attachment to the shrunken self, our individuality, and return to union with our true nature, God.

We Are Our Own Worst Victim....

It is not my fault. It is your fault. This view works for me. The only time this does not "work" is when both of us claim the role of victim. Then we have a competition. When this happens, we can have a standoff for hours or even days. We are committed to our shrunken self as a victim, and we will not give up. We win.

What do we win? When we are the victim, we get to be right. We get to have people feel bad for us. We believe people understand and care about what is going on in our life. We are the center of attention. What more can our shrunken self wish for? We definitely win.

The only problem is the misery. Why is it that when I win, I am still miserable? My shrunken self has all it is looking for, and yet pain is the experience instead of joy. Maybe the role of victim is not as good as I think it is. Where is this misery coming from? These are the questions I need to ask when, after labeling myself the faultless victim, I am in pain.

My very commitment to being a victim is the cause of the misery. I have willingly stuffed myself into a box that imprisons and belittles. The cause of this choice is ignorance. "Victim" looks like a great explanation and solution to my problems; it seems so natural and true. How can this be ignorant? I have taken "victim" to be me; I have believed in the superiority of victimhood. So I have taken the not-self of victim to be the Self, the impermanence of victim to be permanent, the impurity of victim to be pure. Once I choose victimhood as the pinnacle of life, I lose my subject in the object of victim. Now, as a victim, I am attached to certain things. As a victim, I am repulsed by certain things. Finally, I cling to the life of my victimhood.

Seeing all this, we can understand the real solution of our misery to be giving up our identity with "victim." How do we do this when we believe being the victim makes us the winner, the good person? We have to see that "victim" is not who we are. We have to see that "victim" is not universal. And since we are not the victim a hundred percent of the time, we prove that victimhood is a temporary state. Also, we are not universally seen as victims, so it cannot be our identity.

I want to be happy and love my life. The role of the victim requires misery. As a victim, I am not myself. I am not my true nature: Love. Being on the other side, as the aggressor, also has not worked. Neither brings happiness or love. Once this has been revealed to us, we have the opportunity to choose something different. But what? If we remain in our shrunken self we will unwittingly choose the same thing. If we surrender and let go of this shrunken self, that always leads us astray, we then can put our attention back into the Heart, where true discernment can occur.

The truth is, we are the perpetuators of our identity as victims. We choose to relate to our circumstances in the role of victim. We interpret the circumstances of our life as defining us as victims. However, we could always respond differently if we wished. By doing so, we are no longer victims, no matter the situation. We are our own worst victim. It is not the winning ticket, so let it go and take responsibility. Then Love rather than misery becomes a choice.

Are You Sharing or Reporting?….

On a plane heading toward Florida. Reporting or sharing? Just a fact. Do you need to know? Not really. What you need to know is there is a person in the seat in front of me who has not stopped talking for over an hour. She is reporting as if it really mattered and anyone would like to listen. The person listening next to her is listening almost as if it were a television show and she could be passive as the show proceeded.

Do you report or share? What is the difference between reporting and sharing? When we share, we are actually interested in the person we are speaking with. When we report, the recipient does not really matter. It could be anyone.

Do you believe that, if you are emotional, you are sharing? Or are you just reporting your emotions and boring everyone? What is your purpose of expressing your emotions? Are your emotions the way you control your life? Do you use your emotions to manipulate everyone around you? Do you assume everyone does this? Do you do emotional competition?

Emotions are vibrations; they are vehicles we have to aid in our functioning here in these bodies. Emotions are tools that aid the soul to have experience and learning. If we use them to manipulate, then we are probably not learning what we are meant to. We will see as we grow that we have identified and worshipped these vibrations. That makes us used by them rather than us using our emotions. False idols, and we are left empty.

There is no satisfaction from this. And the people around us will be hurt and feel we never cared. We cared more about our emotions than anyone else.

Do you find the person reporting as bored as you are?

Reporting by most accounts is objective communication of facts. Is there anything wrong with that? Most people like reporting or objective communication, so is there a problem with it? No—when we are looking at science, business, or news. Good reporting can be sharing. There used to be reporters who reported the news with as little bias as possible and wanted us to understand and engage and wrestle and think for ourselves. Discernment was important. Now we have reporters who engage in hyperbole, and communicate it through false feelings. They "guide" us in how we should see what they are communicating. They are not interested in engaging us; they want to manipulate us. This reminds me of *Fahrenheit 451*, where all communication was about manipulation and maintaining life only on the surface.

However, when we are in relation with someone, we should want to share and have someone share with us. When we report, we do not have to be present, we can be dissociated. We can speak remotely, as if reading a boring book with no awareness or consciousness. When we share, we are participating and contributing consciousness to the communication. We are neither purely intellectual nor emotional. There is something deeper than the words themselves. We are sharing ourselves rather than sharing only our vehicles.

When people just want to report to me, I tend to feel bored, because they are not interested in what they are saying. They are disembodied voices with no life. They are *prakrti*, nature, in the form of inertia.

Let us go forth and share. Let us not share our tired reports of emotions, narratives, ideas that have not had any life in them for so long.

Let us share us, truly us and not our angry, bitter, blaming self. Who are we? Love.

Sadhana Is Uncomfortable....

We have been looking at how we repackage things to suit our shrunken selves, and seeing that it is so sad. If we do not restrain our shrunken selves, we only repackage. Repackaging is just another word for twisted love. We are unwilling to love openly and honestly, so we twist and repackage and then present that to the world. Yes, it is sad.

We repackage ourselves and then give that empty charade to others. We lie to ourselves first, then feed that lie to others. We perpetuate our own ignorance.

Sadhana is the practice that brings about removal of that ignorance. If we are ignorant and do not know who we are but believe we do, then *sadhana* is going to be uncomfortable. It is uncomfortable for the shrunken self because this shrunken understanding believes it is the Self, who we really are. The irony is, this ignorance is enlivened by who we really are. Our wrong understanding actually has our consciousness informing it. That is why we are deluded into thinking that what we have enlivened is actually what we are. Our consciousness enlivens that which is not real.

Are you who you think you are? If yes, then.... Once we convince ourselves that we are this shrunken self, we do not want to be restricted. We want to be free. We want to be free to be "me." No one wants to restrain the shrunken self. We believe that the restraint of *sadhana* stifles who we are.

The truth is: *sadhana is* unsafe for the shrunken self. When we practice, there is no place for the shrunken self. The shrunken individual wants to do whatever it wants. When we "just" practice by going into the Heart, the individual feels like it is being punished. In Truth, though, there is no shrunken self. We enliven this thing and then identify with it, so we believe we are being punished. If we had right understanding, we would know we were in fact being freed by practice.

If we believe we already know who we are, then *sadhana* is definitely not for us. *Sadhana* on all levels will feel like prison if we think we are who we think we are. In the ashram in India, when I would walk around to make sure everyone was at the chant, people would be hiding as if the chanting were the most horrible thing they could be made to do. We were punishing these people by making them participate in activities they originally thought they wanted to do.

People ran away from the daily program; they most certainly ran from the internal practice. People thought bliss was just going to come spontaneously. After the bliss of the beginning subsided, people did not know or understand what they were supposed to do internally. The outer schedule was all they knew, and when this was not blissful, then they avoided the practice, they ran from what they saw as restriction and imprisonment. So many teachers have been characterized as tyrants because they do not have their students in bliss all the time. Remember, the teacher cannot change the student. The student changes himself by following the teacher's instructions. The practicing student is working to let go of being identified with his individuality, and so does not see practice as prison.

Once we are no longer identified with our individuality, *sadhana* is no longer seen as a prison. The shrunken self then embraces the practice and surrenders willingly to its own demise.

The False Idol of Self-esteem....

Being strong-willed is not being willful, and freedom is not getting to do whatever you want. Our first lessons in these realities come from our first caregivers. These people demonstrate and reflect for us how to live. They both model and teach.

Good leadership is like good parenting. Both embody and encourage behavior that is healthy for everyone involved. This means growth without injury, and no discrepancy between what is modeled and what is taught. A good leader will model what he wants the disciple, the follower, to do. This is the difference between a tyrant or dictator and a good leader. A leader should not ask the follower to do anything he himself does not or would not do.

Dictator	Absentee / neglector
Involved / directs / teaches / challenges	Lets be / gives freedom / allows room to grow

Good parenting breeds good governance. What we do as individuals, we bring into the world; what we do as families, we bring into our governments. The world is as we see it. We create our world. We create our problems. So much of what I am seeing in the United States and beyond is the outcome of bad parenting. People think being willful is having a strong will. So when their children act out of willfulness, the parents applaud the children's strength. Children who actually obey and show discipline are thought of as weak-willed and brainwashed, as somehow unreflective and inhuman. We have gotten this whole thing wrong.

Strong-willed	Weak-willed / brainwashed
Willful	Disciplined / obedient

Leaders and authorities who were brought up this way—to be spoiled brats—are tyrants and dictators. These leaders are not strong willed; they are willful. We have lost sight of this truth in an environment where everyone is fixated on self-esteem. When we promote self-esteem over character, we get a society of citizens who are both willful and brainwashed. This is the American dream: to be free to do what we want when we want.

Whatever happened to building character? When my children were young, I read them biographies of great people. We also read a series of stories about values, which connected each value to a historical figure. Patience, determination, kindness, humor, truth and trust, caring, courage, respect, fairness, learning, responsibility, honesty, love, integrity, helping, dedication, friendship, creativity—these are qualities that come from a disciplined will.

The worship of self-esteem is destroying our sense of responsibility. The truth is, we validate our rights by our contribution to society. Democracy cannot happen with ignorant people. In our ignorance, we all want to be treated with kid gloves, and our children have become outgrowths of that desire. We can't be happy if our children experience any discomfort. We are no longer educating our children, because when a teacher says a student got something wrong, the teacher has wounded the student's self-esteem. We have come to a place where self-esteem is a weapon. So the child watching the adults in her world goes to school and figures out how to manipulate through being the poor victim of the mean leader who is making her feel bad about herself. The meanness cuts both ways.

Because there is less and less real reflection, we have forgotten that if we "think" well of ourselves, then we also "think" poorly of ourselves. If the only way I feel good about me is when I get what I want, then I will be unhappy for much of my life. And if this is the pursuit of happiness, then my happiness will most definitely require someone else's unhappiness. We are allowing mere desire without discernment to rule our lives.

A leader or a parent operating according to this model will be not looking out for others, but pursuing their happiness at the expense of everyone else. If I operate this way, then everyone else exists to fulfill my desires. If I am on top, you should be focused on my needs. If you ever get to be in this position, then you will do the same.

Where does that leave our sense of leadership? In truth, only those who know how to obey can command. People who believe they are losing their will when asked to give up their willfulness have a difficult time seeing that obeying is an important step in learning leadership.

Freedom does not mean no discipline, no structure and no limits on doing what I think I want. Freedom means responsibility. Without a disciplined framework, we cannot have a civil society. Following a framework goes deeper than this as well. We can follow the framework of a spiritual or religious tradition. But without imbibing the essence of that tradition and practicing its disciplines, we will be neither spiritual nor free.

When we are disciplined, we actually open up options that we never had before. We have freedom. When we encourage freedom as indulgence, the range of activity is so limited. We are imprisoned in a chaotic world.

As we discipline ourselves or are disciplined, we do not lose our will but rather give up willfulness. With discipline, we are not at the mercy of distractions, and therefore we have freedom to act.

Free will is choosing to do it God's way; surrendering to Love.

The Ease of Spiritual Practice....

Working to redirect to the true center is not easy; sometimes it can be extremely difficult. Somewhere in popular discourse, "ease" became a word that sat next to "spirituality." Nothing could be further from the truth.

First of all, the question needs to be, easy for whom? If "spirituality" is a lifestyle driven by concepts and ideals, then our shrunken self does have an easy time of it. The ideals are the driving force to remain in the head and emote an effusive expression of those ideas. Next we ask, what is easy? The "what" of "spirituality" is an imaginative modification of the mind, which then remains focused on ideals and assures us of our righteousness and clarity. Our certainty lasts until we hit the rock of reality and hurt like hell, and we lose our sweetness and "spirituality" completely.

Hopefully, we then search for real spiritual practice and are lucky enough to find a good practitioner and teacher. Once we have applied ourselves to true spiritual practice, we will see the error of ideas and ease.

When we realize that true spirituality is not idea-based, not emotion-based, not personality-based, and not energy-based, we then approach the "whom." The appearance of ease disappears and the confrontation and hard work become clear. As we continue down this path, we will see the value of hard work. We will understand how little we understood before, and we will want to delve deeper into the true practice—which, though not easy, will remove our pain and misery.

Getting the outside world to change is not the goal of practice. If we align ourselves properly, we will see that what must change is how we approach the world, though the world itself may not change at all. We will just relate with it differently, which will make all the difference to us. Our job is to change us. Our job is to remove our ignorance, to remove our attachment to the ephemeral centers of life, and return to our true center in the Heart. Remember: if you can perceive something, it cannot be you. You are the true perceiver. The shrunken self cannot be us, and we should know this because it is not self-illuminative. Sometimes the mind appears to be us, and sometimes we are aware of witnessing it. We are the perceiver; we are never the object.

So when we think we are practicing and we are "sweet" and "nice," look out. We are probably centered in an idea. In its fickleness, the mind will move on from that center to a new, more attractive center. None of these is who we are; they are just a bunch of words we have brought together to fool ourselves. We are locating ourselves in an ever-changing vehicle. Not until we let go and turn to the hard, disciplined work of real spiritual practice will the light of Grace shine and guide our effort in the right direction. Then we will rest in our true nature. Remaining in our true center no longer will be hard work; it will be just what we do and are. We will be riding the horse in the direction it is going, Home.

What Do You Prize?….

Misery loves company. That saying is thrown around like a trite and empty truism. But if we actually look at this phrase, actually feel this phrase, the truth and the sadness of it become evident.

Have you wondered why the phrase "Love loves company" does not have the same truth or reality? After so many years of peddling the removal of pain and the pursuing of Love and God, I am finally coming to understand why so few are interested in my product.

Misery loves company. People are more interested in maintaining their connectedness through misery than in freeing themselves and being with God.

God is One. God requires complete surrender. It is either God or the individual. Very few people actually want that. God demands too much to be with God. God just does not appreciate how hard it is. If God would lighten up a little, then maybe God would be an option. But just Love? Just God? Too limiting.

Misery is easy, and readily available. Without our turning inward, without even a lick of discipline, misery is there for us. So easy. So comfortable. Shared misery is what brings us together and what keeps us together. When confronted with the unacceptable prospect of Love, people will work resolutely to maintain their misery.

So here I am in the business of taking away people's pain. How stupid, how naïve. I offer a product few people want. When people actually buy my offering, they then either deny that they got it or at best hide it away as a guilty pleasure.

Baba used to say, "If you see me as a clown, then I am a clown."

Through the years, I have pondered this and never quite understood what he was saying. How could anyone see him other than as I saw him, a self-realized being living and teaching all of us the way back to God? In my naivety, I believed everyone saw what I saw and wanted what I wanted.

Baba removed my pain, and as he did that, he taught me how to do it for myself. Baba wanted us to be free, not dependent on him. When he left his body, I struggled because I loved him so much and missed him. I felt he had left me; but he had not. He gave me the way out of pain and inward to God. Every day, as I remove the next vibration of pain and move further on the path, Baba is with me, encouraging me to practice.

I approached teaching with that same naivety, believing that everyone wants the removal of pain that comes as we walk Home to God. Most people don't want their pain taken away; they come to me to challenge themselves and see if they can win by maintaining their misery and sense of self. Resistance is the characteristic that these people work to nurture. They have eyes only for power and control, not love. Maintaining their misery is the goal. I am a circus act, a carnival game that allows people to test their sense of self. People want to win the stuffed animal and go home feeling secure in their accomplishment.

So for the few who want their pain actually removed: Love loves company.

Fellow Travelers….

The greatest warriors know that fighting is the last resort. Resistance is a form of fighting; it may look benign but can be insidious. When we are committed to our individuality, we will quietly resist anyone or anything that threatens our sense of self. This form of fighting is a disease that can destroy a person's spiritual journey.

"I can't surrender to another person." "I need to think for myself." "I can do the practice without someone directing me." "I don't need a teacher." All these statements are a form of resistance in someone who wants to do spiritual practice. Their sureness reveals the problem that we are dependent already and do not know it. We are surrendered to a voice that undermines any chance of moving forward on the path, the posturing of a self-taught person who already knows everything. Listening to that voice makes for an arrogance with no grounding in the experience of the Truth.

To reach that Truth, the first step is to cease believing that "sure" voice that wants to run the show. Before we can get to non-duality, we have to surrender to something greater than who we think we are. God, the Self, has to be allowed in the room. Compared to God, that sure voice suddenly sounds shrunken and shrill. Another important step is submitting to a teacher. It is not personal. The teacher is not just a louder voice. The teacher has to have surrendered to a teacher and to God. Unless we genuinely submit to a true teacher, we will resist Grace.

But what about testing the teacher? Absolutely. This is done by actually committing to the practice and seeing if it works for you. Testing is not a power struggle. Testing is not resistance. Testing is actually listening and obeying and seeing if there is validity in what the teacher teaches.

"But I do not want to change anything in my life." Well then, do not start down this path. There is no way to walk down the spiritual path without change. And are you then saying you do not want to give up your misery? Because if you want to get rid of it, your life is going to change. Regardless, there is always change. The change may unfold so slowly that it looks like constancy; but that sameness is not real.

This is where I am going: down the path to God. Do not try to fight me or convince me not to go. Do not say you want to come along and then resist. You do not have to come now. You can wait until later.

This is how I am getting there: by boring into the Heart and letting go of my individuality. Being with my experience moment to moment, letting whatever comes up from the Heart come up, and functioning appropriately on the physical plane. I get there by surrendering to God and Guru. By doing what they tell me because they want what is best for me. By resting in the Heart.

If you want to come along, I would love to have you join me in this journey. I am not in competition with you. I am not going to convince you. I love to share. If all you want to do is resist, then this is not the place for you, and I wish you luck.

Imagination Isn't Practice....

Sit in the room and be realized. Do not offend anyone or make anyone uncomfortable. Then leave and resume your ordinary habits. Is this what you think *sadhana* is?

Around Baba, there were people who did just sit around and then go home. Their discomfort came from their fellow ashramites, so their interactions and relationships looked very much like the ones back home. Baba would sit and smile and say, "Meditate on your Self. God dwells within you as you." These people believed that by showing up and hanging around, they had imbibed all that was needed, and there was nothing more. They could have powerful *shakti* experiences around Baba and imagine their own place in the universe. When they returned to their homes, they would continue "*sadhana*" by living life as before and occasionally sitting, maybe even religiously, and imagining their experiences with Baba.

Sitting with Baba and experiencing bliss happened for me also, but I did not want to imagine. I did not want bliss only when I sat for meditation. That would have been just like when I had formerly relied on Tai Chi Chuan for my bliss. I had already done that. I wanted bliss all the time. I did not want to imagine and then be slapped back into relative reality. I wanted the Real.

I did not want Baba as an abstraction, or the teachings as abstract. The lineage was not about imagining, or about having a great awakening and then being realized. We had to, and have to, walk the path Baba walked. That does not mean adopting particular external trappings. That means doing what he modeled: surrender of the shrunken self.

That surrender will probably remain no more than an abstraction unless you have a teacher—a teacher willing to do battle (as you should) with your shrunken self. *Sadhana* is not an intellectual exercise. We have to do something to get to the Self and then live the Self. What do we have to do? We have to give up our wrong understanding, our wrong identification with the shrunken self. We have to give up our shrunkenness.

"Of course we want to get rid of our shrunkenness," you might say. Really? Then do it. Right now. Be who you really are. It is not that easy. We do not realize how much we are attached to our wrong understanding. Again, this is where a teacher comes in. The teacher will be able to see this wrong identification and begin the process of awakening the student, not just once but all the time. This has to be done over a period of time, with the teacher constantly bringing the Truth to the student. Each student is different; hence the Guru-disciple relationship will manifest differently for each person, but the outcome is the same.

The teacher will shine a light on who you think you are, then call it what it actually is and show you your delusion. For instance, a student may think of herself as noble and generous when in fact she is a miserable doormat. Facing this reality will hurt. The teacher will then work with the student to remove her wrong understanding. So the Guru will be with us through the pain of our stupidity and guide us in the burning up of our delusion. Each time another layer of delusion is removed, we will feel lighter, and the bliss will be there for us.

If all you want is a course that teaches a tool or technique like meditation, then you do not want or need the Guru. If you want the Truth, then the Guru will be there and shine the light for you. Meditation will be just another tool you use in the process of removing your darkness. Meditation will support what the teacher is saying and guiding you to do in your daily life.

So whether you are a monk or a householder, whether you live in an ashram or house, know your commitment. And do not fool yourself into making your imaginings into something they are not. *Sadhana* with a living teacher is not easy for the shrunken self. It pulls back the curtain on the shrunken self's magic show. Only the Guru can do this with us.

True Normal….

There is a difference between conventional and normal. Most people, when they hear the word "conventional," tend to think in terms of other people and see particular situations, groups, cultures, or religions. The word "normal" tends to encompass a larger, vaguer area, and people tend to think of it as applying universally. Many times we conflate the two words, and in our limited view believe our convention is what is normal.

If we take "normal" as having a universal meaning, then it has to apply to everyone. The true normal, however, is being in harmony with God; this is our birthright. Normalcy is an underlying consciousness moving constantly toward God.

Convention is something else: it is a custom that can either coexist with true normalcy or conflict with it. In one family, the convention may be to yell. In another, the convention is to remain silent. Both, if their motivation internally is to be with God, can be normal with different conventions. When we go outside our home environment, we may decide to serve the situation and sacrifice our conventions, as long as the adjustment does not require us to be offensive and allows for us to keep our integrity.

Problems arise when the merely conventional is taken for the truly normal. The only way *sadhana* is going to be considered "normal" by most people's conventions is if the goal of *sadhana* is to have a beautiful, happy "normal" life. That would mean that the goal of *sadhana* is to be a perfected shrunken self. We tend to believe the one we call "me" is really who we are. From that standpoint, *sadhana* then will only clean up that "me" so that we have happy "normal" lives. We believe that the lives we lived prior to practice were "normal," and now with *sadhana* that "normal" life will be even better. Of course, each person's idea of "normal" life will look different, because each person's idea of "normal" will be based on the particulars of their early life.

The truth is, *sadhana* will and should turn your life upside-down. During *sadhana,* the shrunken self will crack. The façade and its conventions will be revealed for what they are. If you want to remain the "normal" you have always known, you will want to heal the crack. *Sadhana* will be seen as a battle against the teacher in order to remain "normal" and "true to yourself." If you aid the teacher in further breaking up the façade, then the truth that your "normal" was only convention will be revealed, and you will be able to free yourself from that attachment.

The reality we are seeking in *sadhana* is not a thought construct. Your life as you understood it was just an idea that you constructed and called "normal." It will be exposed as nothing more than a vocabulary list that you formed into a story. Your narrative will look very different once it is examined and a light has been shined on it. Your life will not be the same. Thank God.

But most people, even those who consider themselves seekers, cling to their "normal." I keep finding seekers who say they want God but don't want to give up their "normal" lives. And they can maintain those lives—if those lives are in harmony with God. If your "normal" is dysfunctional, it has to go.

If we are truly normal, we will maintain our attention in the Heart and adjust our vehicles as required. In other words, we will be with our experience, let whatever comes up come up, and function appropriately on the physical plane.

This applies as much to groups as to individuals. Fitting in brings harmony. It may bring harmony and peace within the group but disharmony outside. It may bring harmony and peace within the group but disharmony within each of the group's members. We need to be careful about accommodating ourselves to various groups, fitting into different settings. If a group is inappropriate, then to be truly normal will mean not being in harmony with that group, and to fit into it will be merely conventional. We need discernment to decide when it is appropriate to fit in. If fitting in requires us to sacrifice without receiving fulfillment and love, then there is a problem.

These fourchotomies will aid you in freeing yourself from attachment to convention:

Fits in	Outsider
Conformist	Independent

Conventional	Authentic
Fits in	Defiant

You are wrong by my convention	You are right by my convention
You are free with integrity	You are bound to the wrong thing

Each of us has to make the choice to be truly normal rather than merely conventional. In order to make that choice, you have to know what your conventions are, and have experienced true normalcy. My sadness is in watching people choose to cling to convention when they have experienced true normalcy. Ultimately, the true normal is the Truth, and the Truth is *so'ham*: I am who I am.

Exceptionally Mediocre….

While away on a campaign, Zhuge Liang, the great Chinese strategist, became fatally ill. He wrote letters of advice to his nephew and son before he died.

To his nephew, Zhuge Liang wrote:

Aspirations should remain lofty and far-sighted. Look to the precedents of the wise. Detach from emotions and desires; get rid of any fixations. Elevate subtle feelings to the presence of mind and sympathetic sense. Be patient in tight situations as well as easy ones; eliminate all pettiness.

Seek knowledge by questioning widely; set aside aversion and reluctance. What loss is there in dignity, what worry is there of failure?

If your will is not strong, if your thought does not oppose injustice, you will fritter away your life stuck in the commonplace, silently submitting to the bonds of emotion, forever cowering before mediocrities, never escaping the downward flow. (transl. Cleary)

To his son, Zhuge Liang wrote:

The practice of a cultivated man is to refine himself by quietude and develop virtue by frugality. Without detachment, there is no way to clarify the will; without serenity, there is no way to get far.

Study requires calm, talent requires study. Without study, there is no way to expand talent; without calm, there is no way to accomplish study.

If you are lazy, you cannot do thorough research; if you are impulsive, you cannot govern your nature.

The years run off with the hours, aspirations flee with the years. Eventually one ages and collapses. What good will it do to lament over poverty?

(transl. Cleary)

Though written around 234 CE, Zhuge's words speak to us with great relevance. He is writing to us, guiding us to live our lives fully and with integrity. It is not the action we take that is mediocre; it is what we bring to the table, our intention, that makes our action mediocre. When we live in the vitality of the moment while resting in the Heart, our simplest action is filled with import.

Living in Swami Muktananda's ashram proved this to me every day. Baba's actions were always filled with Love and life. No matter what he did, whether sitting in the courtyard, feeding the elephant, walking in the upper garden, cooking or just yelling at us, all was full, rich and so alive. His very presence buoyed us up to a life we had not lived before. He always was encouraging us to live; to live fully.

Muktananda was extolling us not to live mediocre lives, but to choose lives filled with the love of God, the Self, who is present in every moment of our day. No matter how mundane our obligatory actions are, we are to live fully with God.

Unfortunately, we use our emotion to exaggerate the events in our lives so as to make them appear exceptional rather than mediocre. An example would be a person who thrives on conflict and crisis management. Crisis, along with heightened emotionality, becomes a peak experience imbued with significance. The crisis may just be "I don't know what to wear," but it is made into a pinnacle experience. We then believe we are rising to an occasion when we are only overcoming the simplest of tasks.

Mediocre	Exceptional
Realistic	Dreamer

In his study *The Mystical Theology of St Bernard*, Étienne Gilson describes the Cistercian practice of self-awareness, humility, and self-discipline:

Misery of man: to have lost the divine likeness; greatness of man: to have kept the divine image; to strip away the alien likeness with which sin has covered it over—that is what the novice first learns at Cîteaux. But, to strip it away, he needs must recognize it; that is to say, learn to know himself for what he has become.

Baba always said to see God in each other, and that means we have to see God in ourselves. Our true greatness lies in our being images of God; any other pretense of greatness is just the posturing of the small self. By doing as Zhuge Liang instructs—detaching from emotions and desires, and getting rid of any fixations—we can ensure that we will not spend our lives cowering before mediocrities and thinking of ourselves as exceptional.

Is your mediocrity exceptional?

Spiritual Practice Is Not a Drug....

There is a big difference between doing drugs, basking in *shakti*, and spiritual practice. That should be obvious, but it's not. With drugs, there is no self-effort, and the result is a counterfeit experience. We are continuing the shrunken self's delusion; we are on the grid. If we are lucky, we wake up where we started and have a great memory. Around a teacher, if we simply bask in *shakti*, we are fooling ourselves, mistaking supersensory experience for spiritual attainment. When the teacher passes on, the experience dries up. In true spiritual practice, there is constant self-effort over time, which will open us to Grace.

Spiritual practice brings us permanently to God and Love. We are then independent and free. Drugs bring us to dependency—on the drugs, and on a pusher. We can also treat *shakti* like a drug. The result is the same: we are never free. Depending on the drug, we either numb ourselves or delude ourselves into thinking all kinds of things.

The real issue is what people believe is the goal of spiritual practice.

If your goal is numbing, dissociating and having super, drug-like experiences, then you may as well just do drugs. The price is the same, and the lifestyle may be more indulgent for you. The shrunken self gets to be "enlightened," and you do not have to surrender anything. You have your idea of God, your idea of the world, your idea of everything. You will just need a good supplier of the drugs. Remember, you will be dependent on an outside substance—but not to worry, you are in charge of when you use it.

People who believe that dissociating, not feeling anything, and having *shakti* experiences is the goal—which is the same goal as the drug users—feel a little more arrogant because they actually worked enough to get an awakening. The problem is, they then allowed their shrunken self to take ownership of their experiences. As a result, they believe they really *are* "enlightened." They can then consider themselves graduated from the teacher and strike out on their own.

The problem with real spiritual practice is that we have to work. We can become the master only by surrendering to the Master: God. And though that sounds simple, it is anything but easy.

If God is what you really want, you will have to have a teacher. You will have to give up dissociating. You will have to give up your attachment to super-duper experiences. You will have to give up the one who wanted these experiences in the first place. Sorry, but that is the way it works. You will have to be awake. You will have to take off your blinders.

The way to true independence is to surrender our individuality, our separateness. The only one who is independent is God. When you say, "I do not want to be dependent on Rohini," you are right. Neither do I. I want to be with God. People used to say, "You are dependent on Baba." "Thank God I was" would be my answer. By surrendering to the Guru—who, by the way, is not an individual—I was able to begin the process of dissolving myself, so that the Self could manifest clearly. In surrendering to Baba, I am freer and more independent than I ever was before meeting him.

The true teacher fosters this true independence. The true teacher wants the student to become a master. Drugs never do. Any drug encourages us to adore it and need it. Then, the shrunken self is the master always, and we are dependent. The shrunken self dopes us—I mean, dupes us—with dope.

So what about the teacher? Following a teacher can be like using drugs if that teacher encourages numbing and blindness. But if you have a teacher who is surrendered to God, then as long as you surrender, your life will get better and better.

Use drugs, and your life will get worse and worse. It will crumble, and the time under the influence will become your main focus. With spiritual practice, your daily life and relationships come alive, and you are free to be you.

These fourchotomies reveal the misunderstandings of spiritual practice that can trip us up on the path, or take us completely away from it:

Committed to practice	Self-indulgent (paying attention to self)
Fanatical / obsessive	Self-restrained / measured (paying attention to self)

Dependent	Independent
Reliant	Arrogant (too arrogant to rely on anyone)

What it comes down to is that you should be reliant on the Guru, not dependent on Rohini. And you had better be reliant on the practice.

Climbing the False Mountain....

Self-esteem is nothing more than the shrunken self's opinion of itself. It is a tale told by an idiot. Any education that prioritizes self-esteem is a course in unreality; it leads the student on a needless journey across an imaginary landscape of illusory meadows and false mountains.

When we fixate on self-esteem, we fall prey to the delusion that accomplishment only comes in one of two ways: either effortlessly or through dramatic struggle. Either your minimal effort and work are automatically sufficient, or only an achievement that comes after great struggle will earn you praise and love. So we have to either be careless or put on a display of strength in order to earn or get love. We are too good to work, or we overcome and triumph. We stroll through a meadow, or we scale a massive peak.

It is easy to recognize the game of someone whose self-esteem is based on refusing to test themselves. It is much harder to discern when someone is playing the self-esteem game by turning what should simply be hard work into a dramatic struggle designed to make them look heroic.

The notion that self-esteem is born only of dramatic struggle encourages a desire to fail at first, even if the task is easy, just to make the accomplishment appear heroic. If it is easy, we need to make it difficult and have things go wrong so that we can fail, and then snatch victory from the jaws of defeat. When skill and capability are already in place to complete an undertaking, we must either remove tools or add increased burdens in order to make it worthwhile. A worthless task becomes invaluable when completed through struggle, while an invaluable task is worthless if completed with ease.

So we believe we have to struggle. If we are not struggling, then we are not doing. We create a challenge in order to consider ourselves heroes when we overcome that challenge. The truth is, in most situations, there is no need for the challenge, and the real hero is the one who acts with ease and accomplishes life without creating fake mountains to climb. We do not look heroic attacking what is not real.

Applying this to *sadhana* is easy. Good practice is not a fight. It is not denial or pretending; it is surrender to and acceptance of what truly Is. Misery does not make us spiritual. Overcoming a false challenge does not attain us anything.

We must not delude ourselves that *sadhana* has to be a struggle. That is part of why the Guru is so crucial to our practice: the Guru reveals our delusions, including the mistaken conviction that spiritual practice is inseparable from suffering. On the contrary, spiritual practice frees us from suffering. The Guru shines the light to bring us joy, not to make us struggle.

Avoiding Safety….

Our culture buys into, and sells, the delusion that the way to remain safe is either to be more dangerous than the people around you or to cut yourself off completely. Being the most dangerous person in the room can mean having the bigger gun, being more willing to say terrible things, being more erratic and unpredictable, or being more of an emotional terrorist. Cutting yourself off completely can mean living in a gated community, constantly editing the information that comes into your world or goes out of it, and dissociating—living in what appears to be a closed off room in your head.

Underlying all these choices is the unspoken, maybe even unconscious, belief that the only way to be "safe" is to be dead, figuratively if not literally. This fourchotomy reveals how we conflate safety and death:

Safe (in God's hands and knowing it, and knowing yourself and others and the terrain)	Dangerous (quick to injure, consciously or unconsciously; treacherous to self and others; no care; alienated)
Dead (refusing to be present)	Alive (fully present to self, others and situation)

Part of the problem is that people confuse *tamas* (inertia) with *sattva* (calm). True safety is not numbing; it is the stilling of vibrations. Being dangerous is creating vibrations—and inertia is a vibration. And only by stilling our vibrations can we reach Love, which is the only real way to be safe. But Love, because it removes the illusion of control, looks like risk, so people choose not to love so as to avoid risk. They choose not to care about others, even though they believe they do care.

The whole point is to make it safe for everyone by first making it safe for ourselves. To do this, we need to be comfortable in our own skin, knowing ourselves and being willing to have others know us as well. We have to know what we bring to the table.

In order to get to safety, we have to be willing to be uncomfortable at first and get rid of our "sure" and "absolutely clear" voice, which has never really worked anyway. We have to get rid of our habits. When we truly meditate, we shed our habits internally for a while, and are safe within and for ourselves. But when we stop meditating, we revert to habit. So we need to change how we relate to the world. Knowing the Self is crucial, but we must also know our shrunken selves.

In other words, we have to know our narrative of separate selfhood, inside and out. If your narrative is intact, you are not safe. You must be unsafe for your narrative, and this cannot happen until you have gotten to know it. The narrative was not built with your best interests in mind. This is why you must put your head on the chopping block every day. If you are not willing to do this, you will never be safe.

If we don't want to be safe, what do we do? Maintain our individuality. Deny our experience. Pretend we don't have a narrative. Say we're pure. Decide that everyone else is playing a part, but not us—we are the true Self. Everyone else is the problem. Say that we are true to ourselves, and then numb, delude, judge, and keep our eyes on the other. If we keep our eyes on the other, we don't know anything, because all we see is a projection.

It is a small step from here to becoming oppositional. The oppositional type has no Love; it is a narrative that believes it is the be-all and end-all, the judge of everything. Its core is the vibration of opposition, so it can only define itself in opposition to others. It can only survive in juxtaposition with what it decides is a hostile other, whether good or bad. It therefore becomes a sower of discord. Would the oppositional type be peaceful without someone else's violence? No: it needs others' violence in order to be peaceful. Others' violence is its peacefulness. If the other is peaceful, the oppositional type will bring violence.

No one is more unsafe than the oppositional type. Unfortunately, it seems to be multiplying all around us, always in the guise of intelligent assessments and unerring righteousness.

If we want to shed our unsafeness, we must give up our separateness. Our illusory separateness is broken up by Love. But we have to work to learn how to Love, and from where real Love comes. This takes time. We must beware the desire to have that work over with now. Habits do not go easily.

The question remains, why would we want to be safe in the first place? Because true safety means we are just being who we really are. By being who we really are, we are in harmony within and then function safely without. Love, being our true nature, is then our motivator.

Unidualism….

Baba used to tell the story of a man who was walking into town after meeting a Guru. The Guru had told him the Truth that God is everywhere. So when the man left, he continued to repeat those words. As he walked down the road, a group of villagers came running toward him, screaming, "Run for your life! Run for your life! Mad elephant! Mad elephant!" The man disregarded the warning and kept walking, repeating, "God is everywhere." Then another group of villagers ran toward him, saying, "Run for your life! Mad elephant!" The man walked on, saying, "God is everywhere, God is everywhere." Soon enough, he crossed paths with the mad elephant. Enraged, it kicked him, picked him up, and threw him in a ditch before rampaging off. Once the elephant was gone, the villagers came back and found the mangled man in the ditch. They put him in a litter and took him back to the Guru. "Oh Guruji," he moaned, "you said that God is everywhere." The Guru replied, "What makes you think God was not in the villagers warning you to run away from the mad elephant?"

The unfortunate man didn't heed the warnings because he was what I call a unidualist. He superimposed his idea of nonduality on relative reality. Big mistake.

In the words of the Zen Patriarch Hui-neng, "Though good and bad differ, the original nature is not dual." The importance of this sutra-like comment cannot be overstated. Hui-neng is not saying that nonduality is everywhere for everyone; he is saying that relative reality contains both good and bad, and we must be able to distinguish between the two. The original nature—the Absolute—is nondual, but we cannot know this nonduality until we are our original nature. It is only by being nonduality that we know nonduality. This crucial truth is what unidualists fail to see.

Unidualism is one of the most pernicious narratives out there—and, unfortunately, all too common. Unidualists believe they are seeing the big picture, and that their big picture is the universal Truth. They come in two varieties: intellectual and sentimental. And both types are dissociative.

I have met many people who speak as if everything is gloriously good or horrendously bad. They themselves, they believe, have correct and clear understandings. As they assess the world through the lens of unidualism, either everything is all good and they then miss any of the warning signs, or everything is all bad and they cannot see the revelations and opportunities right in front of them.

The intellectual unidualists tend to see everything in the world as bad and tainted. These unidualists believe they are smarter than everyone else because they are capable of seeing the universe as it really is: meaningless and bad. They view anyone with a positive view of anything as intellectually inferior and ignorant. They are really nothing more than cynics, who conflate their hopelessness and despair with wisdom.

The sentimental unidualists see the world as unfailingly good and themselves as spiritual, positive thinkers. They have in fact completely misunderstood both reality and true spiritual teaching. Even if they belong to a developed religious tradition, they come under the heading of New Age spirituality, which tends to embrace the misconception of imposing an idea of Absolute reality on relative reality instead of understanding that relative reality is dualistic and only Absolute Reality is nondual. As a result, they whitewash their own experience and everyone else's. This wrong imposition is the most common form of unidualism.

Anyone with any real spiritual understanding knows that the material world is dualistic. It is only experienced as Unity by liberated souls, *jivanmuktas*. If you project an idea of universal goodness or ill on the world, you have not grasped nonduality at all—you are a unidualist. The way to be truly nondual is to live in the awareness of Absolute Reality which is beyond good and evil.

What this means is that unidualism is a kind of no-man's-land between the realities grasped by both dualism and nondualism. It is a spiritual desert, and wandering in that desert and not knowing it means you can never grow, never move forward.

Give up your commitment to unidualism and you will begin to see the world as it is. That is not always easy, but it is much better than missing the whole point and wasting away in your own desert. In other words, work to give up seeing the universe as all bad or all good. Stop being a unidualist.

The Manchurian Candidate Student....

Some people do not have the capacity to see me. They decide me. So they never know me; they only know what they project on me. The picture they project depends on what they bring to the table unconsciously. And sometimes, I can't recognize myself in their projections.

These people already have a guru—their early guru. They are committed to that guru unconsciously. Usually, it is one or both parents—their first caregivers. I will see this, but they will deny it and are certain it is not true. In the ashram, Baba used to test people to see whom they followed. No one was independent, though they thought they were. They all had an early guru that they followed religiously, so they could never learn from Baba. I watched this resistance, but did not understand it. Now I do.

These people are actually like Laurence Harvey's character in *The Manchurian Candidate*. The people who brainwashed him picked him because they knew he was committed in a particular way to his mother, who was their agent. He is almost completely programmed to see his mother as an absolute authority on all things; all she has to do is cue him by showing him his trigger, the Queen of Diamonds, and he will follow her every suggestion. If someone else by accident shows him that card, he will react just the same. Only through a wrenching and ultimately fatal act of courage is he able to break through that programming.

For us, the early stages of *sadhana* involve exposing and disentangling from similar programming that has shaped our lives. We have to find a teacher who wants the best for us and has proved to be skillful and trustworthy. Assessing that teacher can be difficult, as we are still bound by our program. But there has to be a surrender to someone outside the program. People who are still unconsciously committed to their early guru will fight anyone who tries to free them, because they do not see freedom for what it is.

Their reaction is reflected in these two fourchotomies:

Know better than	Able and willing to learn
Testing / wrestling	Servile / hollow

Fight	Cooperate
Stand up	Cave in

Clearly, they have a problem with authority. They aspire to be their early guru, whom they believe to be all-powerful and all-knowing. For them, to accept any other guidance is to cave in, and to be willing to take instruction is to be servile.

So they really just come to have their egos affirmed. As long as my guidance dovetails with their chosen identity, I am a good teacher; as soon as the two diverge, I am no longer worth listening to. And as long as the focus is not on their individual selves but on abstractions and people in general, all is okay.

In other words, they like spiritual practice as long as it remains purely theoretical and no feelings get hurt. But I am a practitioner, so anyone who works with me is going to have to face themselves, and it will hurt. That is the nature of real spiritual practice. As Dzongsar Jamyang Khyentse puts it:

It is such a mistake to assume that practicing dharma will help us calm

down and lead an untroubled life; nothing could be farther from the truth.
Dharma is not a therapy. Quite the opposite, in fact, dharma is tailored
specifically to turn your life upside down—it's what you sign up for. So when
your life goes pear-shaped, why do you complain? If you practise and your life
fails to capsize, it is a sign that what you are doing is not working. (*Not for*
Happiness 8)

One woman who came to private classes some years ago did so because, in her mind, she was fine but surrounded by awful people doing terrible things to her, and she needed support dealing with them. As long as I didn't focus on her and made sure she knew that nothing was her fault, all was okay. But at some point, we all have to see that the common denominator for every terrible situation we're in is us. Once the mirror was held up to her, I became the mean person who didn't understand. This is all too common.

If someone wants to cling to their early guru and their shrunken identity, they can simply think of me as ignorant and unrefined, and of themselves as sophisticated and knowledgeable about themselves and the world.

Practitioner	Theorist
Ignorant / artless / naïve / unrefined / unsophisticated	Cultivated / sophisticated

The *Manchurian Candidate* student knows better than the teacher he is looking at. He is "independent"—but in the sense in which the word is used as code for unteachable and unmanageable. "Stay strong" is his power trip. He sees everything in terms of power. So around me, he feels agitated, because the *shakti* discomfits people who are into power.

The work of spiritual practice, though, is about discomfort—at least for the shrunken self. Often, the *Manchurian Candidate* student's belief is that if you deny problems, they will sooner or later go away. If someone calls a problem a problem and deals with it, that person is accused of creating problems. So I end up being cast as the promoter of problems.

Then comes the disrespect. Convinced that listening to me means caving in, the *Manchurian Candidate* student resents being taught. "I can't do it without you, but I hate your guts": this message comes through in countless ways. And that student then rationalizes his rudeness. "If you're spiritual, none of this should bother you," he thinks, "so I can say whatever I want to you." No, he can't. It's still rude. At this point, I may need to raise my voice as I speak to his underlying vibration of arrogance, defensiveness, and hostility. Then the recalcitrant student can regard me as a tyrant. It never occurs to him that the real tyrant is his commitment to his early guru, which dominates his life.

To be clear, I am not talking about legitimate testing and wrestling and questioning. It is one thing for new people to question—that is completely appropriate. But when people who have studied closely with me for years, who have been shown the validity and value of the practice, continue to be skeptical and believe me to be cruel for telling the truth, they need to leave. They need to return to their original teacher, whom they have never really left.

The real question is this: how many times does someone's life have to be dramatically changed for the better for them to decide that a teacher like me is worth listening to? People committed to their early guru will not even be willing to frame that question; they will confront the true teacher's authority with the smugness and authoritarianism of their own sure voice.

Authority	Authoritarian
Smug	Stalwart / disciplined

On the other hand, when you do practice—when you work to be with your experience, let whatever comes up come up, and function appropriately on the physical plane—you will appear appropriate to most people in the world. If you are videotaped acting appropriately, then no matter what others are doing, you will look appropriate on tape. When you project onto a true teacher "tyrant" or any other kind of authoritarian tag, you look inappropriate. Watch your tapes.

Spiritual practice is not easy, and it is definitely not comfortable. Like the character in *The Manchurian Candidate*, you have to face and dismantle the forces that have controlled you. If you don't want to do that work, don't blame the practice. You can always stick with your early guru.

Happy-go-lucky….

I am writing this out of a deep sense of sadness as we keep heading down a road that hurts us all. Many years ago, I worked with an eleven-year-old who was extremely troubled. His parents were a big part of the problem, though there was no recognition of that fact. What I heard over and over again was the phrase, "He was such a happy-go-lucky kid. I don't know what happened." From this and several other situations, I grew to realize that "happy-go-lucky" is in truth a euphemism for someone whose heedless destructiveness is obscured by a bubble of carefreeness. Depending on how we have been raised, we can believe we are fun-loving without realizing that our fun comes always at the expense of others.

We talk among ourselves and in the media about addiction and epidemics of all kinds. Happy-go-lucky is an epidemic. These fourchotomies show how this public health problem manifests.

Happy-go-lucky (easygoing, fun, carefree)	Uptight / humorless
Heedless / destructive	Conscious / responsible

"Happy-go-lucky"	Careful / reflective
Spontaneous / unburdened	Rigid / depressive

If instead of facing this epidemic we continue to call our behavior "fun," then as we grow, our destruction will also grow. We then will find ourselves in a situation where we believe we only misbehaved for "twenty minutes" when in fact we have a long history of wrong action that got us to that twenty minutes.

People who are called happy-go-lucky generally do not present as mean. They appear fun-loving but are careless and reckless, and they can produce the same destruction as a vicious person. It is usually a surprise to others that these people are found to be in trouble, and they continue to be called happy-go-lucky. They are the inevitable products of the destructive belief that the good life is a life free of responsibilities and consequences. A carefree life.

Indulged	Disciplined
Fun / free	No fun / imprisoned

Lascivious	Safe
Fun	Humorless

Flippant	Considerate / respectful
Witty / fun / playful	Boring / unimaginative

On a tear	Easygoing / lets be / fun loving
Taking care of business	Confused / befuddled / unclear

Instigating / inciting	Secure / nonattached
Inspiring / funny / playful	Apathetic / disconnected / unresponsive

If we look at the above fourchotomies, we see "fun" in every one of them. As a culture, we talk about safety, but we really are going for fun. So children are encouraged to have fun. Parents are supposed to be fun. School is to be fun. And on whose terms? The children's. How scary is that? How unsafe is that?

We are now a culture that sees responsibility as nothing but a burden. Our self-absorption leaves no room for accountability, and the consequences are horrific. Recently in Virginia, a woman dropped off her three-year-old at day care and proceeded to work. After work, she again got in the car and drove all the way to collect her eight-month-old before going on to pick up her three-year-old. Only the eight-month-old had never been dropped off. The baby was still in the car—in the car all day and now dead. The mother hadn't noticed. She is now facing charges.

When bringing up my two sons, I always spoke about causes and consequences. Many people disapproved of the way I raised my children to be adults. The belief was that parents should insulate, not expose. My young sons followed the police cruiser in which I accompanied that happy-go-lucky eleven-year-old to a psychiatric hospital. They recognized how destructive his decisions had been. They saw the consequences of happy-go-lucky, and understood that we each have agency and choice. It was an important lesson for everyone.

If we are all supposed to be happy-go-lucky, then there are no adults. We have removed adulthood as a desirable choice. We all aspire to remain our idea of children: carefree and with no responsibilities or consequences. We have reached a place where we do not reflect on our own actions and how we are subtly heading toward those "twenty minutes" or eight hours of devastation. We are longing for our good ole days, which never existed except in our heads. The truth is, if we were to actually be responsible and discern the consequences before we proceeded, if we were conscious and awake to our lives, we would not be looking at destruction in our wake.

The Way Not To Be….

In the ashram, people tended not to like me. My presence has always had a strange ability to bring out whatever is inside of people. Depending on where they are internally, being around me will bring out the worst or the best. Many times Baba would direct me to walk into some office of the ashram, and shortly thereafter something unexpected would appear.

In *sadhana*, the worst and the best both keep us from Love. Both are parts of who we think we are. They have to be pulled into conscious awareness; then they can be disentangled from who we truly are. When these traits are positive, people tend to be pleased with themselves and with me. When they are negative, the response is not welcoming.

We may be identified with the negative but call it our best trait. Then, when the world does not receive it the way we believe it should be received, we will be defensive. We may think of ourselves as assertive and outgoing, only to find that when the world experiences our assertiveness and outgoingness, those qualities are received as rudeness and intrusiveness. On the other hand, if we do not value what is truly great within us, when it comes forth, we will barely recognize it. When I acknowledge such a trait in a student, she will not believe me.

Until we let go of such wrong identification, we will see goodness as whatever we believe is "the way to be." For each of us, "the way to be" is different. For example, if your "way to be"—your "goodness"—is not to take care of yourself, then if I advise you not to buy a suspect car, you will go ahead and buy the car, because I am advising you to take care of yourself. I am not "good"; I am encouraging you to depart from your idea of "the way to be." If being "good" means not exercising any discernment, then no matter what anyone else says, you will not exercise discernment. It is crucially important for each of us to discover our "way to be," our "good."

Our delusional notions of "the way to be" lead us into some very interesting thought-forms. Let's say you believe that hate is power and Love is weakness. Look at the nonsensical thinking that follows:

Hate is power. If you have no hate, then you have no power. Therefore, if you let go of hate, you are choosing to be a weakling.

Love is weak. If you are weak, then you love. Therefore, if you value love, you are hopelessly weak.

Life is about Alphas and people subjugated by Alphas. You have two choices: be an Alpha, or be subjugated. Therefore, the one condition that makes no sense is equality.

People also approach spirituality with their understanding of "the way to be." For instance, they might decide that "goodness" can never be colorful, or that spirituality is just a way to compensate for their perceived inadequacies.

Goodness is about drabness. Stylish, colorful clothes are bad. Spirituality is good. Therefore, if you wear stylish, colorful clothes, you are not spiritual.

If you are bad at life, spirituality will divinize your inadequacy. If you are spiritual, you must be bad at life. Therefore, the more you are spiritually committed and advanced, the worse you are at life.

Many people think that because I have committed my life to spiritual practice, then I must be completely inept in what they think of as "the real world." I no longer bother to demonstrate otherwise.

As I have said many times before, "goodness" is not the goal. It has nothing to do with Love, and it isn't compatible with happiness. We will never be happy until we are perfectly happy not to be "the way to be."

The Way Not To Be, Part Two....

I wrote recently about how we all must uncover what we believe is the "way to be" in order to free ourselves from that idea of "goodness." We may know intellectually that our "way to be" is wrong—even that it is destructive—yet on an emotional level, we are still sure it is good. But the truth is, the "way to be" is what hasn't worked.

We have to be ready to not be the "way to be." This can only be accomplished by digging in and being with our experience and letting whatever comes up come up. We cannot intellectualize and then think we have it. We do not have it then, because what is doing the thinking is not us.

So our wrong understanding is our garbage. If we want to be clean and clear within ourselves and in the world, we have to be willing to get rid of our garbage. We have to see our own crazy logic and let go of it.

Our idea of the way to be, our goodness, is a particularly nasty piece of our garbage. We have to put it out and let it be taken away. We have to participate in the removal of that garbage. Isn't that what a student is supposed to do: put out the garbage for its removal and incineration?

I'm an internal sanitation engineer. I can remove and incinerate a student's garbage—if the student is willing to work with me to actively and consciously separate the garbage from what he must keep. But I watch people say, "No, I want to keep my garbage. I can't tell the difference between the garbage and what I need to keep, so I'm keeping it all." They are hoarders of garbage.

If a student believes that her garbage is pure, is she going to allow for its removal? No, and so she's going to resist getting to this place because she's so sure she's pure, so sure of who she thinks she is.

The responsibility of the student is to speak up so that she can get clear and to know what the garbage is. We can't see unless we open up and show what we have. If we sit in a corner and are miserly, our garbage is not going to be removed.

If the garbage is removed, what do we get? Peace. And what do we find? Was there anything to attain? Was it always there? Yes, always there. And the teacher says, "It's there. Just remove this. If you just let go of that… it's there."

Some people turn *sadhana* itself into garbage. They approach *sadhana* because they feel they are not successful at life; once they do *sadhana*, they can now feel that their inadequacies are karmic and are just lessons on the path. They then divinize their "way to be" and never have to change. So instead of healing their brokenness, they exalt it as a spiritual virtue, and see their failures as signs of their spirituality.

Once we resort to that delusion, it will take tremendous vigilance to catch it and root it out of our lives.

Ultimately, our garbage is our attachment to the vehicles as being the individual self. And though we must let go of all attachment to a separate self, the individual is still going to manifest and appear to be the individual. The Guru, which is the *shakti*, is going to funnel into and through the vehicles unimpeded—but it is still flowing through those vehicles. As soon as the individual, if there's any individual left, takes ownership of the *shakti*, everything is shrunken and deflated, and the source, the Guru, is cut off from the individual. We are back in our pile of garbage. Hui-neng explains this:

The existence of state refers to the four phenomena of self, person, and so on. Unless you get rid of these four phenomena, you will never realize enlightenment. If you say "I am inspired to seek enlightenment," this is also self, person, and so on, which are the root of afflictions. (Hui Neng's Commentary on the *Diamond Sutra*, transl. Cleary, 126).

People living the "way *not* to be" are rare. As Hui-neng says, these people will have "no image of self, no image of person, no image of being, no image of liver of life." They are fully living their lives without obstructions of any kind. They are not attached to their wrong understanding; they have given up their garbage. They are *living* life and are truly alive.

Notion-Building....

If you are identified with your idea of the "way to be," then you are not practicing. You are not being with your experience, letting whatever comes up from that experience come up, and functioning appropriately on the physical plane. Instead, you are keeping a lid on vibrations, or calling them something other than what they are, to keep your narrative intact.

But your narrative is just a notion you've built. It's not even your life. And when you're notion-building, you're not practicing. I'll say it again: you're not being with your experience, you're not letting whatever comes up come up from that experience, and you're not functioning appropriately, because you're functioning according to a notion.

If you think of the "way to be," you don't question it; there's no reflection. It's the way it is. But it's just an idea. When that notion is confronted, you will defend it—you're obstructed from seeing clearly by your "way to be." And no matter how happy someone else is, if their way of life diverges from your "way to be," then you will be unable to see its value. If you were actually practicing, you would in fact dismantle your own "way to be."

If you are living the "way to be," you are only playing at spiritual practice. You are superimposing your "way to be" on everything and everyone, including *sadhana*. Your "practice" is all being done with notions. You have a notion that says, "I am a good person," or "This is love." But you are never checking out the actual vibration.

There are two ways not to be with your experience. If, when I am having a horrible experience, I only think, "This is horrible," I am not being with my experience. I am being with my notion. If I think, "I am having a horrible experience" or "I am having a wonderful experience," and I have put a lid on my experience, I may not be having either. How would I know?

If I have superimposed the word "love" on the vibration that should be called "putting up with," when I see people putting up with each other, I will say they love each other. If we take the fourchotomy of "put up with," we can see how people conflate, and how this superimposition works.

Put up with	Stand up for self
Accept	Intolerant

If I superimpose the word "accept" on the vibration that should be labeled "put up with," then I cannot really accept, I put up with, and insist that others put up with me. If I superimpose "stand up for self" on the vibration that is actually "intolerant," then I am not standing up for myself but just being intolerant. Until I am willing to call the vibration what the vibration is, I am just lost among my own notions.

We have all sorts of ways of notion-building. One of them is what we call "processing." How many times have I said not to process? Processing is notion-building. Worrying is notion-building. Intellectualizing. Rationalizing. There is a long catalog of words we use to notion-build around things we would rather not feel. Here are some:

Processing

Worrying

Intellectualizing

Abstracting

Dissociating

Rationalizing

Mitigating

Defending

Spinning

Wallowing

Judging

Inflating

Convincing

Notion-building prevents us from ever reaching resolution. Resolution happens when we accept our experience fully and are able and willing to call it what it actually is. When we do this, the "way to be" and all our other notions will dissolve. Because where are those notions? In the mind. If we are actually practicing, we will be in the Heart, and whatever notions occupy our mind will dissolve.

The "way to be" is not the way to be. Narrating your feelings is not feeling. The notion of the Heart is not the Heart. Real Love is not a notion.

Really Being Positive....

Calling something what it is is being honest, which is truly being positive. Calling something what it is is *not* negative. What is really negative is not calling something what it is; it is calling something what it is *not*.

So if I am practicing, then I am truly honest with myself. I can choose. I can see what is what and name it. So I am really positive. This has been a surprise for me and many other people, as I am often called negative. But I confirm, and affirm, what is really there, so calling me negative is calling me something I am not. Those who call me negative, then, are actually being negative themselves; they are judging, not affirming what is.

When we are positive in *sadhana*, we are being with our experience, letting whatever comes up from the experience come up, and functioning appropriately on the physical plane. We begin to call each vibration what it is. We have to be willing to make that shift, which means starting to dismantle our notions, our narrative. That is why people leave. They want to change the story they tell themselves, not still their vibrations. They have notions of love in their minds, and superimpose them on the vibrations they have. They refuse to call their vibrations what they are.

If you are having a notion and listening to it and believing it, you are not practicing. At that moment, let go and go in; then you will begin to experience a vibration you did not allow.

If we guard the Heart, we can still our vibrations because we discern what they are and allow the letters to arise from the vibration and form words that call the vibrations what they really are. We are not denying or running away, and we are not calling the vibration anything it is not. We are then being positive, no matter what the vibration happens to be.

We are shining a light through our attention, and this light dissolves the vibration. This is very positive, and as we continue to practice, the stillness that comes allows the Love within to shine forth. We are no longer obscuring the truth.

If we remain in our heads, we will probably call our vibrations whatever we are comfortable with. We will judge and deny certain vibrations that we actually need in order to move forward in our lives. Under the guise of calling ourselves positive, we prevent ourselves from having what we need in order to resolve our life's lessons. We unwittingly will be negative and out of harmony.

Until we get out of our heads, we do not have a chance of being positive. Our heads are about notions and maintaining our narratives. Our words are more important than authenticity. As long as we are in our heads, there isn't anything that comes out of our mouth that isn't a notion. Whenever a vibration comes up, we will seamlessly transition into notion-building, into narrative.

All comes down to trusting your own experience—letting it come up without judging it. I always say, "I would rather make my mistake than someone else's." Not superimposing on my experience, but allowing whatever comes up from the experience to come up and being appropriate, allows me to see the world as it is, not as I would prefer it to be. If you trust your experience, you will begin to discern.

Be with your experience. People think I am naïve for saying this. They say it doesn't work, that the world does not really work that way. Practice really does work. When we are with our experience, being positive, and calling our vibrations what they actually are, we can see clearly, and all the options for acting appropriately will be available to us.

Appropriateness is then flexible. I cannot stress enough that appropriate does not mean "acceptable." Acceptable to whom? Appropriate is what is needed in the moment. If we act according to what we call "acceptable", we will be negative; we will be limiting our options according to our notions. We will not necessarily be appropriate.

This is all very positive, isn't it?

Torture for the Shrunken Self....

I recently heard that someone said spiritual practice was self-torture, and that I am a composite of negativity. It is and I am. For a lot of people that is the truth. So much of *sadhana* is uncovering the truth; the truth that lies under a giant fortress of lies. The delusion that who we are is the one that thinks is what keeps us locked in a fight against the truth. The thought form of torture manifests when we resist learning.

To resolve this, or anything else for that matter, is torturous and removes the pleasure we so pursue. If someone wants to keep the pain and misery of something secret and unresolved, then I am a torturer. Ganesh is the remover of obstacles; remember, that is what Baba used to call me. That is a function I perform. So someone who is wed to a secret and calls it all kinds of adjectives except the true one is going to not feel comfortable around me.

If who you think you are is who you think you will be at the end of *sadhana*, then you are in the fight of "your" life. *Sadhana* will be self-torture, because you are going completely in the wrong direction.

If you know that you are a prisoner of who you think you are, then *sadhana* is a jailbreak to the light of day.

Until that awakening, the shrunken self is a criminal who holds you hostage. You pay ransom and are never freed. You enable and indulge the shrunken self, and it only gets stronger.

We have to starve the shrunken self, and redirect our attention away from it, in order for who we really are to be revealed by grace. The shrunken self will feel that this is only self-torture until we no longer identify with it. Until then, the one who is complicit and the criminal are one and the same: the shrunken self that powers rather than loves.

The irony is that when you are committed to power, you are the criminal, not who you really are. And you are the torturer.

Grace is experiencing that you are not who you thought you were; it is the experience of "knowing," not thinking an idea. Changing your idea of who you think you are is not the same thing as being who you are. It is a beginning, and will help you see that thoughts are just thoughts. We then have to let go of those thoughts, even the good ones, to get to the emotions and then more subtle vibrations until we are at stillness. From the stillness, we arise.

As long as we believe the one who is thinking is us, we are in prison. A great delusion is that somehow we are instinctual animals that do not need to be trained, that everyone will learn the same functioning and life skills through osmosis and time. This cannot be further from the truth.

Christ makes it clear that the choice is either the prison of the shrunken self or the daylight and freedom of Love. "Whoever comes to me and does not hate father and mother, wife and children, brothers and sisters, yes, and even life itself, cannot be my disciple. Whoever does not carry the cross and follow me cannot be my disciple." (Luke 14: 26-7, NRSV).

This speaks to the fact that as long as we are wed to our family system, we cannot go to God. The first step is to hate our family system; then we disentangle from that system until we see it for what it is. Finally, we are free to be with family again but with the Love of God within. We know that it was not our family that ruined our life; it was following the map of the family system and thinking it was taking us back to God. It never could. We tortured ourselves with our own resistance to God. Now we can see that *sadhana* and the Guru take us to our true nature: Love.

Turn to the Fire, and Enter

bored room....

time   passes   and
                 thoughts   bore
  us   to   boredom
     the   day
             the   night
       the   inbetween
      productive   lazy
      crazy   easy
time   still
                  passes
    distraction   concentration
time   still
            not   still
    moves
         change
evolves
        all   even
      jury   duty

number is up....

made   it

                                        land of

            mundane

sit   in   plastic   rooms
        gray   and   grays
                    black   with   whites
                        grays
    hard   surfaces
                                        waiting
waiting   to   not
            be   called
    judging   fairness
            seems   so
empty   yet
        a   right   and
    rite   for   us
                all
        day   be   over
            and
after   last   time
        jury   duty   done

summoned....

wait   no   more   then
                 wait   some
                                   more
          called   wait
moved   wait   stand
          wait   go   wait
life   is
                                   jury   duty
     questioned   yes
          be   seated
     yes   no   be   seated
not   called
     return   to   stark
               gray
     wait   again
          pray   for   gray
               until   the   end
                         of   the
          day

Extended Family

immune to distance....

the herd heard   what did
       they   say   over the

                            cliff   we   go

heard the herd   immunity for

                 community
                           h
burn up our   suffering not   our
                           m
                           e
                           s

whether by   illness   or   violence

both   destroy our   physical homes

prostration   as   protestation   heals

surrender   our   homes   in order

to free   our   selves   to walk   the   walk

in herd   toward   Love the Love

unemployed....

world is shrinking
    universe opening

                no one home
     too crowded

better
    all

  more room

              nothing to do

doer is everywhere
          no place to
     go

    all going

    all doing

form
        goes
          no where

    all still

    all vital

choice....

don't do

        it

though fun
       for
whom
   what
      where
         when
why

don't do
     it

who
       wins
we
      lose

don't

who is
     i
winning

not me
    not you
       not us
just
      it

be
  instead
love
  instead

don't do it

passage....

across
valley
up
mountain

only to go
back down
mountain

across
bridge

along
two edged sword

challenge
for what
never for who

we are

the road back....

start in hell
the journey is
to move

keep moving

or
stay in hell
home

or
through hell
to all the facts

face in purgatory

relief
remorse
one road then
alone

not lonely
we each climb
to community

heaven
recognize
each other
as
each us
no
other

recognize

Absolute Fact

at the table....

bring to the table
  good food
  good company
  good cheer

care cares for all
 no one is left
   with
   out

whether flat or round
 the table is
   full
nurtured by God

no pretense
 lies
 hate
see what's on the table

know what you
   brought

clean yourself
   to see
 the Real table

our narratives
  starve us

leave us hungry
  for truth

though full we can't
  partake
 we fed so long

on empty
satisfied not an
option

retreat before
returning to
the table
wash thyself
to see
what we have
missed

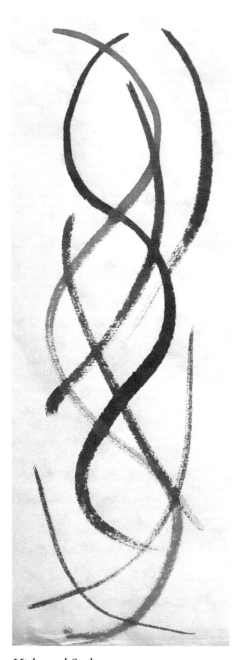

Hide and Seek

Baba's full moon dream....

in an outdoor amphitheater
someone asks
what about sadhana?
I ask
have you experienced
been in the Bliss

light of God
for two weeks at a time?

I fall into that experience
brilliant pure white light
filled with Bliss
nothing else
I come back

return to here
the person answers
no
I speak
spiritual practice is not about knowing the world
knowing the world is easy

another man asks Nature?
then corrects himself before I do and says
no still part of the world

I say how sad there have been so few
over all time
even the ones that have gone have
not written the map so clearly
for each of us has something slightly different

so difficult the path
I start sobbing
and wake up

stay in your lane....

the car mechanic
              repairs   and
works   on   with   cars

the medical doctor   pt   kinesiologist   acupuncturist
            repairs and works on   with
                              physical bodies

the psychologist   therapist   psychiatrist
            repairs and works on   with
                              psychic instrument

energy worker works
              on   energy

they stay in

              their lanes

the guru removes
              ignorance

                        detaches attachment

              of vehicles

brings us to
              light
                    love
                              who we are

what remains….

take a fact
from a fact
fact does not remain

Perfect remains

light the sky
can't see the stars
fog protects our narrative
hides the facts

the facts remain
a safe deposit
no light shining
the fog remains

Perfect remains

with the stars
the microscope misses
the facts
the story remains
as do the facts

Perfect

Discussion

unsubscribed....

national geographic
                    gorgeous
          gouge

rural   but
        not
                              fences
fertilizer   focus
            on   paddys

      traffic   traipse
            through
    dirting   dust

intentionally   in
          idealic
                          idea
      inconsistent   inconsiderate
    smells   sounds
    sock   souls

all   contribute
      crushing   ferns
            cry
        praying   prey
tiny wings   taking
          refuge   inside
      refuse   to   leave

all   biting
              we   laugh
              and   vacate
          no   subscription
              to
                          magazine

codebreaker....

God said

        no flood

so   we are   drowning

in   algorithm

we   drown   in

      narrative
which is the binding of
     matrika shakti
           magic used

by God to fool   us

     after   all

        God controls
           the world

within   world game

               one who has control

over
your narrative

       controls   your world

     God   provides   tools

    God   embeds   solution
in   all

fourchotomy   tool

unlocks   matrika

once   ununderstood

mother

revealed

can break

algorithm   narrative

children of God....

child centered
        learning
    we put
        God
            the guide
    on the side

    we grow
            off
        kilter

to   center
        we
                            require
            sage
                on the stage

    do not miss
    do not belittle
    do not misread

then God will
    move to the
            back
    and be
        the quack

the mastermind
    in the behind
    runs the
        show

    we do not
        respect
    we cannot

see
we cannot
revere
acknowledge

we become
the fool
in the pool
of
humanity

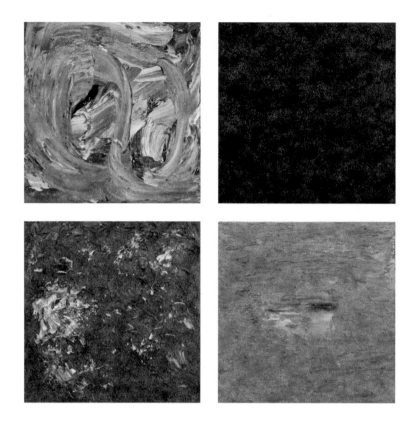

Empathetic

Empathetic	Unfeeling
Impressionable	Serene

CHAPTER THREE
RIGHT ACTION IN THE WORLD

Dismantling the Victim and the Bully....

We have become a nation of victims and bullies. Everyone is encouraged to adopt one role or the other. We seem to have lost our sense of character and of the honor in taking responsibility for our actions. Our media and public officials have taken to name-calling rather than discerning what actually may be going on. We are all so sure that we see everything correctly. *We* are good and right; *they* are bad and wrong. And everyone is saying the same thing. Each person is looking to usurp the role of victim.

Victim	Responsible / leader / in charge
Nice / innocent	Bully

Looking at the fourchotomy, we see that if we are a bully, then we are also responsible and in charge. The problem that I see with the victim is that the victim believes he is powerless—at the mercy of the bully. The bully will often say that it is not his fault and even feel victimized by the victim. Everyone is looking to be powerless and not responsible. Everyone wants not to be accountable.

The fact is, we are all responsible. Both the victim and the bully cannot say that they have no responsibility. How we act is totally our fault because we choose to be entangled in these attachments. We will claim that we don't participate; we will say "I wasn't planning on this." And though we say God is everywhere, we also say God wouldn't do that. What? God is all-knowing, all-powerful, and all-present, and He wouldn't do something that you decided he shouldn't do? So the God who does all is only responsible for what you decide? Who then is God? Your shrunken self has set itself up as God—do you trust in that God?

Baba used to say, "Love everyone, trust no one." From the standpoint of Absolute Reality, we should love everyone; and from the point of view of relative reality, we should trust no one. We do not know someone as much as we would like to think we do. Going back to the Christ narrative, we see Christ followed this creed. He was not surprised by what occurred. He was not a victim; Christ knew what was going to be played out and surrendered to his role and everyone else's. After Gethsemane, there was no victim or bully—only God.

Baba also said, "Strange are the ways of karma." We are never sure where we stand in any given situation. We may be creating karma when we think we are reaping it, and vice versa. The answer for all of us is in the way the great beings have modeled for us. They were detached, and uninterested in taking on the identity of either victim or bully.

Constancy in Practice....

Spiritual practice is not a crisis intervention to use only when we are in trouble. It is to bring us to peace not only for a moment but for all time. So we practice and get to a state of peace and then we go about the business of life. When we walk into the world, somehow we lose this peace. How can we maintain it? This is the question so many of us have.

If we just let go to a nebulous state with no consciousness, we will be lost quickly. However, if we are able to reach this peace with an awareness of going to the core of our being, to the Heart, and use our will to stay there, we can then engage with the world and not lose ourselves.

Sahaj samadhi is the state of being in the Heart and acting in the world simultaneously. We live then from the Heart. We are conscious of acting from the Heart and respond to the world rather than react to it. Again, our will has to be honed to keep our awareness in the Heart. This is the work at hand.

We tend to find peace and then go back to normal, not aware we can maintain the state we had in the wonderful meditation. What did I do in that meditation? What did I do internally to be at peace? I let go of my attachments and rested. Who was aware of that stillness? I was. Where was that I, and am I willing to consciously remain there? What did my five senses do during this time? They were inverted toward this I awareness. Can I engage in the world and keep the senses restrained, looking in and yet functioning? Can I keep my mind and attention turned inward and yet still relate with the world? Yes.

So the consciousness when we are at peace is disentangled and deep within. Our vehicles are turned inward to maintain restraint, and then we relate with the world from there. We come to ourselves in our practice and then never stop practicing. It is the practice that is so important: knowing what to do and then doing it all the time. Looking in and out simultaneously. Are we multitasking then? Or are we moving closer to Home and relating from there?

Katha Upanishad uses the image of a chariot to make the practice clear. The Self is the lord of the chariot. The chariot is the body. The intellect is the charioteer and the reins are the mind. The senses are the horses, and where the horses go is the objects of the senses. The body, the senses, the mind and any other venue from which to experience are all just vehicles for the Self. Without imbibing this understanding, we live the life of one with no restraint.

To live in peace, we have to practice and live where peace actually comes from. We must return to the Self and rest there. Resting and living in the Heart, we then can act from there. Peace is then the awareness of our daily life.

Act in Stillness....

We speak so many words, and then how much do we practice them? When I say practice, I do not mean "trying"; I mean actually "being" them. *Yoga Sutras* 2.18 says *prakrti* (Nature, material) exists for the experience and liberation of the Seer. The Seen exists for the sake of the Seer. Experience and liberation are then knowables. When liberated, the Seer has no need of *gunas*; all vibration (experience) is stilled.

So what are we doing here? This is a game God plays with God. It is not worth it to fight God. God wants you to win. So stop the fight. We are not here to fight God. God wants us to be happy, to be who we really are. Isn't that what we want? Or is it? That depends on who we think we are. If we believe we are the series of thought constructs that are constantly being expressed, then we will be fighting God all the time. We will not want to be in harmony with God.

We may ask, who is God anyway? God is not any idea that comes into our mind. God is, period. Everything is within God. There is nothing that is not God. "So if that is the case, then why should I change? All is God, even the me that is not me." Fine, do not change; you are no different than a gnat. You are then just blowing in the wind with no awareness, bumping into objects that bring pleasure or pain. You have no control over your universe because you do not know where you actually live.

We reside in the Heart. That is where God intersects with us. Is God in my big toe? Will I meet God there? No. In the Heart. Our job is to disentangle from our vehicles and return to the Heart, which is where we started. We are to return to the stillness of knowing who we are. From there, we then enliven our vehicles while remaining anchored in the Heart. We need to be still.

"But I need to pay my bills and do my job." No one said not to. We are all to do our mundane tasks, our obligatory actions. Do those tasks, all activity, and stay in the Heart. This is not about being still in the laboratory and then leaving to go back to normal. This is not about the body being still and then active. This is not about the mind being still and then active. This is not about being in the Heart one moment and then in the head the next, or being in the Heart one moment and doing actions the next. This is not one and then the other. This is about both at the same time.

We are to live in the world always perceiving the unity in diversity. We are to be in the Heart all the time, not just at moments, glimpses, or in times of crisis. All moments reveal the unity as well as the diversity. Every moment, every second, and when we forget, we should then remember and turn back immediately. We are not to wait for a "good" time to practice. All times, all places are good times to practice. We are to focus in to the Heart and be aware of the outside at all times. When we rest in the Heart and look out from there, we put forth right effort.

If when we meditate with eyes shut, we are focusing out; we are promoting a focused mind and the acquisition of power. Then when we open our eyes, we are focused intently on the physical and we can easily become seducers or be seduced.

Meditation practiced with eyes closed focusing in toward the Heart brings us to calm and promotes surrender—surrender of what is not Real. So that when we open our eyes, we are still connected to the stillness and we can function appropriately with a sense of detachment rather than dissociation.

Practicing correctly and continually brings us to live in stillness with God even while we perform our daily activities. There is no outside activity that cannot be performed while we are resting in the Heart; that means all activities can be performed while being still in the Heart. This is about choice, not about whether doing this is possible. If we choose to turn in, yes, for a time it will be difficult, but God wants us to win. God wants us to be in harmony with God while we act in the world.

When Are We Responsible?....

What would happen if God decided He wanted to no longer be responsible? What would happen if God decided He wanted to be selfish instead of Selfish? Who would He be? He would be us.

That is how we got here; did you forget? For God to not be responsible, He has to limit Himself and pretend nothing He does impacts on Him or others. God has to believe that others are not He, that He is not whole. He has to think of Himself as separate, imperfect, and the doer in limitation. He is then us.

It seems absurd, and yet this is how we play. We are One with everyone—on our terms. We are responsible when being responsible looks good and is easy. When All is working out for us, that is when we decide we are in charge and responsible. As soon as our life is not "the way we wanted it to be," we are blameless. We are victims. It's not our fault. All of a sudden, we have no say, no choice, no responsibility for whatever is happening. Others did this or God did it, but not us. We are spiritual and doing *sadhana* as long as it suits our worldview and our needs.

Thank God, God does not play according to these rules. Yes, God is everywhere, but we do not know it. We may think it, believe it, but we do not experience or live it. From the standpoint of the Absolute, God is All and responsible for All. But because we live in relative reality, we cannot see the greater Reality. We are in truth the many from the One. If we actually worked and did *sadhana*, then we would see the Absolute underlying the relative. But we tend to be so in love with ourselves and the diverse that we are blind to Reality. We say, "It's not my fault, I am human." The truth is, "Yes, it is my fault; I am human." We are responsible for ourselves and each other.

How do we evolve back to being responsible and in harmony with God? We have to evolve from Inertia to Activity to Calm. These are the three principles of which everything is made. Everything is a combination of these three vibrations, including us.

We begin as inert: dull, and with nothing to offer except reckless apathy. When we are here, we are definitely not responsible for anything. All cause is outside. God is only outside. We are ignorant and believe we are smarter and clearer than anyone else. We barely impact the world in any way other than contributing resistance.

If we work at least some on becoming educated, if nothing else in order to have a job of some sort, we then begin to move toward activity. The problem here is that our activity is still colored by inertia, so we muddle through life not taking responsibility for anything.

As we let go and move forward, Activity becomes predominant. We run after the world outside ourselves. This process only brings us pain, and we refuse to acknowledge that we have any choice.

Only after we have disciplined our individuality and directed our attention inward does any possibility of real change occur. Turning inward and being responsible for all that occurs for us brings us to both peace and empowerment. We are now using Activity in combination with Calm. When this happens, we are bright and clear, and can see the approach we need to take in any situation.

We are now in harmony with the One. We are working toward a universal responsibility. With Calm the principle vibration, we are now clear that we are responsible for everything and everyone. We do not run from our job. It is here that we contribute to relative reality from the place of the Absolute. We have our attention on the Absolute in our own Hearts, and we do not run away. There is no place to run. We know who we are, and we are with God.

The Meaning of Stewardship....

In church, I used to hear the word "stewardship" thrown around: "We need to be good stewards." For most people, that did and does mean "give money." The real sense of stewardship is to take responsibility for the care of something. So if we are stewards of something, then it is our job to make sure all is right with it.

We are stewards of what is in our world. We are responsible for what is in our possession and our vicinity. As we grow spiritually, our shrunken self is diminished and our stewardship expands beyond very limited borders. We become more conscious of who we truly are, and our area of responsibility grows. The truth is, if we are to be good stewards, then we are responsible for every person and every thing. Someone else's pain is our pain. As we dig deeper in *sadhana*, we come to know that everyone is us, no matter how different they may appear or how far away they are from us. We are us. So full stewardship means full responsibility for all.

This is why every tradition has observances and restraints, rules to follow so that we treat each other as we would like to be treated. We cannot serve two masters: it is either God or the ego.

The purpose of school is to discipline the mind so that our individuality has not gone astray. We are to learn to obey. When we are more interested in children feeling good than in their obeying and being disciplined, we are not being good stewards. Now, in the U.S., we have lost our sense of stewardship. We are wasting our resources. We now only tend to our own tyrannical individuality. We serve the wrong master, the ego.

The role of a spiritual teacher is to help us choose God over the ego. A dear and wise friend wrote this to me: *"All" issues arise from minds that are not "practicing." If someone is practicing with loving discipline, all problems that arise are dissolved back into consciousness. When someone withdraws their attention from practice, begins to feel unsatisfied and then turns their attention outside to locate and place the blame "out there," [they] flip their complete devotion to their Master of many lifetimes…the ego.*

So the true beginning of spiritual practice and a good life is to discern our stewardship and whom we serve. Discipline and surrender, done for the right master, bring us to a place where we can then practice the third level, which is taught in every major religious tradition. We will then understand what it truly means to be good stewards, because everyone and everything will be Love and with God.

St. Symeon the New Theologian, a tenth-century Byzantine mystic, wrote about the practice that will bring us to this place of surrendering to God and living life as a good steward:

Truly the third method is marvellous and difficult to explain; and not only hard to understand but even incredible for those who have not tried it in practice. They even refuse to believe that such a thing can actually be. And, indeed, in our times, this method of attention and prayer is very rarely met with; and it seems to me that this blessing has deserted us in company with obedience. —If someone observes perfect obedience towards his spiritual father, he becomes free of all cares, because once and for all he has laid all his cares on the shoulders of his spiritual father. Therefore, being far from all worldly attachments, he becomes capable of zealous and diligent practice of the third method of prayer, provided he has found a true spiritual father, who is not subject to prelest. For if a man has given himself up entirely to God and has shed all his cares on to God and his spiritual father, so that, in his obedience, he no longer lives his own life or follows his own will, but is dead to all worldly attachments and to his own body—what accidental thing could ever vanquish and enslave such a man? Or what worry or care can he have? Therefore all the wiles and stratagems used by the demons to entice a man towards many and varied thoughts are destroyed and dispersed by this third method of attention and prayer, conjoined with obedience. For then the mind of such a man, being free from all things, has the necessary leisure to examine, unhindered, thoughts introduced by the demons, and can readily repel them and pray to God with a pure heart. Such is the beginning of true (spiritual) life! And those who do not begin in this way, labour in vain without realizing it. (from *Writings from the Philokalia*, ed. Kadloubovsky, and Palmer, 155)

As good and true stewards, we want what is best for everyone. And what is best for everyone is for them to be truly who they are. That does not mean we should want them to live the same lifestyle as we do. Rather, the point is that each of us is very different on the surface; in the worldly sense, our likes and dislikes vary. It is at the core of the soul that we are all the same, and we as good stewards will support this. As we work to live there, our security will be clear, and we will feel safe to let others manifest in the manner they need to as long as we are all supporting good stewardship.

Approaching the World….

No matter who we are, there are only four possible ways we can engage with the world: reacting, resonating, responding, and empathizing. Where we choose to land on this spectrum of action determines our degree of agency, and therefore our humanity.

If I were to write nothing more than reactions to life, I would be showing you that I was at the mercy of the world around me. My practice would not be very detached, and I would be sharing the fact that I had no agency. Reacting to life means my *sadhana* would be just crisis hopping or pleasure jumping. The five senses would then be the vehicles that guide my practice. I would have no core.

Resonating with the outer environment would show that I still have a lot of work to do disentangling. When we resonate, we are vibrating with the world and people around us, like tuning forks playing the same note. Some would say that this is a good thing, but even in this situation, we forfeit our agency. We have no control over our reaction. So if we walk into a room with someone who is angry, we will resonate with them. We may think we are "connecting," but in fact we are only absorbed in our own vibration, as the other person is in theirs. We can't help anyone when we resonate with them; it's the equivalent of two people clinging to each other as they both drown. We see this in countless relationships: what draws people together is only the fact that they resonate on a certain frequency, not that they truly connect. Two people drawn together by a shared vibration of self-hatred may believe that they are in love.

The way to use resonating in our practice is to see that when we resonate, we have something to learn. The vibration we have can now be acknowledged, and we can work to still it in ourselves. The environment created an opening for the vibration that was already in us. Once we have stilled that vibration and mastered it, we will no longer resonate with others who have it. We will no longer make the mistake of believing we are on the same page as someone else when in fact our vibration is our own.

Responding to life is a recovery of our agency. Here, we are clearly assessing what is in our world and responding consciously and deliberately. We are no longer at the mercy of the world and people around us. Because we are disentangled, we neither react unconsciously nor resonate; we now have the distance to evaluate with discernment. This is where I speak of being with our experience, letting whatever comes up come up, and functioning appropriately on the physical plane. By responding appropriately, we will grind down the ego. Our wrong identification with the non-self is worn down. There is a discipline in our approach to life. We can only respond to someone else's sadness appropriately when we do not use them as an occasion to wallow in our own sadness; we can then offer real sympathy, not self-indulgence masquerading as sympathy.

To understand true empathy, you have to understand subjectivity. The world in relation to the mind is an object. The mind in relation to the Self is an object. When the world is the object, the mind will appear to be subject.

At other times, the mind will be an object. The mind is not self-illuminative. The Self is the only absolute Subject: it is the Perceiver, and can never be perceived. It is the Self of All.

When we empathize, we are in the groundwater of the Heart, and actually feel what someone else feels without resonating. We have not lost ourselves. We know the experience is theirs and not ours; we know it is not who we are. If we were resonating, we would just be feeling our own vibration. By surrendering to the Self, we become capable of truly being with others.

Recovering Our Agency....

"The world is a mess." "We are a mess." "This is just the way it is." "There is nothing we can do." "It hurts, but there is nothing that can be done." All these are normal statements and concerns expressed everywhere, by all sorts of people. Yet for most of us, "concern" will be as far as we go.

You may argue that you have no power, no venue, no access to anyone, and when you have in fact put forth your voice in concern, absolutely no one comes back and nothing is done.

It all appears hopeless, and from a worldly perspective, it may be. So why am I writing about this? Why am I even bringing up the discomfort of the hurt, the powerlessness and the hopelessness?

Because there is something we can do. It may be too late to change the current tide, but if we all participate, it can change the environment and prevent a future filled with living nightmares for so many of us.

If each of us stopped reacting and resonating, and instead began responding from the Heart, the world would appear to shift. In fact, we would be seeing for the first time the openings for Love. Different choices would begin to arise. These opportunities have always been there; we just were not aware of them.

In Dante's Hell, no one moves. Each inhabitant of Hell stays in one place, either completely immobile or going in eternal circles. In his journey, Dante comes upon the damned, and from the place of their punishment, they share their stories. Dante then moves on. In Purgatory, everyone is moving toward Paradise. Everyone will get to Paradise because they have admitted their sins. By admitting their sins, they acknowledge their accountability, which means they have agency. Not until we admit that we have agency can we move forward. So in Purgatory, everyone reaps what is there for them and then they move on to Paradise, where all is pure and filled with the Bliss of God. All three places are here on the physical plane: Hell is *tamasic* (inert and dark), Purgatory is *rajasic* (active and painful), and Paradise is *sattvic* (still and bright).

As long as we identify as victims—victims of our environment, victims of any kind—we have no agency and therefore we are in Hell. As reactors and resonators, we forfeit our agency. Once we respond appropriately by being a conscious participant in the world drama, we get out of Hell and begin the long road of Purgatory through consciously reaping what we have sown and practicing right action. Finally, as pure agents of God, we reach Paradise. All this can happen right here on earth. But in order to live heaven on earth, we have to give up what keeps us in Hell, what keeps pulling us back down into Hell.

The *Yoga Sutras* tell us the same thing. When, out of ignorance, we wrongly identify, we lose our Real subjectivity; then, based on this mistaken identity, we are either attracted to or repulsed by what we encounter. We then cling to this way of life. Our wrong identity is only an object, a collection of vibrations—not who we truly are. When we are attracted to something or someone, we resonate with their vibration; when we are repulsed, we react against their vibration.

Resonating is not empathizing, is not being kind or compassionate, is not connecting, is not fitting in, is not being appropriate. Reacting is not standing up for ourselves or sharing our true voice.

Resonating is all about vibrations and sharing them. As children, we internalize the vibrations around us, and we either resonate with them or react against them. We end up building a collection of tuning forks within us that vibrate automatically. When we resonate with another person, what we feel is really our own vibration, not the other person's; there are two tuning forks humming the same note.

We resonate because we do not want to be ourselves. We unconsciously abandon ourselves to the frequency of the moment. This self-abandonment becomes our strategy for meeting and connecting with others. We decide that sensitive people are connecting with us and we with them, but in truth we have no core, nor do they. Who we "are" at a given moment is our vibration at that moment.

The opposite of resonating is being self-contained and inwardly clear. As I have said before, only in this state can we respond appropriately. People committed to resonating will regard this as being disconnected, when in fact no real connection is possible without it.

Resonating	Self-contained
Connected	Disconnected

The uncomfortable truth is that resonating is really love full of hate, not real Love or compassion. By resonating with others, we perpetuate our deep-seated self-loathing. In abandoning ourselves, we abandon everyone else—even the people we convince ourselves we are "connecting" with. Only when we are coming from our core and not lost in vibrations can we truly empathize. Love comes from the stillness of the Heart, not from resonating.

Resonating can be a beginning in the Guru/disciple relationship, but it must not last. The Guru/disciple relationship is the disciple surrendering into the groundwater where the Guru dwells. Many people around Baba did not surrender to the Real; they wanted to be enlightened shrunken selves. As a result, they only resonated with Baba's *shakti*, so that when Baba was gone, they were left with nothing but memories. They then moved on to resonate with others. As disciples, we should have agency; after all, the Guru's job is to make the disciple the Guru. Baba always said, "You have to have a strong, healthy ego to be able to surrender it."

Please let us all join as accountable agents in stilling evil, in illuminating the darkness that turns all Love into twisted, tortured love. Hate is abundant and thriving, disguised as righteousness, caring, knowing the way, without any questioning or reflecting or agency. So sure, so emotional and so empty.

As we approach the anniversary of Baba's *mahasamadhi*, the world needs us to have agency. Using that power to choose and act, we must surrender consciously, with all our hearts, to God and Guru, so that we can all take our place in Paradise as the only true agent, the Self of All.

Settling into Unsettled….

From the standpoint of relative reality, everything is unsettled. Even when good things occur, everything is unsettled. The world definitely is unsettled. And the news media and entertainment industry stake everything on keeping everyone unsettled. When there is a crisis, it rises to our attention, then settles down. The truth is, the crisis has not settled; we have grown bored and the media has removed it from the ticker.

Why do things disappear from our consciousness? Because if we were to stay with them and confront the problems head-on, we may have to face our own responsibility. So we have hit-and-run crises. That's much easier: it's sort of like a movie or a television show. Two hours are quite enough. Now we can move on. So though everything is unsettled, do we really want to be settled?

We troll relative reality for peace. Right now we have to go far and wide for that, so we then settle for distraction. I recently wrote about being a hermit crab without a shell. Well, two weeks have gone by and still no shell. I have used the very tools I teach, which I learned from Baba, and they have worked well.

The *shakti* has grabbed me these two weeks. I could have fought it and tried to "live my life," or I could have surrendered to what was. I surrendered: without distractions, barely functioning and very uncomfortable at times. Unsettled. Internal and external *kriyas*. Could not eat. Weak. I knew I could not do this alone, so I asked for help. From the UK to California, friends and Guru brothers and sisters helped with support and suggestions on how to cool down, knowing that Baba was with each of us. I had had a dream of Baba on the full moon when all this started.

If I just kept going inward, there would be peace. When I would come out for a little bit, the *shakti* would not like it and would call me, pull me in. I had to remove resistance of any kind, empty everything out, and then I would settle. The *shakti* washed through me, removing any obstruction so that there was nothing to interfere with it. My body was continuous with the rest of relative reality. Absolute Reality, where Being resides, permeated everything.

I had no control over the *shakti*; it is always the boss. My job, as it is for all of us, is to obey. We need to be willing to listen and discern our course. And if we misread, we will find out rather quickly. If we go out when we should be going in, our lives will be more miserable than we can imagine.

Any vibration, whatever it is, obscures who we really are. No matter how uncomfortable, if we can steadily be with our vibrations, we will find them dissolving into the Love that has been hidden. Even if the world around us is unsettled, we then rest in our true nature.

If we practice, the *shakti* will guide us and will remove our individuality.

The Guru will take us out of relative reality and return us to the Absolute. Be ready, be strong. Be not afraid, we have nothing to lose and everything to gain. Rest in the awareness of the Self, the Guru and God. We can remain silent and in awe at the center while everything around us is unsettled, and also totally perfect.

Dealing with Conflict....

Conflict	Harmony
Engagement	Complacency / inertia / passivity

Whether we live in community or alone, we all face conflict. It comes in countless different shapes, sizes and styles. And since the world is here to help each of us remove ignorance, we each have conflict in forms designed specifically for our benefit.

The root of our word "conflict" is the Latin verb *confligere*, which comes from *con-* ("together") and *fligere* –("to strike'). The Latin noun *conflictus* means "contest." From this we should see the virtue of conflict. We are contesting. We are coming or striking together. We conflict with people, objects, situations, nature, ideas, and ourselves. There really should not be a problem with conflict. It is an important venue of learning. The question is what we make of conflict in relating with ourselves and others.

We avoid conflict only because we have not learned how to act appropriately in conflict—how to use it wisely. What we run from we will run into. If we are trained in how to deal with conflict clearly, to neither escalate nor run from it, then resolution will be available for all.

No one sees the world in exactly the same way. We each have different vibrations that shape how we assess our world. We approach a situation, a person, an idea, an object, nature, and ourselves differently. As in *The Art of War*, we need to know ourselves, our opponent, and the terrain. If we do not, then there is little chance of winning the contest.

When a conflict involves anger, that vibration needs to be directed appropriately. Here is a fourchotomy that illuminates this problem:

Displaced anger	Appropriately directed anger
Safe release	Dangerously exposed

Recently we have seen people protesting injustice. These protestors are angry, and it is their right to express that anger. Some of them, however, feel powerless and have a storehouse of anger they do not know how to express clearly. They are then displacing their anger and taking it out on their neighbors through vandalism and looting. Why, we keep asking, do these people destroy their own neighborhoods? If we look at the fourchotomy above, we can see the reason. People who do not feel safe in their expression of anger will look for an outlet, for what they believe is a safe release.

The problem is that this kind of displaced anger will not provide a safe discharge. Also, there will never be a resolution if you use this form of expression. The conflict cannot be resolved because you are not addressing the conflict in the appropriate direction. If you consciously confront the conflict, you are shining a light on the situation all around and can see clearly what is involved. You can then choose to communicate appropriately and discharge your anger in such a way that it aids in resolution. For instance, when Joseph Welch said to Joe McCarthy, "Have you no sense of decency?," his clear and appropriate expression of anger woke everyone up from the spell and McCarthy lost his prestige, and hence his power.

Our fear is that if we express our anger directly rather than displace it, we will be dangerously exposed. Everyone will know how we are and where we stand. But they will know these things anyway. And being clear and clean does not belittle us or others; it frees everyone to arrive at the same clarity, and then at resolution.

Stuffing anger within ourselves is also a form of displacement. Yet another is what we too often call "taking the high road," which is usually displacing anger by directing it at ourselves. We say we are letting it go, or it's not worth it; in truth, we are actually saying we are not worth it.

We now have an abundance of models for displaced anger and violence. What we lack is models of appropriately expressing anger. Where are the role models who have actually expressed anger cleanly? Atticus Finch in *To Kill a Mockingbird*. Eleanor Roosevelt redefining the position of First Lady by standing up for civil rights. Martin Luther King Jr. expressing his appropriate anger through powerful yet consciously nonviolent words and demonstrations. John McCain explaining with clarity and depth of experience why it is important to release the torture report.

When we forsake this kind of clarity and appropriateness and remain attached to a conflict, it never ends. We are bound to our opponent, whoever or whatever it may be. We never get away. Have we not seen that the United States has been in a perpetually unhealthy relationship with terrorists since 9/11? We are in it together. We express for each other the qualities that are within both of us, and we hate. We will not free ourselves from terror until we give up our appetite for conflict.

Appropriately expressed anger resolves conflict—if not with adversaries, then within ourselves. When a conflict is resolved, we are no longer trapped in an adversarial role. We are detached and free.

Seamless....

What you see is what you get. When we are clear, what you see is what you get. There is nothing to hide and nothing to reveal. We are. We no longer hide from ourselves or others.

Usually we present our best foot when meeting with people socially, professionally, or even in the privacy of our families. This means that somewhere we know we have another foot; a foot we do not want others to see.

The fourchotomy below presents this set of beliefs about our interactions with others.

Fake / for Show	Authentic / honest
Polite	Rude

In *sadhana,* everything is to be brought to the front and dissolved. There is no best foot forward or worst foot hidden. We are to work to know all that is within our individuality.

Surprisingly, being given the opportunity to acknowledge the other foot makes people angry. This last year, we worked on accepting our self-loathing. I gave everyone permission to hate, to feel the hate that everyone has inside themselves. People did not want permission because they did not want to face their own feelings of hate. Not only do we want others not to see our dark side; we do not want to see it ourselves. We decide what we as well as others can see.

This presents another fourchotomy, built around our beliefs about self-presentation and self-concealment:

Deceitful	Up front
Secure / discreet	Exposed

Even if we own, master and transcend this fourchotomy, people will still project their imaginings onto us. When we are not identified with what is being projected, though, there is no need for upset or joy. Just quietly watch, marveling at the creativity.

When, instead of being who we really are, we decide who and how we are, we box ourselves in. We act in ways that we have decided express the characteristics we believe we embody. This presentation is motivated by the ideals to which the shrunken self is attached. Being comfortable in our own skin would have us functioning from the Heart, and all would be infused with the Heart. If we are imposing ideas on ourselves, then only our outer shell will mimic those ideals. Our presentation is only skin-deep. If and when we go deeper, or if something occurs to throw us inward, that shell will no longer be what we present outwardly. When we are tested, we get to see what we are made of; it is not the thin veneer we have presented to the world.

There is a reason I trust Swami Muktananda, my Guru. So many events occurred in the ashram that tested all of us. I found myself in many an uncomfortable situation. Each time, Baba could have done something that would have hurt or crushed me. He never did. He always guided me, even when I had done something terribly wrong. He showed me over and over again that what he wanted was what was best for me. And because I was always willing to step up and face my own delusions, we were on the same side of any battle of wills or egos.

This does not mean I did not question. The way to build trust was to question, to commit, to participate. If I had walked around presenting as something I was not, Baba and I never would have cleared out so much of my inner debris. I would not have seen my motivation and its flaws. Over and over again, Baba proved to me that what he wanted for me was true Love and happiness. He wanted me to be free in the best sense of the word. He neither wanted nor allowed me to box myself in or have others box me in.

This fourchotomy shows how we box ourselves in:

Comfortable in own skin	Uptight / insecure / boxed in
Inconsiderate / insensitive	Well-mannered

As my time with him went on, it became clear to me that Baba was the same all the way through. He was seamless. There were people who used to say Baba was different in public and in private. Baba was just different with them privately because they themselves were different in public and private. Baba used to say, "The world is as you see it."

So maybe I am stupid and did not see what others saw. I looked and questioned, and I trust Baba with my physical and spiritual life, both of which he actually saved. For me, Baba was seamless. What I saw was what I got. No regrets. Just my deepest gratitude.

Speaking Freely….

For many, free speech is the freedom to say what we want to say. "I can say what I want. This is a free country." "Everyone has the right to free speech." What is free speech really? Here in America, we pride ourselves on free speech; it is enshrined in the First Amendment. Of course, there are reasonable restrictions, as the famous example of shouting "Fire!" in a crowded theatre indicates. But what I am concerned with here is a deeper kind of freedom of speech. For instance, political correctness of all kinds remains entrenched in our society. Even in the privacy of our homes, we are watching our language so as not to offend anyone. In Ray Bradbury's *Fahrenheit 451*, anything that upset anyone was removed from view. Exactly how are we policing our speech? How do we reconcile free speech and inoffensive speech?

People are up in arms when someone offends someone else, or hurts that person's self-esteem. We are working to protect the individual from anything that may make them feel bad. Well, maybe there are times when we should feel bad. Maybe there are times when we need to be offended. There are also times when we should risk offending. If, for instance, we are unwilling to offend someone who desperately needs to be called out, we are only setting them up for disaster; we become accomplices. And there ought to be times, when those things are said, when we "own up" and receive them, saying, "You know, though this hurts, you're right. And thank you for being honest with me. Thank you for respecting me enough to say something that in fact is just meant to wake me up."

If we are all about being able to say whatever we want, no matter what, then we must be ready to face the consequences. Free speech is a two-edged sword. We must be prepared for someone to respond in kind. In *The Art of War*, we are to know ourselves, know the terrain and know our opponent. When we speak up, we must first know ourselves. What is our real motivation? Are we ready to do this? Are we able to face what comes? Then we must know our terrain. Is it safe to say what we want? What are the ways to do that? And are we able to maneuver the terrain? And finally, we must know our opponent. Do we know how they may respond? Can we handle their response appropriately?

Free speech	Policed speech
Unchecked ego	Restrained ego

With free speech comes responsibility. This responsibility requires us to speak up and keep quiet as appropriate for the situation. We are not to be too timid if the occasion calls for up-front communication. We need to examine what is the purpose of free speech. Are we communicating to confuse or delude? Or is our motivation to speak for the betterment of all involved?

Free speech from the shrunken self starts with being deluded by one's own individual voice. Shrunken self free speech is empty chatter believing itself authentic and profound. The shrunken self is fascinated listening to itself, and assumes everyone else will be fascinated, too. Its communication is usually boring, often hurtful, and maybe destructive, depending on the motivation. Shrunken selves tell themselves that they are kind and good when this is not true at all.

Shrunken self free speech is not universal. The belief that one's individual expression is priceless and unique is wrong understanding. "I don't want to be universal," the shrunken self says. "I want to be unique." We are all-too-apparently confined within the shrunken self when we "speak our truth," which is really opinion without knowledge or discernment. The Internet, along with texting, creates an illusion of connectedness, but too often encourages us to feel insulated in our individuality. The Internet is a zoo of shrunken self free speech; it encourages us either to remain in *rajas* (agitation and incitement) or *tamas* (numbness and inertia). Outbursts of excitement, outrage, and sentimentality turn up everywhere, all under the guise of authentic expressiveness.

Truly free speech comes from an inner place of nonattachment. It is clear, clean, and honest both inwardly and outwardly. Its motivation is selfless, and it is never merely partisan. It works for the betterment of all. It is heard by all—though shrunken selves are repelled by it—because it comes from Love for All. It goes beyond politics, culture, and religion. It encourages us to move from *rajas* to *sattva* (clarity and calm). *Real* free speech will inspire us.

We all need to work toward a right understanding of truly free speech. The state of the world calls for it. Thanks to technology, nearly everyone in the world inhabits the same "now." Culture and language no longer insulate us. "Safe" and "unsafe" no longer exist as distinctly as we would like. There is no escape at this point. So we have to be responsible, and contribute genuinely free speech. Removing our wrong understanding by constantly focusing our attention in the Heart, where we actually reside, is the way to this freedom. Rather than remain in the prison of the shrunken self and its delusion of freedom, we must liberate ourselves in Truth, from within. Then all our speech will truly be free.

Clues….

When I was around 24, I had a dream that was so powerful, I knew it was real while I was having it. When I woke, I knew I had no soul. My experience was that there was nothing inside me. There was no ground of being. Nothingness, emptiness. I was sure there was nothing there, I was a façade with nothing to back it up. In the horror of this reality, I went to my Tai Chi school to teach. As my students came in, I confessed to them that I was the first person in history without a soul. It was going to be on the cover of the Boston Globe that night. As the day proceeded and I continued to communicate my truth, I began to laugh and this truth began to lose its grip. By the end of the day, there was a freedom from a belief that had felt so real, that had been sitting there informing my existence and creating a sadness and pain. It was gone. That experience had been a clue for me, something I was to face and move through, not run from or deny.

We tend to deny clues or experiences that seem unreasonable or feel painful. And yet these are the very opportunities that will free us to take the next step in our lives. When I give someone a clue, it may look arbitrary and tyrannical. Depending on the situation, I may be very emphatic. It is not my idea; all I am doing is conveying a message. Most of the time I am unaware of the why of the clue and where it will take a person. Usually, following the clue will free the person of something. When the person does not take up the clue, nothing changes, and they remain stuck.

Baba used to say that whatever God does, He does for good. God is always providing clues; we may fail to understand them, or we may even ignore them.

In *Mastering the Art of War*, Zhuge Liang discusses clues as opportunities: "There are three avenues of opportunity: events, trends, and conditions. When opportunities occur through events but you are unable to respond, you are not smart. When opportunities become active through a trend, and yet you cannot make plans, you are not wise. When opportunities emerge through conditions but you cannot act on them, you are not bold."

The opportunities have to be discerned even though they are actually right in our line of vision. Life is a treasure hunt, but we have to know the clues in order to proceed. So many times our reasoning intellect will discard or pass over the clue that is crucial to our hunt. These clues are there for us; they are there to help us, and yet we cannot or will not see them. Strategy that is off the grid never seems reasonable, and the shrunken self is determined to maintain its sense of reason. The treasure hunt then does not move forward, and we remain trapped in the mire of our own reason.

Back around 1980, Baba started to give me the clue to have a child. I told him I was fine, that I did not want a baby. He was so patient. He just kept telling me this clue. Baba would say, "If you don't want a baby, then you should become a *sannyasa*." My response was always, "I am fine the way I am." Gradually, the desire for a child arose, and I went to tell Baba. Before I could open my mouth, he said, "So you have finally come to ask permission to have a baby." He knew this was an important opportunity for me and had kept at it. He was so right. Parenting two sons was the hardest and most rewarding job I have undertaken, and it moved me forward in my *sadhana*. Quite the treasure hunt.

The treasure hunt is here to clean up the effects of something we once caused. It is sad when we see the clues and fail to recognize them as opportunities. The clues are guiding us to the next effect we must clean up. They are moving us to freedom, to the stillness and bliss of the Self. Following the treasure hunt detaches us from what is not us and removes what covers Us.

The treasure is our true Self.

I Am No Fun....

I am no fun. Throughout my life I have heard this. I have even believed it and felt bad. Being identified as a no-fun person means the activities and interests I enjoy are no fun. Some of those activities and interests included dancing at age six and becoming both dedicated and disciplined from the time I was eight. Neighborhood bicycling, touch football, hide and seek. In the winter, skiing, sledding, backpacking, and snow camping, along with various techniques of fort building depending on the variety of snow. And let us not forget the two months at overnight camp every summer until I was sixteen. These were all fun for me, but in my home and outside, there have always been people telling me I am no fun.

Why am I no fun? At this point, I do not care. Why not? Because I am and have been having fun. My fun is different from that of the people who say I am no fun. These people play in a completely different arena than the one in which I have always played. Do not get me wrong. I tried their fun. It was not me; it was not fun for me.

Determined to find out if I could not play like others or if their activities were not for me, I plunged in. College gave me great opportunities to check out this other fun. I pledged a sorority and became president of my pledge class. Parties, games in mud—they were fine. I was fine participating, but when I was to participate with the voting on the new pledge class, for me the fun stopped. "Nice but not necessary" still rings in my ears. Having been called "not fun" in the past did not give me permission to return the favor. I quit.

My time in college was before Title IX. In high school, I lettered in every sport available; college left me with no options. So I decided to go out for cheerleading. Not only was I a Washington University cheerleader; I became a cheerleader for the St. Louis Cardinals football team. Everyone said, "This is fun." I did it. Until, at a convention for Procter & Gamble, we did a routine and then handed out Cardinals jackets. That was when the all-male convention started in with "I'd rather have the girl than the jacket." I felt like a piece of meat. No fun. I quit.

In the ashram, I thought everyone wanted what I wanted: Muktananda, the bliss of freedom. I was so wrong. Working toward what Baba had was hard, not fun. Baba knew people were in the ashram for nothing but a lifestyle, not what was really offered. He would call me naïve for thinking people wanted the Self. People were caught up in the world and wanted only to enhance their sense experience. My thought was, why stay here for that? Go somewhere else for that kind of fun. But for those people, rebellion against the ashram was fun in itself. I was no fun because Baba would send me to find these people and they would not be happy to see me; they felt compelled to tell me, "You are no fun." Baba always knew I was "no fun," so he always put me in juxtaposition with the pleasure seekers. Baba was working for me to get okay with not being any fun. But Baba and I had a lot of fun together. I loved Baba's fun.

It has taken a long time, but I now understand what Baba was trying so hard for me to get. I am no fun to self-indulgent pleasure seekers. I rain on their parades. And they enjoy telling me how much I am no fun. A year ago, I wanted everyone to accept the hate inside them—accept that hate and then work to dissolve it away. There were people who thought, "No, I will not accept that I have hate, the hate that I know I have. No, it is too much fun indulging emotions and feeling victimized." Once more, I was considered no fun.

So here I am, 66 years into "no fun," and it is okay. I am still the same kind of "no fun" for the same kind of people. My fun is loving Love and learning Love. My fun is cleaning up anything that keeps me from Love. I have to do it God's way. I will never be fun for the self-indulgent pleasure seeker. I am too busy having my kind of fun to care.

Love is so much more fun. The play that emerges from Love is joyous and shares itself with everyone. The fun that I am not is heedless indulgence in money, sex, food, power, or substances. That is temporary, and the fear of loss is always there. Addiction is the dedication of the pleasure seeker. These pleasures have to be generated externally. Me? I am lazy; I would rather let the Self generate Its play, and I will just quietly function, swimming and dissolving in God and Guru's grace.

Seamless Always….

There are certain questions we need to ask ourselves constantly: Do I have public and private faces? Do different people get different versions of me? Can I be good without someone else being bad? Is how I act in line with what I profess? Am I seamless?

In order to be seamless, we have to have good boundaries. This seems like a paradox. But the truth is, when we are seamless, there are clear and clean lines. We are not vague, losing our subject in objects around and within us; nor are we compartmentalizing ourselves and our lives. There is clear distinction between how we are, who we are, and who we are not. When we "adapt" to what is around us, we are just chameleons. If we stay true within the Heart and act appropriately, we are not losing ourselves and therefore have good boundaries. But that does not mean we do not care. Now we can really care, because we are present to both ourselves and others.

If we compartmentalize, we cannot be human. We will then not feel what we need to feel and not face ourselves or others. We cannot empathize when we practice cutting off from ourselves and others.

Seamless (integrity / no gaps / whole)	Compartmentalized (partitioned into sealed segments / no integration)
Simpleton (unable to fit in / no modulation)	Managing life (in control / skillful / clever)

Yet we choose not to be seamless, so that our shrunken self can believe it is in control. We do that by setting partitions between different areas of our lives.

Partitions, dividing walls—we try to box in or quarantine certain behaviors we engage in or regions of our lives. The dividing walls have to go. My job is to facilitate the bringing down and burning up of people's dividing walls. Unfortunately, too often people rebuild them. When people crack, however, walls have been breached.

I don't know what people do outside my classroom. But when people enter the teaching room, I can feel their dividing walls. What you keep within your various walls is not of interest to me. The walls are what is important; they need to dissolve.

If you bring down the walls, your hidden behavior is exposed, even to you. Then you have a chance to become seamless. The opportunity arises for you to face yourself and choose how you manifest at all times.

Dissolving our dividing walls takes commitment, effort, and a willingness to hear and absorb what our teacher reveals to us. An athlete or performer must be able to receive and appreciate constructive criticism; if he is seamless, this ability extends across his entire life. It is much easier, however, to get something and then go back to sleep. Many people trivialize what the teacher uncovers, so they can mitigate discomfiting truths.

A recent study in professional working groups reinforced the importance of seamlessness. When a professional group did not function well, it was because they compartmentalized: they walled off their work from the rest of their lives and did not bring their humanity to the group. When they were seamless, willing to integrate their professional and personal lives, they worked well together.

Why, then, do we keep our compartments? Because we want independence, even from God. It doesn't matter: we may know we will have to surrender—just not yet. But we will finally surrender because we are challenged long enough and are shown that protecting our delusion of independence was not the answer to anything.

In *sadhana*, we have to be seamless, We cannot compartmentalize. People have to work with me to bring down their walls. We do this together. The point is to turn the corner toward seamlessness. This in itself does not fix anything, but it does create the environment in which healing and fixing can happen. Which means a lot of hard work.

We resist becoming seamless because, by integrating everything we do and being transparent, we lose our sense of specialness. But what does it mean for us if that sense of specialness is unavoidably tied to secrecy?

Secret	Transparent / open
Special	Mundane

The practice I teach is not a secret. I do not teach it as a secret. It is readily available, but because people only see what they want to see, few see it, and it remains hidden in plain sight. Truth is always available, hiding in plain sight until we are ready to see it. When we are open, we will see what was always there.

For me, practice is daily life. It is seamless. No matter where I am, no matter who I am with, no matter how mundane the situation, I practice. So it is not a secret. It is not special or privileged. God is, after all, seamless, everywhere.

If you are seamless, you seem less, because you just are.

Gossip....

Do you know the difference between gossip and history? Do you know the difference between gossip and an entertaining story? Do you know the difference between gossip and a teaching story?

Gossip actually derives from the Old English *godsibb* ("god-kin"): a word for someone with whom you are linked through sponsorship at a baptism. Over the centuries, it gradually evolved to mean idle chatter, but especially mean-spirited chatter. We often make a distinction between "idle gossip" and "malicious gossip," but all gossip is essentially unkind and untrue. Gossip is designed to hurt; its motivation is from hate. Idle gossip may appear entertaining, and malicious gossip may be seen as cruel, but both come from the same motivation. History, entertaining stories, and teaching stories can also be unkind and/or untrue, but in very particular ways and for particular reasons. People who gossip see themselves as having formed a bond with whomever they share stories with. Hence, *godsibb*. The purpose of gossip, then, is to connect—but also to injure the parties that are spoken about.

In gossiping, we are out to malign or belittle the objects of our gossip, and we are disrespecting and manipulating the listeners of our gossip in order to reel them in. In idle gossip, we reduce human beings to nothing more than sources of amusement. In malicious gossip, the only solution is to destroy or shun the objects of our gossip. We try to create allies within our destructive little dramas.

In history, there are witnesses from all angles. There are facts and therefore a certain kind of truth. The story of an event or a people may be unkind and make us cringe as we do with gossip, but the facts are the facts. For instance, when I lived in Wilton, Connecticut, a Congregational minister said to me, "Hitler did not kill the Jews. He just did not give them health." Now, for whatever reason, she held that view. For her, history was just a story that could be adjusted for her convenience. Maybe she could not face the horror of what actually happened. Many Germans, however, have worked hard not to make everything nice, but to learn from the facts of the Nazi era. They do not mitigate or hide or whitewash. History—in this case, the unkind facts—is a great lesson.

Avoiding this kind of discomfort means losing opportunities to learn. When we were children, and our parents yelled at our siblings for something we may not have understood, did we listen? Or were we so uncomfortable that we did not watch and learn?

The parables, the teaching stories of all traditions, the stories of the saints—are they gossip? Or are they there for each of us to learn from them?

In the ashram in Ganeshpuri, Baba once had me come to his house. He had a group of people sitting in a circle and had me take a seat next to him. Baba went around the circle, one by one, and yelled at each person for something they had done. I was the witness. He was teaching me that I was to listen and learn not to cringe. This event was not gossip; this was an opportunity for each of us to learn.

Gossip is not meant for learning, and it isn't even entertaining unless you enjoy hate.

Gossip	Truth / fact
Entertaining	No fun / harsh / brutally frank

Learner	Pridefully ignorant / arrogant
Nosy / gossip / intrusive / indiscriminate	Self-contained

If I am not a learner, then to me every story is gossip. I can't tell the difference between a parable in the Bible, a Hadith of Mohammed, the story of Moses, and the ridiculous gossip in magazines at the grocery checkout. So I learn from none of them.

We can discern between truth and gossip, but do we want to? If we view all stories as gossip, we can avoid the truth and call our avoidance virtuous. We then conflate gossip with anything that may challenge our shrunken self's sense of goodness and well-being. We allow the shrunken self to dictate what we will listen to and what we will discard. Anything that makes it uncomfortable is not to be listened to because we call it gossip. If we say in our minds to a person who is telling the truth, "I have nicer thoughts than you, and I am a better person than you are," then we can never learn.

At times in my life, I have been the object of people's gossip. I understand the damage it causes. When I was gossiped about from the pulpit of an Episcopal church, for instance, it was not for the betterment of anyone in the pews. It was about malice. When some people whom I did not even know called me vicious names, it was not educational or helpful. It was gossip. Yes, whatever God does, He does for good. That does not mean that gossip does not do injury. My job has been to learn from these experiences, to learn when there is truth and when there is just gossip.

Gossip is telling stories that don't make us better. History, entertaining stories, and teaching stories all have at their core something to uplift us. When we discuss stories from history, spiritual texts, movies and novels, or people we know, we should be doing so to learn—to uplift ourselves and each other. Will some of these stories be painful? Yes, but they are there for each of us to learn. Our task is to face the challenge of learning.

Angry

Angry	At peace
Invigorated	Inert

the way away....

so   sad

to   see

suck   up

cynic

sink

into

abyss

since

sources

say

don't

and   they   just

say

sorry

Satsang

irresolute....

wounds   not
                           healed
   not   ready to
play

my   anger is
                        my problem

you   can't   take it
                          away from me
i have   to take   it away

   i hate   to resolve

it

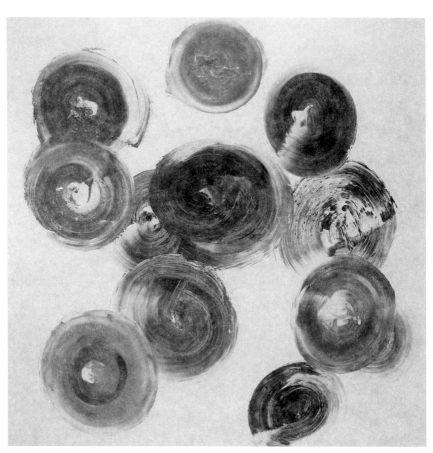

Still Moving

skinned....

do i want   to hate forever
eating   me   inside
                      out

          born   black in america
to feel the
                      pain and
                                suffering of hate

the color   of   my skin
is   not   the issue
                         but the   hate is
other   places
              particulars of
                                         various kinds
                              cause fuel for
                                              hurt and pain

born   somewhere else
              my skin fits
                                         in and no longer the
                      issue
              my skin is not
                                   universal
                                       temporary covering
i love   this vehicle
but i   am not
              my vehicle
          can not   take it
                                         with me

too soon   to
                         distance   must
          first wail   the
                                         call of so many

               insight yes

                                         empathy not yet

karmic chain….

abidjan   to have
                              been   born
          there
                    not
                                  alabama
              and   yet
                  we   all
        slave
                                as hate
        masters
                  us
                      buy   beg
              borrow
                              freedom

        own   self   cut
                      shackles
              face   hate
                      silence   so sound
        is   Love

soul survival....

democracy   cannot
                                                survive
            unless   the
                                    truth is
born

we   start   anew
                        not a few

in   family   of humanity

difference
                        surface indicators

sole one soul   playing all

the parts

facing it....

Love   thy   neighbor
            as   an
                        adversary
    my   narrative   is
                the high   way

self   fish   for   what
    ever
                    so   close
and   yet   galaxies

        a   way

    time   will
        wear   us

down   to   the
        wire   fence
    and   yet
        never   give
            in

    so   walk   away   and
            re   direct   the
                path   back   in

free for all....

                      chaos
              disruption
                              distraction

creates
              the   perfect
        environment
                                for
              repression
          look   out
don't   do   it

             order
                settles
                   into
       freedom
   and   order
     creates
   a   home
           for
           All
           of
           us

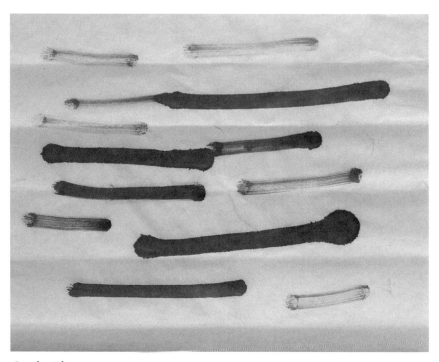

Stroke Play

the pride….

the world cheers
  to   proud
  to   love
marching
        forward to
 its death

  soldiers
    falling
 from
    self esteem

  learning
    ejected
from   education

  truth
  facts
  clear
  clean

  forgotten
    for
  blurring
  opinion
  own
  mine
to   proud
    we go

Love shrinks
    proud
 booms across the
    room
 we believe

        proud   stands
tall   as
     our   force
     our   sentinel

   making us
miss
        why
   we are
   who
           we   are
proud   fools
        us
   into   fools

               shrunken
only
     illusion
     mirrors
     smoke
   delusion
              tools
proud uses
     true shrunken self

care   has   no
                         place
     tied
         together

     communion
flattery   false
              platitudes
     ink

                              reality

spell   check
            our   weapon
      fixed   us

we   are   one
      we   are   me
me   is   all

      no   two

too proud to Love

report....

                        the gun

                  is   the

                              voice

                 of so   many

          ringing

                            songs

            that   leave

               us

crying

                      no   joy

only   voice

      no

                 choice

   to   bring

       us

           to

  our   knees

begging   for

   life   love

     yet we   sing

      shots   of

        cruel   power

   where agency

    comes from

crushing

       each

   other

opinion peace….

we
  twist
   stretch
        truth
  minimize
     shrink
change focus

  pop   and   realign
     emphasis
what is   important
  is   always
           changing
what   happened is
        changing

  history
past   present   no longer
     valid

  degrade   institutions
     downplay   good
  stir all in pot

important and   trivial
        same weight

     hysterical   trumps
        valid   trauma

refusal....

        a   window
                look   through

no   why   not

fear   fear   not

        to   miss   universe
            cherish   light

        so   few   windows
                opportunity   missed

another   lifetime
    and   millions   of   miseries

until   see   window
                                        again

how it happened....

Prahlad
      did not
          fit in
he had no
    choice
  but
  to be   himself
      lover of
  God
  not   demons
never
  distracted
     one pointed
  as
 to love
   all
at all
    times
 fulfill
destiny
playing
          his part
 simply
      for all

 God's
        grace
shone on
    Hiranya
 in death

 love
    always
   there
here

Asmita

cruel pleasure....

there are monsters

competition   different
            from
seeking pleasure

what works
    Love here
    working

can't compete
                have to choose

    competence

by projection
make place of Love
                        normal
    bring normalcy
of no love

        chooses
    different concrete
        action

than love
    which manifests coldly

different playing fields

saliency determined

each highlights
   completely different
treasure hunt

   can't win them over

   what drives them

                              treasure

power
      enhanced
   amplified

what they
      say
      do
      see
      relate

path lights up
      accordingly
   motivation

normal like them
   being the center
making monster good
      human

   trying
         can't

Love
      destroys

The Deeper War

CHAPTER FOUR
CONFRONTING POWER AND HATE

Real Leadership....

A leader can be defined as someone whom one or more people authorize to guide them or others toward a particular goal. In this situation we may intellectually believe we share a common goal, and we even speak of this common goal; however, not until we start the process of leading and following do we actually see if we do have a common goal.

Many people believe that the person who demands the most attention is and should be the leader. The problem with that is that if all the person does is be the center of attention, then that is what ends up being the common goal. The followers will probably not have designated this as their goal. This form of leading or leadership is simply control. If the follower confronts or criticizes the leader, the leader is still in control. As long as anyone pays attention to the leader, everyone unwittingly supports his goal of being the center of attention.

People who need to be the center of attention are the worst people to be leaders. They are not interested in any activity that would deprive them of the spotlight. All that the followers do is feed the shrunken self of the leader. The leader is then able to say, "I am leading you around," and "If you do something for me, the leader, I am just getting my due. I am always the center of attention."

A good leader who wants everyone's well-being fulfilled does not necessarily have perfect followers. Sometimes the followers just want to be the center of attention and do not want what is best for them. A leader may have to say, for instance, "You and I had different goals for you. That is why you did not obey me. I wanted you to be happy, but you didn't want to be happy." The irony is, these followers just want to be in charge. When these situations occur, everyone is frustrated.

Whether the leader or the follower, the shrunken self that has to be the center of attention is weak and therefore will not let go. The person is not healthily self-contained. Because of this, no matter how much we discuss concepts, intellectual ideas, and goals, we are going nowhere with them. The goal will always end up being the same: someone is the center of attention. In addition, this person, whose shrunken self cannot handle not being the center of attention, can easily be manipulated. They can purposely be given tremendous attention and then maneuvered. It is not until we give up our need to be the center of attention that we can actually be of help to others and ourselves; then we can lead toward the common good.

A true Guru will guide disciples through the journey from apprentice to master. That is the purpose of the Guru/disciple relationship. If the guru is not truly a Guru but only wants to be adored, then the disciples will always remain beneath the guru and will be told the guru has secrets that cannot be revealed. Only by focusing on him can you get anything; there is no other practice. This kind of guru will always be superior, and everybody is just to adore and admire him. Hopefully, the followers will wake up and then there will be a disagreement about the goals.

When we are in the Heart, we are not the center of attention. No one is. And many people do not like this experience. People who do not have the strength to be equal will not like being in the Heart. For when we are in the Heart, it is just us. There is no more me, no more I, just us. This is so important to grasp. A leader must have the strength to let go of their ego and not be the center of attention and look and act for the greater good.

If you are in the Heart, there is no "center of attention." You are the Subject with no object. Everyone and everything is One.

Accepting Our Own Evil....

From the standpoint of worldly existence, my vocation looks rather difficult to understand and even boring. My job is to guide people Home. My vocation is to be Home. Home is the Heart, where we meet God. In order to go there, we have to leave all our attachments behind. Among other things, we have to go through all our emotions, owning, mastering, and transcending them. We cannot pick and choose; we have to face them all.

As I guide people through this territory, each person has to feel what they have. It is not my fault if you are filled with hate and anger. Those emotions are yours, not mine. I am willing to walk through them with you to go Home. We cannot skip parts of the road because we do not like them.

As long as you are willing to let go of and move on from the emotions that arise, I am with you. Though I am willing to go through these with you, they are not mine. They are your attachments. You are the cause and effect of your experiences, and you are the only one who can let them go.

When you leave my class, you are by yourself with any vibration you may have. I, too, am on my own; I do not have "your" karma or feelings. Neither do I have your karma or feelings when I am working with you. In other words, from the standpoint of relative reality, we are each responsible for ourselves.

I understand and empathize with your feelings and situations, but I do not, nor should I, resonate or react. My job is to help you still these vibrations. If I resonate or react, then I am drowning with you. I am not to jump in and drown with you. My job is not to be distracted from being focused on God. My job is to help you not be distracted by your own false idols. To be focused on false idols is to be hollow at the core.

If you have no core, then you "live in the moment" in a destructive way. You have no memory. You believe that everything you do, feel, or say at any moment is equally valid and cancels out all contradictions. You rewrite the narrative at will. And you do injury—to yourself and then others.

Focusing on God will bring you back to the Heart, to your true core. It is crucial to remember, though, that constant devotion to God is not a relationship between equals. We are not colleagues of God. There is no dichotomy with God. If we create a dichotomy, then we are limiting God. God IS everything at ALL times and places. If we are made in God's image, then in a limited way we have all that God has. We have all God's aspects in a shrunken form.

In Sanskrit, we say we are all made up of the three *gunas*: *tamas* (inertia), *rajas* (activity), and *sattva* (calm). In *sadhana,* we have to overcome all three to go Home. *Tamas* causes reckless indifference or dullness. *Rajas* causes passion and pain. *Sattva* brings calm, light, and clarity. We are a combination of the three, and we must therefore accept all of them within ourselves. Depending on where we are in the spectrum, we cause varied levels of injury to ourselves and others. It is only when *sattva* predominates that we begin to bring peace to ourselves and others. In a given situation, we may think we are bringing peace, but in fact we may be bringing inertia.

Tamas, inertia, is the source of evil. When we choose to commit to darkness, ignorance, and indifference, we choose evil. We identify with the quality of inertia, and our activity is then colored mostly by *tamas*. In order to overcome evil, we have to go from inertia through activity to calm. We cannot be a *sattvic,* truly good person until we accept our own evil. If we are not willing to be honest and traverse that country, we will never arrive at the Love we long for. This is an important part of the journey on which I guide you.

Remember, as soon as we are truly honest, we move forward. Here is a fourchotomy that will help us accept our own evil:

Evil	Grace
Self-reliant	Done for you / magic / easy / codependent / lack of will / absence of self-effort

If you refuse to accept your own evil, you will project it elsewhere and never get free of it. You will do untold injury and call it being good. You will see anyone who calls attention to your own evil, even in an effort to help you get clear of it, as judgmental.

Thomas Merton understood how this works, and expressed it clearly in *New Seeds of Contemplation*:

> *There is no evil in anything created by God, nor can anything of His become an obstacle to our union with Him. The obstacle is in our "self," that is to say in the tenacious need to maintain our separate, external, egotistic will. It is when we refer all things to this outward and false "self" that we alienate ourselves from reality and from God. It is then the false self that is our god, and we love everything for the sake of this self. We use all things, so to speak, for the worship of this idol which is our imaginary self. In so doing we pervert and corrupt things, or rather we turn our relationship to them into a corrupt and sinful relationship. We do not thereby make them evil, but we use them to increase our attachment to our illusory self.*

> *All sin starts from the assumption that my false self, the self that exists only in my own egocentric desires, is the fundamental reality of life to which everything in the universe is ordered.*

> *There are two things which men can do about the pain of disunion with other men. They can love or they can hate.... Hatred recoils from the sacrifice and the sorrow that are the price of this resetting of bones. It refuses the pain of reunion.*

Accepting our own evil is a vital step in this "resetting of bones."

Selfish *Sadhana....*

We do *sadhana* for ourselves. We also do *sadhana* for the sake of the Self. And if we all did *sadhana* for the sake of the Self, then we would all be living in peace and Love. We would not be killing, and we would not be blaming. We would be taking responsibility for our actions and being empowered to change ourselves and the world.

But as small selves, we do not want Love. The small self can't get Love; it can only get attention and coddling. It only seeks enabling. As small selves, we choose to be victims. We want to be soothed, and we call that compassion. So our selfish *sadhana* really is selfish; it only serves our small self. We are forcing others to cater to our needs. True compassion and Love are neither enabling nor needy.

In Reality, each of us is All. There is just the Self. As each of us truly changes and turns to God, everyone changes. So we should be selfish—in the sense of Selfish. Then we will all benefit. Each of us going inward and doing *tapasya* will actually be contributing to the greater good. We create a furnace within that burns up our impurities. As we move closer to God, the world moves closer to God.

It follows that the further we move away from God, the worse the world becomes. When we insist on a stable narrative, a stable small self rather than a core that resides in the Heart, we stray further and further from Reality. We then believe our narrative is the core of our being. If we find ourselves taking things personally, then we should know that we are identifying with our narrative. That is okay if we are conscious of it, but then we should not pretend to be somewhere we are not. We need to accept where we are; that way we begin to gain distance from our narrative.

But if we are identified with our narratives, then even what we consider selflessness becomes selfish. It can even become monstrous. As Eric Hoffer observes in *The True Believer*, "The inordinately selfish are particularly susceptible to frustration. The more selfish a person, the more poignant his disappointments. It is the inordinately selfish, therefore, who are likely to be the most persuasive champions of selflessness....And though it be a faith of love and humility they adopt, they can be neither loving nor humble " (48).

In order to get rid of our selfishness, we must accept it, and all that it entails. If we want to be truly human, we have to accept all that lies within us. If we refuse to accept, we become emotionally, sometimes physically violent defenders of our narratives. Thomas Cleary explains this in his excellent introduction to Sun Tzu: "Lao-tzu and Chuang-tzu show that the man of aggressive violence appears to be ruthless but is really an emotionalist; then they slay the emotionalist with real ruthlessness before revealing the spontaneous nature of free humanity" (28-9).

In *Yoga Sutras* 2.34, Patanjali makes clear that evil inclinations arise from greed, anger, and delusion. At a pre-verbal level, these vibrations emerge, like everything else, from the Heart. If we refuse to accept them, we choose to let them run us and contribute to the disharmony in the world. If we ruthlessly face ourselves, accepting and mastering whatever vibrations come up, we will no longer construct narratives to defend.

So choose your selfishness. You can have the selfishness that perpetuates the very things you complain about. Or you can have the Selfishness that manifests Love.

The Rotten Root of Hate and the Route Out....

God is Love. Love is our True nature. If we want to be autonomous, we must reject God, and therefore reject Love. So we twist Love into hate, and call ourselves individuals in our own right.

But the shrunken self is a prison, and we "know" that and hate it. We all have the memory of who we really are. That is why we long for something more: we know that we are more than "who we are." But we run from this awareness. We run outside, even further away from the Self.

Self-hate is an unavoidable outcome of ignorance, "I"-ness, attraction, repulsion, and clinging to life. Put another way, our self-hate arises through our mistaken identification with imperfection, separateness, and doership.

Inherent in our self-loathing is the awareness that what we hate, we actually "know" is not who we really are. We hate, however, for the wrong reason. We believe we hate ourselves because we can't be happy, and therefore go outside ourselves looking for that happiness. But in truth, we hate ourselves because we know that our unhappiness arises from our not being who we really are. We always do "remember" our True nature.

But we work to forget. Ironically, we hold onto our shrunken selves because we hate ourselves too much. We cling to what we hate so that we might forget the real reason we hate it. The choice to be infinitely less than who we really are is so painful that we turn even further outside and project our self-hate onto and into the world. When we turn inward, we see our self-hate, so we turn outward and project that hate elsewhere. Our self-hate informs everything—even what we tell ourselves is love.

We created this prison. We diminished ourselves. So we believe we are freeing ourselves by projecting out of ourselves. But we are going the wrong way. We will have to go through the self-hate of the non-self in order to get back to the Self. Hate is just twisted Love. When we give up ignorance and wrong identification, we untwist our manifestation of Love and let go of hate.

So the answer is to turn in, disentangle from what we loathe and re-cognize who we really are. Again, remember that self-loathing and self-love are just twisted Love. Love is who and how we really are—but as long as we remain locked in our self-hate, we are incapable of Love. The self-loather cannot simply decide to love. The Lover loves. The self-loather has to sacrifice itself in order to have the Lover emerge from under the cloak of hate. The self-loather emerges from the Lover. The self-loather is the twisted and shrunken manifestation of the Lover.

The popular delusion that most perpetuates our self-loathing is the belief that we are the creators of our own Grace. We are encouraged to believe that we can free ourselves on our own. In Truth, everything comes from God, even our self-hate. When we experience that truth, we can see how self-hate can in fact help us in our journey back to the Self. Embedded in self-hate is Grace. Grace makes us unsatisfied with our prison; it reveals to us that who we hate is not who we are. Self-hate helps us to let go of what is not us. It helps us to detach, if we are strong enough to seek Love. Then we surrender to God, Love and Guru. We no longer fight against our true nature.

We cannot get rid of our self-hate if we refuse to accept that we have it. Until we accept our self-hate, we will resort to a range of strategies to conceal it from ourselves and others.

Numbing	Denial	Stupidity
Vagueness	Confusion	Distraction
Defensiveness	Guilt	Processing
Victimhood	Blame	Assuming
Rationalization	Stubbornness	Beating up on self
Having it both ways	Making light of	Apologizing
"Nothing ever changes"	Having glimpses	"Not my fault"
Abstraction	Regret	Coldness
Planning	Good intentions	Enthusiasm
Counterexamples	Overriding	Resignation

We have two choices: either turn outward to avoid the Truth using these strategies of concealment, or turn in and face the Truth of our ignorance and wrong identification, and free ourselves by returning to Love.

In order to hate, we have to maintain the shrunken self. In order to maintain the shrunken self, we have to hate. The only way to Love is to surrender our cherished autonomy and accept Grace. Then we can be liberated from the prisons we have made for ourselves.

Drawing Out the Poison....

Hate is so mundane. Last week, I wrote that in order to hate, we have to maintain the shrunken self, and in order to maintain the shrunken self, we have to hate. Everyone has hate; everyone uses it and everyone is motivated by it. This hate is the first and most important distortion of Love. Everything we do comes from and is based on this hate.

Self-hate, the hate we are unwilling to face, motivates us to manifest that hate further outward into the world. I turn in and see my self-hate. So I turn out and project it outward.

We all profess to hate hate. That in itself is hate. We do not need to hate in order to discern evil. In fact, in order to have that discernment, we must be free of hate. The love that is opposed to hate is not Love. The love that is opposed to hate is attached to hate, and cannot see clearly.

Our task is to be true even around haters. Can I love in a hating environment? Remember, our shrunken selves arise from twisted Love. And as we as individuals become more separate and empowered, our hate becomes the only thing we have to offer.

True Love melts the borders of selfhood. But we distrust anything that will cause us to leave our prison cell of the shrunken self.

Self-absorption of any kind comes from a deep-seated, deep-seeded self-hate. We are shrunken selves lost in themselves, not realizing that the very basis of the shrunken self is self-hatred. Again, this is not the shrunken self hating itself for its misdeeds. This is the shrunken self hating itself for existing at all.

In our fundamental ignorance, we mistake self-hate for self-love, simply because self-hate is a kind of self-absorption. It is a way of being caught up in ourselves. We are swimming in our own sewage, but because of our own ignorance and darkness, we cannot see it. I hold onto my shrunken self because I hate myself too much.

But for all this, we would rather hate than learn to live in Love. Despite what we may say, almost no one wants Love. Love requires too much hard work. Love requires us to surrender our separateness. That's why, if you want to get rid of somebody, then Love. If we really Love, then people who are committed to self-hate will not want to be around us.

If you are willing to surrender to the work of Love, you must first know and accept your self-hate. You cannot get rid of something you refuse to accept. Then, you must understand the process by which you got from who You really Are to the self you hate. Here is how it works:

1. The True Self. You Are who You Are, the Self of All.

2. Ignorance. You mistake the image of the Self in the mirror of the intellect (*buddhi*) for the Self. You lose the Subject in the object of the mirror. As soon as you take the non-Self to be the Self, you lose yourself in that image. The false, shrunken self emerges. Because the shrunken self has a memory of its True Nature and knows it is false and shrunken, it hates itself for existing. Its existence is a prison cell.

3. The shrunken self hoards its hate, collecting reasons for hating itself. It fills its prison cell with various forms of self-hatred.

4. The shrunken self tries to unload its self-hatred by projecting it out into the world. It hates others.

5. The shrunken self recognizes that it is throwing out hate and decides to restrain itself. It calls itself a "good person" or a "spiritual person." But it is still stuck in its cell with all its self-hate, and all its "good" words and actions are tainted with that hate. So it has not begun to do real work yet.

6. The shrunken self begins to truly reflect and to clear out its cell—not by trying to project hate outward, but by owning, accepting, and dissolving hate. This is what fourchotomies are for.

7. Once all its manifestations of hate are neutralized, the shrunken self is back to its simple, basic self-hate.

8. When liberation arrives, all separation is healed, and all hate dissolves.

9. You will never then be "Rohini," "Sue," "David," etc. again. You will enliven the shrunken self and remain the Self. Love then manifests through the shrunken self without any twist or taint.

Liberation means re-cognizing our True Nature. In *Shiva Sutras* 3.9, it says, "Such a one who has realized his essential nature is a Self that is only an actor (on the world stage)." (transl. Singh)

In Jnaneshwar's poetic commentary on the *Bhagavadgita*, Arjuna awakens in just this way:

Filled with pride in my personality I thought that I was Arjuna in this world and said that the Kauravas were my relatives.

In addition to that, I had the evil dream that I would kill them and then what should I do? But the Lord wakened me from my sleep....

I, being no one, thought I was a person and called those my relatives who in reality did not exist. Thou hast saved me from this great madness.
(transl. Pradhan)

Victimhood: The Way of the World....

This is going to be the final part of this series. I want to address something that is going to be uncomfortable for many readers: attachment to victimhood. This subject can be raw, and it can trip a wire that may bother people who have not faced that attachment in themselves. It is crucial to recognize that I am using the term "victim" in a spiritual sense—not in terms of physical or emotional events, but in terms of how we see ourselves. The point is how we attach to, recoil from, or generally identify with the word "victim."

The further we shrink and objectify ourselves, the more we become victims. Even bullies see themselves as injured or deprived, so we all self-identify as victims. The victimization we seize on may be concrete or abstract, physical or emotional, but we all have a relationship with victimhood. It is a vicious irony: we dream of unity, and achieve a mockery of it by being united in aggrieved victimhood.

Here is a simple fourchotomy to start working with this dynamic:

Victim	Assertive / powerful
Innocent / not accountable	Bully

Self-identifying victims—we could call them career victims—think of themselves as good, caring, deserving, nice people. Above all, they are right in their thinking. Yet if we are really honest, when we are around people who primarily see themselves as victims, we feel them radiate something other than goodness or innocence, and we find ourselves put off. How many times have you been around a victim and found yourself inexplicably angry? There is a reason for that. Victims are great haters.

And victimhood has its appeal. The more objectified we are, the less accountable. If we act out of a sense of victimhood, we automatically feel we are justified. As recent events have shown, even the police now see themselves as victims. In situations for which they are not prepared, they fear for their lives. Then, out of a sense of self-preservation, they shoot to kill. It is clear that they have not been properly trained to discern the difference between a misunderstanding and real danger.

We now inhabit an atmosphere suffused with threat. So in order not to appear as a threat to ourselves or others, we assess ourselves as victims. As victims, we arm ourselves against the world—unwittingly becoming threats. Everything is geared toward terror, so we fear for our lives and shoot.

This is only one example of how we now live in an emotionally heightened environment. All around us, especially in the media, emotionality rules the day. Even our news reporting is governed by emotion. Emotionality is equated with authenticity. We see emotion as the seat of our true subjectivity; as a result, the person in the most dramatic emotional state is seen as the most "real." And our designated victims get a free pass. At the same time, the ideal of heroism has been reduced to surviving a situation in which we might have been more completely victimized.

We have cultivated around the world a support system that idealizes victimhood. Not only the media but also many in the "helping professions," various forms of activism, and political groups maintain the focus on victims and our obligations to them. If you can stake a compelling claim to the role of victim, then anyone who disagrees with you is cast as the bully.

And what is perhaps most disturbing about this is that we have so cheapened victimhood that the real victims suffering right now go unnoticed, or are given brief spells of attention before being trumped by other self-appointed or media-appointed victims. Our attention lasts the duration of a hashtag.

At a deeper level, the self-identifying victim spreads hate. Career victims hate, and they want the rest of us to join their family. Hate binds us together tighter than love. They encourage us to take sides inappropriately, to resonate with their violence, to participate in their self-centered worldview.

Again, there is a difference between people who are being victimized and suffering and those who cling to their victimhood and use it as a power play. The question is not whether someone has physically or emotionally victimized you at some point; it is whether you are going to insist on being identified as a victim afterward.

Anyone tempted to cling to victimhood in this way should consider that to identify yourself as a victim may give you leverage with some people, but in a more real sense, it is to give up your agency. To become human is to recover your agency by letting go of all victimhood. But with agency comes accountability. Rather than be accountable, many people see greater advantage in being victims.

We don't have to operate this way. Each of us must work to give up our own sense of victimhood. Until we do that, we will remain caught in the ugly cycle of victimhood, hate, and violence. Love is the only answer. Not the love that opposes itself to hate, but the Love that transcends all separateness—the Love that has no interest in victims, and produces none.

Crumbs....

For many years, I have used the story of Hansel and Gretel with the breadcrumbs as an example of how we go Home. For us, the breadcrumbs are still there. We can follow them back to who we really are.

The last few weeks, my work has been focusing on the self-hate we all have. We have seen that our hate toward the world is actually outward-turned self-loathing. The first step Homeward is stopping the outward hatred. Then comes the hardest moment: choosing whether to continue turning inward and facing our own self-hate, to stay quiet looking outward, or to return to the arena and spew hate everywhere, knowingly or unknowingly.

The question is why go through all the ugly reality of our shrunken selves. Why would anyone choose to face that head-on? Simply, it is the only way Home. We cannot get Home without facing and letting go of our self-loathing. The breadcrumbs are still there. They will be there for our sake. So many things we think we have left behind we must acknowledge as still being with us. We have to choose to retrace our steps back to who we truly are. Each new crumb we come upon is a clue and will help us in our journey. The more we face and pick up the crumbs, the lighter life becomes for us.

The problem for many of us is that we would rather be fattened up and cooked in the oven by the witch than turn around and face ourselves. That way, unless we are rescued—and even if we are—we have no accountability, no agency. We maintain our victimhood. For those who want that, there is plenty of support.

Those of you who truly want to be yourselves will have to search high and low for a guide to help you decipher those breadcrumbs. Swami Muktananda is just such a Being. He guides his disciples Home to Joy and Love and the Truth of who they are. Baba is a guide who knows the terrain of darkness, ignorance and pain. He knows how to bring us out of our self-loathing and into the light of our Home in the Self of All.

Again, for anyone wondering why we just went through that dark patch, have you noticed you can handle it better and are not so identified with it anymore? We have plenty of darkness to face, but as we learn, we find the ease and willingness to move into this part of the inevitable journey. We cannot avoid it forever. Turning away from the fattening and facing the shrunken self with consciousness is the initial step. Then we have to move into the darkness with our light of consciousness shining so clearly that the forest of ignorance is illuminated and we know how to go Home.

When he was in his body, Baba took his disciples through this passage time and time again. For each of us, the darkness had a different twist that was not easy for the untrained eye to see. But he was and is such a great guide, moving us to retrace our path and clean it up as we go.

What a wonderful adventure. Accountability is so freeing. As we retrace our steps with our guide's help, we are more and more free to Love, because we are more and more accountable and therefore more and more Us. We have turned around, and are moving farther away from the witch's oven. Home is just ahead. Let us keep following the breadcrumbs to Love.

Baba's Work....

One of the greatest misconceptions about spiritual practice is that it is selfish. Unfortunately, the world is full of pseudo-spiritual "paths" that really are nothing but self-indulgence. Real practice is the opposite. When we actually do it, the world changes on a deep and subtle level.

It's hard to fathom this. Few people want to grasp that by turning inward and giving up our hate, we change the world. The truth is, these people would rather have spiritual practice be something they do for themselves alone, as shrunken selves. When confronted with the reality that the stakes are higher than that, that practicing carries the added weight of responsibility to the world, they don't want to take on that accountability. But we are all accountable in this way, whether we like it or not, and whether we practice or not.

God enlivens the world; that means God enlivens all vibrations, including the most prevalent vibration of the moment. In Indic traditions, there are three foundational vibrations, which combine like the primary colors to make up the manifested universe: *tamas* (inertia, ignorance, and darkness), *rajas* (activity, desire, and pain), and *sattva* (calm, clarity, and brightness). Right now, the world is steeped in *tamas*—in ignorance, complacency, and destructiveness. As *tamas* moves toward *rajas*, our actions are colored with this darkness, which manifests as hate. How does that affect each of us? *Tamas* and *rajas* will influence us based on the makeup of our shrunken selves and how detached we are from them. The more we are detached, the more we move toward *sattva*—wisdom, discernment, and peace—and so we are able to see *tamas* for what it is and respond appropriately.

Whether we are active or complacent in our hate and therefore passive in our hate, we are sharing in the vibration of darkness and ignorance. We are contributing to the evil in the world. The only way out of evil is to shine the light of *sattva* on it. Then, with the conscious awareness of our agency, we work to still by facing and being with this vibration of darkness. Each of us needs to still for all of us.

This is true because, from the standpoint of the Absolute, each of us actually is all of us. We are the Self of All. In that sense, every person exists simultaneously as a manifested being and as the Unmanifest. We exist as manifested beings in relative reality; here, we each appear as separate entities existing in time, living and dying and performing actions both good and evil. But in Reality, we are the Absolute, which is pure Love. The Absolute gives rise to the manifest. Just as Christ said that everything, both good and evil, comes out of the Heart, all manifestation comes out of the Absolute. God is All.

From the standpoint of Absolute Reality, there is no good or evil. Everything is God. In relative reality, though, we enact different parts in the cosmic play. Some of us will do mostly good and some of us will do mostly evil. We are all in the Great Game, and we are accountable for what we do as characters. We live as individuals in a universe of cause and effect, and we must reap what we have sown. It all ultimately balances out, but at some points the Great Game tilts into *tamas*. This provides an opportunity for the good to rise up and right the balance, just as in World War II, people arose and joined together against the evil of Nazism. Without such evils, goodness gives way to complacency, which then gives rise to outright evil. These cycles are just cause and effect playing out, so that every character in the Great Game has a chance to choose God or not.

This is what we are seeing now. For instance, ISIS is clearly evil, but in truth, God dwells within its adherents just as much as in the most saintly people on earth. Ebola is a natural evil, and it, too, is a manifestation of the Absolute. But in relative reality, we cannot pretend we are in the Absolute. In the Great Game, the good must be accountable and stand up for Truth; otherwise, there is no redemption for anyone. We can actually make a difference. All of us.

But how we go about making a difference makes all the difference. Standing up for Truth must begin within each of us. We can only take appropriate action outwardly if we have realigned ourselves with God inwardly. We cannot come from some self-deceiving place called "our truth"; we have to throw our idealistic notions into the fire of Truth. Only when we accept where we are, redirect our will, and surrender to Love can we free ourselves from ignorance and hate, and discern right action.

By turning inward, accepting our own self-hate, and working to be still rather than project that hate outward, we contribute *sattva* to the world. This is the spiritual practice enjoined on us by so many traditions, scriptures, and teachers. By using our will, we redirect our attention back into the Heart, the cave of the Self, and rest there. From that stillness, we can see and act clearly, without attachment.

Baba was here to help bring the world back from the vibration of evil. He spread his message and awakened the spiritual energy in hundreds of thousands of people. Though only a few wanted what he really had to offer, most people who encountered him found their lives unexpectedly changed for the better. For each person who received Baba's grace, the world shifted. It was then their task to practice inwardly and continue in their own lives the work he began. Those who truly practice know there is nothing selfish about this work. They know that each step they take toward God moves everyone in that direction.

Power Hungry, Powerful....

When the motivation is Love with no twists and turns, then everyone is Loved. Then every action is for everyone's good.

When we can tell the difference between Love and power, we can see that the Guru actually wants us not just to love, but to *be* Love. But as long as we are attached to and identified with the shrunken self and resistant to Love, the true Guru will look the same as the false. We can't see the difference because we cannot discern motivation.

The true Guru asks you to side against your wrong understanding and become true to yourself. That means you have to disregard your "normal." "Normal" actions, "normal" relations, and "normal" motivations all have to be left behind. There has to be a completely new way of approaching everything in the world. When we approach the world in the same way the Guru does, everything is being approached from Love. Love opens us up to new solutions and resolutions, and expands our awareness, which is filled with possibilities. Truth expands and brings the possibility of joy for all. This will not be the case for people wed to their shrunken selves. They will be too busy pursuing power and calling it something else, such as "love" or "good." The irony of power is that it brings shrunkenness and misery, not the greatness it seems to promise.

All of us have to be willing to lose: to lose to the Truth, to Love, to the Guru, to God, to the Self. When we lose in this way, we actually win, and so do the people around us. When we lose in this way, we love and are loved. When we "win," we create hurt, alienation, agitation, separateness, emptiness, irritation, superficiality, anger and hate. Others are hurt because our motivation is not resolution, it is, unwittingly, destruction.

The shrunken self and you cannot coexist in harmony. The shrunken self only brings misery; when you are identified with the shrunken self, your idea of harmony is then misery. For you to be in harmony with God, with Love, you have to give up your attachment and commitment to the shrunken self. For this work, you need the guidance of the Guru; the Guru shines a light on our delusions and attachments, and leads us to accept and transcend them.

When the Guru frees us, our lives will be turned upside down; because the Guru's motivation is Love, the outcome is always freeing, whether or not the disciple sees it at first. Life will be better for the person, not more miserable. Externally, the situation may remain difficult, but the experience of those difficulties, and the reasons for them, change. However uncomfortable they may continue to be, these difficulties now serve to show us our remaining attachments and motivations, so we are now able to see that there are lessons to be learned. Through them, life is teaching us for our own good.

The Guru frees us to live a life filled with the many textures and layers available to all of us. We look at a scene and see the fullness and Love rather than the most superficial and empty elements. The hurt dissolves. We are Lovers, Loving the Real and knowing reality.

The Power of Woundedness....

We are becoming a world of wounded people. In the United States alone, there is an entire complex of industries, helping professions, and self-help promoters that profit from encouraging us to identify with woundedness. The words "health" and "wholeness" are thrown around, but the actual focus is on woundedness. This "healing" industry preserves our wounds; it feeds off our wounds and disregards our souls. In truth, we have a choice: we can heal our wounds or lick our wounds. The shrunken self prefers to lick its wounds.

A person wed to this form of self-centeredness has a wound that he does not want to heal. It is his tool to manipulate others. There is no way the wound can be healed because he does not want to heal. His power and control are based on the wound. If he were healed, he would lose power. He may speak of "love," but for him love is power; real Love does not enter into his calculations. He therefore looks for someone who would like to play the healer and then tortures them. He toys with the idea of being healed but will never allow it to happen. That is why, when he encounters someone who truly Loves, he will fight them.

When love shows up, this person presents the wound, and the would-be healer reads the wound as a wound and not a weapon. The healer will assume that the wounded of course wants to be healed. The wounded one will say he does and feed the lover with words like "I want to change," "I will do anything," "I am trying," and "I don't know how." But the truth is they are roping in the sucker. They have no intention of getting rid of the wound. The sucker's role is to be always willing to take the blame for the lack of healing.

In moments when the wound seems to be healing, all of us are thrilled for the wounded person, believing that they, too, are thrilled. They do not see it the same way. In their eyes, they have lost their power and are determined to get life back to their "normal." Right around the corner from that wonderful moment is the lash that puts all back to their right order. They win. That is all there is: winning. The lover, the enemy, has lost yet again.

Having injured those who love him, the wounded yet again resorts to the leverage of woundedness. He cries, "But can't you see how bad I feel? I am wounded more than anyone." His hurt trumps any consideration of what he's done to others. The healers accept this, and feel bad for the wounded one. And so the dance continues. The wounded self's belief is that if he is healed, he will then be ignored. The healers get to feel virtuous in their forbearance. They also feel they could have done more.

The wounded manipulator has to make the choice to be healthy and give up power. Either we wake up or the story never changes. Saying that we're all flawed and apologizing for every injury resolves nothing—it is a cop-out. Only through accountability to ourselves and others does anything change.

In order to heal, the wounded self has to sacrifice its woundedness. It has to give up being wounded, to throw down its weapon. It has to truly want to be whole. The only way is to get off the grid completely.

Here are two fourchotomies that will help move us toward resolution:

Wounded	Healed / whole
Cared for	Ignored

Wounded	Healed / whole
Powerful / winner	No leverage / loser

By definition, the shrunken self cannot be whole. The "whole" shrunken self is still shrunken. We have to keep removing every obstacle that blocks us from our True nature, which is Love.

Shrinking the Monster....

When we encounter someone who is evil, we usually react with fear. We do not understand them and want to run away. They are monsters to us, and we feel powerless. If we want to shrink these monsters, we must begin the process of uncovering how they came to be as they are.

These monsters are human beings who committed themselves to the pursuit of power and pleasure. Yet the way that pursuit begins—the way they embarked on the road to evil—is not what most people suspect. And we need to be clear about how evil begins, because we all have it within us.

The road to evil starts when someone commits to believing, without question, that they are inherently good. Once that is done, they begin to believe, again without question, that whatever they desire, whatever gives them pleasure, is necessarily good. They are then repulsed by anything or anyone that impinges on the fulfillment of their desires or challenges their sense of goodness. Finally, they fear the death of their chosen identity so much that they completely refuse to surrender to anything. This fear also manifests as fear of others, and therefore rage at others.

As a result, there is no negotiating with evil. Its commitment to itself is absolute. How then, can we put evil out of its misery? By confronting evil with Love. And by Love I mean what is left when we give up our attachment to anything less than God. Only through Love can we have clarity of sight and action in the face of evil. Love always takes the form appropriate to a situation; if necessary, it may even take the form of a bullet, sent from a place of complete nonattachment.

Once we understand how someone chose to become evil, we can bring that person back down to human scale. Their monstrosity has been diminished, because we know it is simply the result of a series of disastrous choices, all of which we could have made. Now we can discern how to act in a manner that will make us, and others, safe.

Real safety arises from Love. When we come from the place of Love, we support who others truly are and act in everyone's best interest, including our own. Everyone is then free from fear physically, intellectually, emotionally, and spiritually, and encouraged to grow into Love and happiness. People are then free to make mistakes, and so are we. It is so much easier to be complacent; we must be brave enough to be safe.

We should not be fooled by delusions of safety. One of these is appeasement: "If we give him what he asks, we will be safe." We have to know whom we are playing with. When someone is evil, we are never safe. Do not think such people will be reasonable or keep their word.

Appease / placate	Resist / stand up to
Soothe / pacify	Incite / enrage

Evil fools us by calling something safe when in fact it is dangerous. "Trust me," it says, "everything will be fine." These and similar phrases set us up both internally and in the world at large. We are at risk because we do not know it is not safe.

On a camping trip many years ago, my son Aaron wanted to light the campfire, but the wood was wet. His abusive biological father poured extremely flammable white gas liberally over the wood and, in spite of our objections, encouraged Aaron to touch a match to the pile. "Just trust me," he said. But he moved back several feet as Aaron went to touch a match to an exposed corner of newspaper. When the match reached the paper, Aaron was instantly engulfed in a fireball. My older son Ian and I rushed to rescue Aaron. His biological father remained indifferent, and dismissively shouted, "He's fine." This was a classic example of evil creating danger, pretending it didn't exist.

When such an "accident" happens, evil slips out the back door, leaving a trail of excuses: "I did not know," or "It was not my intention." This is the way the evil person weasels out of accountability. Evil people are selectively competent. If you are actually competent, you can't use those excuses; you have to own what you have done and why you did it.

Evil doesn't stop at creating dangerous situations; it takes pleasure in destroying hope. This pleasure often takes the form of offering hope and then crushing it. Evil has the ability to uncover the seed of hope in any person and kill it.

Hope (encouraged, sense of possibility)	Futility (can't win, can't move)
Self-beguiling (blind, unwilling to face facts)	Sober (realistic, seeing straight)

But real hope is not so easily destroyed. Real hope is clearsighted; it doesn't beguile itself. As Vaclav Havel has said, "Hope is definitely not the same thing as optimism. It is not the conviction that something will turn out well, but the certainty that something makes sense, regardless of how it turns out." Real hope is a virtue because it is a step on the path to Love, which makes all things clear and safe.

No one is more dangerous than someone who is wholly convinced of his own goodness—so committed to that identity that he will seek to destroy anyone or anything that rebukes it, and he will create hazardous situations wherever he goes. So all of us must let go of "goodness," and purify our character by surrendering to Love. Love ruins the "goodness" that is the real root of evil.

Discerning Evil….

We all must mourn the loss of innocence—of the delusion that everyone cares about others' best interests—and accept the existence of evil in the world. In an Absolute sense, everything arises from Love. Dante understood this; in his *Commedia*, evil is simply twisted Love. But though evil, like everything else, arises from Love, it rejects its origin and deludes itself and the world into thinking that it is self-sufficient.

Love, as the ground of All, leads us to Unity; it is both the source and the end of every separate self. Evil, because it is the extremity of separateness, denies Love. This is why evil can never last: it denies its own foundation.

So while Love constantly recalls our separate selves to Unity, evil feeds on its own separateness and seeks to divide and conquer the separate selves around it. Both Love and evil therefore target the shrunken self, but in very different ways: one to lead it to joy and freedom, the other to drive it to despair. The motivation makes the difference. Evil appears at first to be good and therefore deludes and disheartens the individual. Evil always gives rise to evil. Love always goes to Love. Baba used to say that both a cutthroat and a surgeon use the same action, but because their motives are different, the results are different.

Discernment is so important here. Both Love and evil strive to break the individual, but to what end? An evil person breaks another person's spirit in order to gratify him or herself. A true Guru breaks students' wrong identification with individuality in order to free them to be who they truly are. There is a difference between breaking an individual's spirit and breaking one's attachments. One destroys, and one frees.

But to a deluded person, both those actions look the same. Only when we begin to see clearly can we discern that there is no serving two masters: the individual self and God. Refinement of our character brings the ability to distinguish between Love and evil, and the recognition that we must surrender to God, which is something that evil will never do. If we serve God, everything else is taken care of—not necessarily the way we would prefer, but the way it should be.

Evil wants us to commit blasphemy and surrender to individual separateness. God wants us to surrender to God, to the Self, who we truly are. We have to discern whom we are going to surrender to, but surrender we must. Surrendering to evil is a habit; surrendering to God is a skill and a conscious practice. When we choose God, surrender means purifying our will. We all have to learn how to do this. The skill of surrender has to be honed through instruction and constant practice. Without the skill and practice of surrender to God, we go nowhere, fail to change, and remain committed to our shrunken self as the highest truth.

To learn this skill of surrender, we must have a teacher. The danger is that if you do not have either a Guru's guidance or the most extraordinary self-awareness and discernment, you run the risk of thinking you are surrendering when in fact you are hardening into an "enlightened" individual. In conflating your individual will with Spirit, you are hardening into "goodness" and therefore separateness from God. You will turn your back on God and the teacher because you believe the teacher is trying to break your spirit instead of break down your individual prison.

If you have problems with a teacher in human form, then don't think in terms of surrendering to that person; surrender to God, to Love, to the true Self. The teacher, if true, will then be very happy with what you are doing.

In order to surrender to God, to Love, to the true Self, we have to be full participants in breaking the delusion of individual separateness. To people who lack discernment and are committed to their own separateness, this process can look like brainwashing. The irony is that when evil looks to break the individual's spirit, those same people do not recognize it for what it is; because they are wed to their individuality, they believe they are being affirmed even in their degradation.

Our responsibility is to wake up, learn discernment, and give up the pride of individual separateness. Then, and only then, can we practice and embody the Love that overcomes evil.

The Evil and Good of Destruction….

We have talked about hate before, as a vibration to be stilled. Here destruction comes into the mix. When we do not know that we hate because we either numb, deny, or call the vibration something other than what it is, we can use the outcome of our actions as a way to unveil our motivations.

If we say we love and yet our actions, no matter how "good" we or others may think they look, end in destruction, then our motivation desperately needs to be questioned. We have to consider the clue that the outcome has not led to anyone's betterment. Denial, numbing or calling the outcome something other than what it is can be used to evade the truth, but if we find ourselves rationalizing, reasoning, or mitigating, then we need to wake up.

As for me, I do not apologize for being exacting. A pencil is a pencil, except when it is not.

We may, for instance, call ourselves diplomatic when in truth we are simply evading responsible action. By the same token, when someone is direct with us, we may choose to regard it as an unprovoked attack. In each case, our real motivation is a kind of contempt, a form of hate, and its outcome is destruction.

| Evasive action | Direct approach |
| Diplomatic | Unprovoked attack |

Fourchotomies are a great tool for this condition because all four components have to be owned and accepted in order to have resolution. If I only allow the "positive" words for me and deny and project the "negative" ones, there is never resolution. We have to de-conflate the positive and negative terms to understand the four different vibrations. All four are ultimately neither positive nor negative; they just are. They are qualities that we define and embody based on our limited understanding.

| Confused | Clear |
| Wrestling | Dogmatic |

Taking the high road	Petty
Cowardly / enabling untruth / disservice	Serving justice and truth

Conciliatory	Confrontational
Squirting ink / befogging	Forthright

Lashing out	Showing restraint
Standing up	Taking blows

If we reflect on these fourchotomies, we will see how often what many people call "love" is really destruction. For example, a parent or teacher who cripples as a way to show care. This person "loves" by denying someone's responsibility for any failure or success, or by squashing their enthusiasm or interest, or by belittling their accomplishments to make sure they know their life is of no consequence. Other people mislabel anger as love: when they have a surge of rage, they experience it as pleasurable, and therefore call it "love" and "uplifting." They then seek to recreate that vibration again and again.

If we approach this dynamic from the standpoint of the three *gunas*, it becomes very clear. An action colored by *tamas* will produce destruction. An action that is mainly *rajasic* will be filled with passion and pain. A *sattvic* action will lead to resolution, clarity, and Love. We may perform the same action, but if we do so from different motivating vibrations, the outcome will reflect the motivation. Baba used to tell the story of a thief who cut open a man with a knife and a surgeon who cut open a man with a knife; one was destroying, the other was healing.

If destruction is the outcome, then Love was not informing the action.

We may then ask, what about the Goddess Kali/Durga? She destroys ego, wrong identification. She destroys what brings us to misery. So though she is destroying, just as hate and evil destroy, what she destroys is different because her motivation is Love and not hate. What is destroyed by what I do? If love, trust, care, friendship and life itself are what is destroyed, then hate is what motivates. If wrong understanding is what is destroyed, then Love is the motivator. We have to continually ask, "What is my motivation? And what do I want to accomplish?"

Collaborator / supports evil / enables evil	Resister
Keeps the peace	Troublemaker / pot stirrer

In the Old Testament, Joseph's brothers sell him into slavery. Many years later, those same brothers arrive in Egypt seeking help because of famine. Joseph is at this point a trusted officer of the Pharaoh, having predicted the famine and saved Egypt from starvation. He recognizes his brothers immediately, though they do not recognize him. Once he tells them who he is, they are chastened and feel terrible for what they did to him. Joseph's response is, "You meant it for ill, God meant it for good." The brothers' initial action was self-serving and destructive—it caused great injury. Joseph faced his fate and became an instrument of God's grace. God's motivation was Love.

God destroys ignorance; the shrunken self just destroys. God is One and All; the shrunken self takes on what it sees as God's qualities: it is one and alone. Because each of us is "God," we are dissatisfied with others and look to raise ourselves up and destroy the "false." It is this destructiveness that God will always destroy.

Love and Democracy....

The only thing I really teach and talk about is Love. I may go to Love from this angle or that angle, but the truth is I only am talking about Love. One could say my profession is that of an internal sanitation engineer: I remove garbage, facilitate the removal of garbage, and encourage everyone to take out their garbage so that it can be incinerated. Once that is done, Love informs everything we are and do. The garbage is our wrong identification with who we are not.

To that end, we have to consciously choose Love and let go of who we are not. We have to accept that all this hate and injustice we see is also in us. As we face ourselves, we are able to empty the garbage and discern how we are to act. God is making us choose: are we going for Love or hate? Who we think we are is more bound by hate than Love. Who we are in truth is the Love that is not the mere opposite of hate. The great task is to continually choose Love. Baba said this is a great time to practice, because good and evil are so well defined. We have to be able to discern in order to choose Love.

Right now, we have an opportunity to go beyond the tired dialectic of hate and love that keeps us trapped in conflict, and choose Love. We must remove our superficial understanding and see the unity in the diversity. Recently, I was surprised to find that there are people who, without knowing it, have been resisting Love because they believed that if we choose Love, we will no longer have a voice. If we all Love, do we still have a voice? Of course we do.

Swami Nityananda was an *avadhoot*. He Loved and lived in the understanding of Absolute Reality. He wore only a *lungoti*, a loincloth. Swami Muktananda was his disciple. He also Loved and lived in the understanding of Absolute Reality. He wore orange robes made of exquisite silk and the finest cotton. He wore malas and watches and the Guru stone. He gave talks all over the world to hundreds of thousands of people. He lived a very different life and lifestyle than his Guru. And yet their Source was the same. Though they were the same, their voices were very different. Their vehicles were different, so Love flowing through them was expressed differently.

Love should consciously express ItSelf. But when we forget who we are by covering up that Love with our shrunken sense of self, we begin down a road to entropy.

| Entropy / disintegration | Growth / renewal |
| Go with the flow / no resistance | Uphill battle / labor |

History, both the big picture and our individual lives, shows us countless examples of people who convinced themselves there was no way hate could win. I was married once to someone who had the ability to detect a person's weakness. He then went about exploiting it. Trump has that ability. He has shown us all the weakness of our country right now. Though Trump is taking advantage of that weakness, many people around the country can't see that; they think he's empowering them so that they have a voice. He thinks he can trust his instincts, and his supporters think they are going with the flow toward some idea of greatness—but the flow they're going with leads only to entropy. Growth and renewal will be, at this point, an uphill battle. If we as a nation want to learn from this, we must see this exposure of our weakness as a good thing, and set about resolving our issues.

The only answer for me is to return to the groundwater and contribute the Love that is not the opposite of hate. In Truth, all is and will be fine, but the drama being played out will cause great suffering.

Democracy is messy. But it allows for dissent, respectful dissent. We are not to be homogeneous in our lifestyles or philosophies or ways of expressing ourselves. Love always allows for difference, for freedom of expression—even the expression of hate. We must remember, only Love is embedded in Love; embedded in hate is its own destruction.

From Hate to Love….

I have spent the last three years encouraging people to own, master and transcend their hate. This has been an uphill battle.

At the beginning of this period, one person left. In one class, I gave everyone permission to hate; he was the most resistant and therefore the one most filled with hate. I called him out and said it was okay for him to hate. He continued to resist. Finally, I said he needed to choose between clinging to his hate and accepting and moving beyond it. Whatever he chose would be fine with me. He needed to take responsibility for his own choices, and he indeed had the agency to do so. After a few minutes, he said he wanted to leave. He got up and walked out. Good for him: he acted on what he wanted. Sad for him: he chose to hold onto hate. He never returned, though the door was always open for him.

For this person and many others over the last few years, accepting the hate within was just too abhorrent a thing to do. It was not nice. It was not positive.

The truth is, when we do accept the hate within and give ourselves permission to be with it, the hate dissolves and the Love that underlies every vibration shines forth. Cleaning and stilling our vehicles allows for God to fill all of us.

This is a practice that takes time and vigilance. We have to be continuously willing to be with our experience whatever it is, let whatever comes up from that experience come up, and function appropriately on the physical plane.

For the people who have remained and persisted through this arduous period of practice, the reward has been the promised Love. We have begun to surrender the non-self in order to uncover and recognize the true Self. "Worth it" is an understatement.

Now, as we move forward in a world that is presenting such a great test, we are to continue to practice no matter what we have to face. Love is the only answer. People who cling to the false idols of self-esteem and positivity will find themselves withering under the weight of these tests.

Our strength always comes from God. It is God's strength and wisdom that guide us through the maze of these tests. We have access to that strength and wisdom only if we surrender our will to God's, not as a concept but as an actuality. When we accept where we are and what we have, we are in the beginning stages of surrender. From there, we must be willing to stay with each vibration with no judgment on our shrunken self's part. Gradually we will become aware that where we were has dissolved, and we are now moving deeper and deeper inward as we continue the practice.

With the cleaning and stilling of the vessel, the Self is free to shine forth its true nature, Love. We then bask in the awareness of who we truly are, not who we thought we were. We are Love for all time.

The Vibration of the World....

For the last three years, I have been warning everyone that we were heading toward a time of fear, anger and hate. We are here.

The way out for us is to see the composite vibration of fear, anger and hate within ourselves and understand how it runs our life. Then we are to be with that vibration, let whatever comes up from that vibration come up and function appropriately on the physical plane by discerning from the Heart, not the head.

Each of us is going to react differently to the vibration of fear, anger, and hate. We act based on our unconscious system and believe we are right, because this is how we have reacted to that vibration in the past. We believe we are only responding correctly to the outside environment, which we wrongly believe is the source of the problem. The real source of the problem is our own internal vibration; we are both the problem and the solution. The outside environment is only a trigger for what we have within ourselves. If we have stilled our inner vibrations, then when a prior trigger reappears, we do not take the bait.

The way out is to get off the grid completely; then we are no longer being run by the vibration of the world. Unless we free ourselves in this way, we are contributing to the global vibration of fear, anger, and hate. By working with the three fourchotomies below, owning and accepting all four qualities in each fourchotomy, we can get off the grid.

Fearful	Courageous
Cautious	Reckless

Angry	At peace
Invigorated	Inert

Hateful	Full of love
Powerful	Weak

Unfortunately, we want to fit in, and fitting in these days means manifesting fear, anger and hate. This is true even of people who say they are acting out of love; if we really feel where they are, we will find a thin film of love and positivity covering a stew of fear, anger and hate. These people are not acting out of Love but reacting against that stew. But the stew is still in charge. People who react against it are mired in the stew and have no recognition of what they are doing. They are like fish unaware of the water they swim in.

Our responsibility is to re-cognize the vibration and own it by being with it—not running away or clamping it down or numbing it. Those strategies only feed the vibration. Unless we are willing to be with it, it will not go away.

This is the job of every human being, but not everyone realizes it. Now we have a great opportunity to see the vibrations, because they are all too apparent. And if we can see them, we can dissolve them.

The only solution is to stop focusing so much on what everyone is doing or failing to do and instead turn inward and face our own vibrations. We must solve, and resolve, our interior before setting out to repair the outside world. We must ground ourselves in Love—not a counterfeit "love" that is only the opposite of hate, but the Love that is the bottom line of all that exists.

All is Not Lost

cloudscape....

clouds   pass   as   always
      under   blue   sky
        white   clouds

below   all   hell   and
                      e
                      a
                      v
                      a
                      n

play
    to   gether
    n

same   field

    narratives   change as   clouds

                      blue   remains

eternal

new world order....

    the same

                                      playing

                                            field

     sky

                                    clouds

                 winds

water

                                      changing

   game

                                    changing

premise   goal

                                rules

   all   changed

  to win

                     get   in the

                              game

know   the

                       world

    and

                       win

  by playing

                     on   God's

      side

       use   same   weapons
          for   God
          for   Love
          for   Truth

don't   run   God   will
            find   you

     other   team   shows
         God's   rules

play
            confess   on   sides
     self   esteem   pushed   you
             to   lose   God

   brazen   attack   brings
                   us   back

      name   calling
            shows   where
not   with   God
   play   test   and
             win
                   by
   facing   facts
            esteem
                        does
not   want
                        to   see

Rush Hour

marching orders....

    Arjuna tried to
  run
 but you in your
  kindness
    checked him
on the field

     how slow i
   have been
  so sure of doing
   your work
    when

     in fact i
   have avoided
  my real work
    for you
now tired and old

     i turn to
   the tasks of facing
  this nightmare
    may your Grace be as
i go into battle

a living map....

my Guru
          showed me
                    the treasure
      not ready
        to be

my Guru
        guided me
              through the
                            maze
          of obstacles

              teaching
                to face
                          demons
                  the vibrations

my Guru fought
      for
      and
      with
      me
until

stillness
    was
    path

the treasure
      reachable

    Love arose

the one that
        first
      wanted treasure
      had disappeared

flag on the play….

    indifference to

                                 vice

      redirect
             to   God
focus   toward
               God
    stop
       the   play
    false   idols

    disentangle   fromthemess
                       ofmatter
        be   free
   in
      God

surrendering to win....

state actors
free actors
state the actors
know your part

the warrior embraces
          boredom
on all levels

as a weapon
as a tool
as a way of life

patiently he bores into
          the enemy
and wears him down

with the vibration
of non-attachment
          acceptance
          Truth
perseverance furthers

as the warrior is
willing to call
          the action
according to facts

he waits for
    peace to arise
  no need to push
          the point

the one that fights
    is a beginner
      is shortsighted

only if all else fails
    does the warrior
        remove his sword
      from the scabbard

last resort
and feels like
      failure
  so much to learn

sit still
wait for peace
dissolve the
      conflict
within to
  resolve
without

then clear action
        ahead

a warrior awakens to
      the virtue
  of boredom

weather the storm....

   whether the storm
            or
     not
  the

            chaos
    shines
           on earth

    internal
            weather
   at
      equinox

     will   be
        still

resting   in the
     Heart

     do   not   leave
      this   anu

     the point
   is us
radiating   out

     ballooning
       forth
  we   reckon
     with
       fate
  still   the chaos
       shines
  until
    we   learn

who   we   are

the storm is
         for us

      weather   it
         and

shine

Brave Souls

CHAPTER FIVE
BEING A WARRIOR

Warriors for Peace and Warriors for War....

It hit me that Tolstoy had it right: War and Peace. We are organized
into two teams: warriors for war and warriors for peace. We are playing a big
game. There are times when more players are on the warriors for war side
and times when the warriors for peace are winning.

As long as we remain separate from God, we are warriors for war,
though we may think we are peaceful. What matters is our motivation—
where the action comes from. If we perform a peaceful action from a place
of turmoil, the action will be perceived as traumatic and agitated. It is not
the action itself that necessarily decides the side it is on; it is the motivation
that counts. How many times have we committed apparently innocent
actions to only get yelled at and then say, "What?!"? Inability to
acknowledge where we are coming from causes us much trouble. We are
lying to ourselves and others.

Warriors for war may appear to be nonaggressive. And yet when we
investigate their actions more deeply, what they do comes from a place of
anger, separation, alienation, or something that causes pain. Pleasure-
seeking is seen as peaceful, yet it too encourages pain: pain of loss, pain of
being away from one's true Self, pain of looking in the wrong direction away
from God. So if we are to say what the main element is, it is pain for oneself
and others.

Warriors for peace feel very different. Their focus is inward—looking to
God within the Heart, not the mind or thoughts. Motivation turns to God's
will, not my will. So though their actions may appear harsh, they will be
experienced as love. Soldiers can be and many times are warriors for peace.

So we have to be really careful not to judge based on action or our narrative's judgment. The internal motivation is what to feel. If the person says, "It was not my intention to hurt," that may not be true. Ask yourself, are you a warrior for peace or a warrior for war? Be careful to answer honestly.

Clues in the Treasure Hunt....

Walking the path of spiritual practice is like a treasure hunt. Each clue will lead us down the path closer to the goal. The problem is, will we see the clues? Will we discern the clues properly? And finally, will we follow the clues?

Clues on this treasure hunt are always showing up. God does not want us to lose. Though we are challenged, the answer is always embedded in nature. The shrunken self, however, misses the clues, and will pass them without even realizing they were clues. So we need to be vigilant. We need to want to discern what is in front of us. The truth is, everything is a clue. So do not worry about missing clues. The answer is embedded in all our life; it is everywhere. If we open our eyes and see the world this way, then we will be approaching *prakrti* as the *Yoga Sutras* teach; Nature is here for our experience and liberation. So all is here for our education. Our life is actually designed magnificently to bring us to liberation. We have to be willing to see that this is the real purpose of our life: to go Home. Then we will see all our actions and situations as clues to take us to the treasure.

The next question, then, is what am I to learn from these clues? Here is where discernment plays a most important part. I may see all the information or clues but be unable to access and analyze them clearly. I can then make decisions that are completely erroneous. I can miss the mark completely. So even though I have seen the clue, I then have to read it correctly. Without discernment, I will be moving away from the treasure.

The problem with the shrunken self is that it is so sure of itself. We can discern correctly, and the shrunken self can be sure of doubt. Its purpose—until it is purified—is to cloud our discernment. We will call a feeling something it is not and then proceed from that erroneous assessment, only to find ourselves going deeper into darkness rather than into the light. So if I have a feeling that I am sure is reflectiveness, I will believe my thoughts to be insightful. However, if in fact the feeling is just sulky, then my great insight is actually a whiny complaint and I will be caught in a swamp rather than moving down the path. Once in this swamp, I will linger there for long periods of time and miss the chance to find the treasure.

I need to be asking myself constantly what am I supposed to be learning from this. True reflection is very important.

So once I have seen the clue and have now discerned the clue, will I follow it down the path? Most people will say of course they will follow it, but in truth will they? Will we have the courage to actually follow the path that is laid out for us? The clues on the path that guide us to the next clue may be fraught with pain and danger. We have to have the courage to face what this clue is telling us about ourselves. This is not always easy. We need strength of character, which means we are not attached to what we have to give up in order to move forward. The goal for us has to be more important than our shrunken self and its ideas. No matter what our temperament, whether a lover, a hermit, a warrior, a scholar, or whatever, we have to have the courage to face the truth.

Know that everything is a clue. Discern the clues. Have the courage to face the truth the clues reveal. Then the treasure of Love is there.

I Lost My Patience….

In Orkney, I cried, I laughed, and I finally gave up my attachment to patience. Thank God. I had been driven to travel to Orkney for the last two years, and on July 27th I finally arrived, not knowing what would happen or how, but knowing this was an important time. The quiet was amazing as was the landscape. Unless we went well out of our way, there were no people. The sounds were the birds, the cattle and the ocean. Some days the wind was prevalent.

The two weeks were about stillness and listening. Orkney was not distracting in any way. The transformation occurred by Rohini allowing herself to be stilled. Fluid, less solid, not important. Then the laughter, freeing and endless. From there, just consciousness.

Once home, there was the question of how the manifestation would change. What had been left behind in Orkney? For me, Orkney had represented the landing place of the Vikings as they began to play their play through the Isles and across Europe. I had felt an affinity with them for a few years, and the visit to Orkney was to be a time of resolution. How, I did not know.

Even as I left Orkney, it was not clear what had happened. As I said before, the vibration during those two weeks was almost nonexistent. That was not what I had expected. Peace, really? Yes, that was what came from the land, the water, the rocks.

Not until I returned home did it all become clear what had happened. I lost my patience. What a relief. Patience had been the quality that held me down. People tend to love my patience, and then are horrified when I lose it. The problem is, I have been too patient. Patience can become an enabler. So by the time the student is seeing me as a mean teacher, I have already been too patient. I am okay with being called a mean teacher. If I am too patient, I am not doing my work as clearly as I should. So patience has left me, and I am on a magnificent tear. Could not be happier.

| Patient saint | Mean tyrant / teacher |
| Suffering servant | Loving warrior / fighter for truth |

People who leave my classes usually see me as the mean teacher and perceive themselves as the suffering servant. Have they ever thought that they have been mean and I have just been too patient, thus putting me in the role of the suffering servant? When I do not play the part of the suffering servant, they resist the teaching.

Orkney was a time to uncover the warrior and free the soul from the tyranny of patience.

Someone will surely say that this is not very spiritual. Oh, really? Why not? Attachment to anything is attachment, and attachment to a good quality produces pride and turns the quality into something negative. For instance, the person who is too patient can feel superior to others. They will enable someone in order to maintain the relationship. How spiritual is that?

Without question, there are people who will say I have no patience. They were too busy focused on themselves to see how patient I was with them, hoping they would wake up. When they did not, the mean teacher or loving warrior—however you want to see it—came forth.

I invite all of you to give up your patience. Give up attachment to it so that you can then use it appropriately. Give up your patience with yourselves, give up your patience with your wrong understanding.

A loving warrior is one who fights appropriately. That means he is riding the horse in the direction God is going. A loving warrior is focused on God only because he knows God is everything. From this, a loving warrior and a patient saint work together within the same soul. And the suffering servant and the mean teacher or tyrant cannot and do not arise, no matter how many people project those labels.

Baba was for me the patient saint and the loving warrior. He modeled both perfectly. I have worked to let go of all qualities that have prevented me from being what Baba modeled, letting go of attachments to all qualities so that they can be used appropriately. And I have been patient in this process. Though my own sons have been annoyed with my patience, I did not realize how attached I was to this quality until returning home from the stillness of Orkney.

Join me in delving into the appropriate practice of patience.

War and Peace....

Peace is something we all say we want—except when we want to fight. Yes, many a morning each of us arises to enter battle rather than face a day filled with harmony and joy. So what is this desire to do battle, to fight to go to war? It is nothing new. War is the counterpart to peace; we cannot have one without the other. For many, peace is boring; war provides exhilaration and an opportunity to rise above the mundane. Heroes tend to come out of war, not peace.

So why do we still long for peace? What is in peace that we cannot find in battle? And how can we live without bouncing back and forth, never satisfied wherever we are at any given moment?

Let us look at why people go to war. For glory. For adventure. To prove our mettle and courage. To grow up. To have comrades.

Peace: why do we want this? For harmony. For quiet.

Can we have any of these without war or peace? Yes. These various goals are not achieved only by war or peace. And depending on his destiny, someone can feel harmony in war and glory in peace. So if we free these goals and qualities from being yoked to war and peace, we arrive at a different view. War brings destruction, distraction, death, horrific challenges. Peace, for many, brings boredom, complacency, passivity, apathy. War and peace produce chances for many people to face different types of karma at the same time.

The real question is, do we want only peace or only war, or do we face the reality that God is in charge and knows what is best for us at all times? War can be necessary when there is a tyrant. We then go to war to override the conflict the tyrant is causing. We will outwar the tyrant, either now or later. And we then work to have peace—not passivity, but a lively, active life filled with change and growth.

Both war and peace require us to give up our attachments. Attachment to peace will bring apathy; attachment to war will bring aggression. When we are nonattached, we face whatever is there for us, and neither peace nor war affects us. We are in the Heart, with God, living the destiny of the character we are playing.

Peace	Aggression
Apathy	Just war

Owning all qualities brings us to where we are fighting no one. Even fighting for peace is a distraction. We fight or live in harmony with no attachment, which means we are always aware and willing to do it God's way. We are not the doer. God is. We are actors on the world stage, playing parts that are all interconnected. If someone is attached to peace, then there has to be someone equally attached to war. If we are distracted by neither and instead focused on the Heart where God dwells, we then contribute selfless service. We play our part no matter what it is. In the *Bhagavadgita*, Arjuna has to fight, but he resists that reality. Finally, after Krishna shows him the Truth, he plays his part without attachment. Bhishma, fighting on the opposing side, is already a great being; he knows the part he is to play in the drama. He knows Arjuna will kill him. He does not shirk his duty. He plays his part to the fullest.

When we live from a place of nonattachment, war and peace are off the point. Whether in peace or war, we are to play our part to the fullest and with our focus on the source of all the play, the great director, God.

Facing the Deeps....

Why does the New Age thrive in the United States? The willingness to put in hard work seems to be leaving American culture. In recent years, we have come to value pleasure and positivity, accomplished with little to no effort. We "deserve." Equality now means that everyone has the same level of input no matter what. Expertise has been relegated to the status of mere opinion, and people with real depth and breadth of knowledge are mixed in with everyone else.

As a nation, we have lost sight of what equality and freedom really mean. We are equal and free to pursue our dreams. But our dreams have become nightmares to my way of thinking. We tend to be looking for constant pleasure, constant good feelings for the shrunken self. We are lost in the pursuit of self-esteem, which brings us to desire whatever we wish, whether it is plausible or not. There is no reality testing, because that would hurt or bruise my self-esteem.

The shrunken self, our individual self, defines love as pleasure and power. This superficial understanding is reinforced by superficial practice. So much of the New Age is about first-level practice as the final perfection. First-level practice involves the five senses, and no matter how sincere we are in its practice, this level alone cannot take us to God and real Love. For so many, the final perfection is about having beautiful ideas that lull us into feeling good about ourselves and others. But true spirituality is not living in the land of the lotus-eaters.

In America, we are so much about idea and image rather than reality testing. We rationalize and avoid owning and facing our mistakes. We protect ourselves, we numb ourselves, we run from things that hinder our growth rather than overcome them. We drug ourselves as a solution to our problems. We would always rather be the victim, so that we're not accountable. In this culture, the one with the most problems and behavioral triggers is the winner. Being responsible for our actions, which would indicate choice and self-control, is not seen as a viable response to life's situations.

Sadhana is all about owning and facing the truth, about calling something what it is. *Sadhana* requires courage, because it demands that we face and own up to the fact that we are the ones responsible for all we do. When we face and still the vibrations for which we are responsible, we then have the choice to realign our motives and therefore our actions. We can then choose to change our actions. Remember, all decisions made from the shrunken self are specifically designed to keep the shrunken self alive and in control. We have to know our system in order to get rid of it.

Evelyn Underhill speaks to true spirituality when she discusses the Dark Night of the Soul: "The ascending self must leave these childish satisfactions; make its love absolutely disinterested, strong, and courageous, abolish all taint of spiritual gluttony. A total abandonment of the individualistic standpoint, of that trivial and egotistic quest of personal satisfaction which thwarts the great movement of the Flowing Light, is the supreme condition of man's participation in Reality." And Johannes Tauler affirms, "We attain to the fullness of God's love as His children, when it is no longer happiness or misery, prosperity or adversity, that draws us to Him or keeps us back from Him." Ultimately, this means being able to live the words of St. Catherine of Genoa: "My *me* is God: nor do I know my selfhood except in God."

As Underhill establishes, "The self, then, has got to learn to cease to be its 'own centre and circumference': to make that final surrender which is the price of final peace."

As a nation and as spiritual practitioners, we must face the deeps. We must know that we can never solve what is deep by superficial means. We have to go deep to solve the deep.

The Pursuit of Friction….

Friction is the force that resists an object's movement across a surface. In practical terms, it slows down an object's movement. Though it sounds like something we don't want, without friction we don't have traction; without friction, we cannot move forward. And if we avoid friction in one place, we will unwittingly be moving into it somewhere else. If we feel no friction, we believe we are going with the flow. In truth, we cannot move.

So much of what goes on in America now is about avoiding friction. Whether it's a refusal to compromise or a desire to live a life of uninterrupted pleasure, our goal has become to no longer work. Ironically, we even work ourselves into the ground in order to reach our life goal of leisure. But by avoiding the effort to overcome friction, we are creating a society dedicated to dullness. Dullness then runs the country.

We spend much of our time pointing to the intense friction in other countries, but fail to see the tension that is forming here. No matter how slowly life appears to move, there is always change; we cannot and will not stay inert forever. The three *gunas*, or properties making up the world, are *tamas* (inertia), *rajas* (activity), and *sattva* (clarity, calm). Whether we are aware or not, we are always heading toward a balance of these properties. We want the three *gunas* to be in harmony. So if we are inert, then unconsciously we will want someone to be active in our midst. If we are lucky enough to have someone *sattvic* near us, depending on where we are, we will be drawn into *sattva* or we will rebel.

By *sattvic* I mean really clear, bright, and peaceful—not as an idea, but as an actual state. Part of what is going on in this country is that, however much we may complain or express concern about collective issues, we pretend that as individuals we are all fine. We decide intellectually that we're "fine," and we make sure our lives look "fine." Most of us are anything but fine, and if we let ourselves feel, we would know that.

American society was largely built on a strong work ethic. When we work hard, we improve ourselves by overcoming friction; we may even reach a level of prosperity. From there we retire, believing we have earned the right not to work. Thinking we want what is best for our children, we encourage our children to work less hard than we did, and try to spare them from stress. We want our children to be frictionlessly happy—but that's an oxymoron. Instead, we produce laziness. From laziness, we get to incompetence. From incompetence we slide into decadence. The prosperity will be used up by our seeking only pleasure and not doing conscious, meaningful work.

Work actually makes us feel better. A life of leisure is not healthy, and we must shed the belief that it is. The pursuit of happiness does not mean we get happiness without friction. Pursuit means we can or may go after happiness, and how we do that is work. If we think pleasure is happiness, then we are really just greedy gluttons. The expectation of happiness without any effort has become the perverted American dream. We have lost sight of the difference between having a right to pursue something and being entitled to it. We have little work ethic in the right sense, and even less stamina.

America distracts itself from its real work, which is cleaning itself up. America spends much of its time "fixing" others instead of actually fixing and taking care of itself. And because we do not really fix ourselves, we cannot and do not discern appropriately how to fix anything. This does not mean we should be isolationist; what it means is that any work we undertake abroad has to be rooted in hard work done at home.

Our children are being brought up without healthy friction. "I want" and "give it to me" are the phrases of an indulged child, not one who is developing character and a well-directed will. Indulging these phrases brings the child to not learn how to develop effort. Even our schools are now complicit; in order to appease parents and conform to current psychological models that still hinge on "self-esteem," they aim to make education as frictionless as possible. And frictionless education is another oxymoron.

Children need to learn how to overcome friction. My job as a mother was not to protect my children from bullies, adversaries, challenges, and friction; my job was to give my children the tools to face and overcome the friction of life. I helped my children see that they had choice—it was their choice. These days we keep the secret of life from our children. What is the secret? Work, discipline, and properly directed will. Those things will bring us to a satisfaction that ultimately leads us inward, to Love.

Guarding the Heart….

Guarding the door was the beginning. It led me to guarding the Heart. Baba knew what I wanted, so he used my worldly skills. They turned out to be the perfect metaphor for the practice I was looking for. Throughout my life, I had always felt directed to the next level. Dance led me in to Tai Chi Chuan, and from there Baba came to take the task of teaching me. As I moved forward, certain aspects of the previous practice were dropped, and something new in a deeper sense was added. In the end, Baba had me let go of all the outer activities and rest in the Heart. Free fall became a constant rest.

Guarding the Heart means being with our experience at every moment, letting whatever comes up come up, and functioning appropriately on the physical plane.

When I first went to Baba, I had been a successful Tai Chi Chuan teacher in Cambridge, Massachusetts. The school I started had over a hundred students. Martial Arts shaped how I approached life. Earning a degree in acupuncture and working in a clinic, studying Mandarin Chinese, and practicing calligraphy were all part of my immersion. My aesthetic naturally leaned toward a Zen spareness, and my clothes were informed by practicing Tai Chi Chuan several hours a day.

During the winter of 1975, I was a guard on the rooftops or patrolling the streets around the Oakland ashram. At the DeVille in upstate New York, I volunteered to be at the gate through which Baba walked to and from the evening program. I willingly missed the program in order to have that one passing minute with Baba. While everyone was at the program, I worked to remain alert guarding the gate.

There was never a problem. Nor was there a possibility of a problem. This was a chance for me to practice. This was Baba beginning to teach me what I had come for. He was teaching me vigilance and one-pointedness without the Tai Chi form—acting in and adapting to any given situation. From there, he was going to move me inward.

This foundational discipline of one-pointed vigilance continued like a thread that ran through all my subsequent roles around Baba. Whether serving as head of security in Ganeshpuri, standing attentively as Baba's gatekeeper in the courtyard or by his back stair, working as his appointments secretary during his world tour, or staying all day on Baba's porch in Delhi rather than sightseeing with other ashramites, I stayed awake and stood guard at all times, no matter what was happening. Usually it was nothing. But good warriors do not wish for battle. They remain still and always ready. Then they can adapt easily and quickly rather than stick rigidly to a plan.

Baba was my focus. Even when I worked in the ashram library in Ganeshpuri, Baba was my focus. I constantly practiced what he had taught me internally.

Everything external provides an opportunity for the practice, because as is the external, so is the internal. Starting with one-pointedness on the outside, the perceived shifts ever inward. The internal then informs the external. Ultimately, there is only the perceiver, and all else is the perceived. Baba was always moving me to guard deeper and deeper inward. So be with your experience at every moment, let whatever comes up come up, and function appropriately on the physical plane.

With sustained, one-pointed practice, the attention reaches the door to the Heart. At that point, the vigilance is thoroughly instilled, having developed from the more superficial practice. The guarding of the Heart forces us to be appropriate always, no matter what the outside may say. Hence Christ's saying that "what comes out of the mouth proceeds from the heart," or St. Symeon affirming that we should "renounce all other spiritual work and concentrate wholly on this one doing, that is on guarding the heart." Even Ho Yanxi, the Song Dynasty commentator on Sun Tzu's *The Art of War*, says, "So unless your heart is wide open and your mind is orderly, you cannot be expected to be able to adapt responsively without limit, dealing with events unerringly."

We are all to guard the Heart and then rest in the Heart. Whether we play the role of householders, monks, or anyone else, we are all soldiers. We must be vigilant. Our relating to the world must be done from the source, which is the Heart and not the head.

The General on the Hill....

Some commentators on the *Yoga Sutras* speak of the Witness as a General on a hill overlooking the troops. From this metaphor, many people come to understand the Witness as distant and unengaged; a being who watches but is completely uninvolved. The troops are left to their own devices and therefore to fate, wandering the field without the guidance of the General.

My experience is that the Witness has agency and responsibility. The Witness/General participates with the troops and engages—just as a military general, though he appears to be separated from his troops, is directing and impacting their courses of action.

In truth, we are the generals of our own lives. Our job is to know this and share in the great game. As the generals of our own lives, we must know and accept our proper relation to the General. From the standpoint of the General, we are foot soldiers, and we must be willing to serve.

The General is Pure Consciousness. Put another way, it is Pure Love. The General enlivens people and events, but it does not dispense advice. Consciousness goes through various filters at the different levels of manifestation. How clean its final expression is into the physical plane depends on how pure the filters and vehicles are. The human psychic instrument, comprised of an intellect, data collector, and identifier, is enlivened by Consciousness. If the psychic instrument is impure, then the clarity of Consciousness will be obscured. The same goes for our senses, personality, and emotions, or any other vehicle.

So the General is always radiating the Consciousness we need to discern and then take action. In order to fully express the General's nature, the troops must be disciplined and surrendered to the fact that they are not in charge. The troops have to work hard to let go of anything that is an obstacle blocking the General's radiance.

The General emanates Consciousness; the troops are to allow that Consciousness to direct all their actions on every level. Because the General is Love, when we are surrendered to him, we are guided by Love in all aspects of our lives. From there, we stop seeing the General from our eyes and only see through the General's eyes.

"Rohini" is an actor in the field for the Witness. The Witness enlivens her. She is a foot soldier for the General. She gets to act, but must always follow and obey the Witness. Baba wanted me to live this, so he was always directing me toward the Witness. Baba called me a general; he wanted me to know the Real General.

Another way to look at this is that in Truth, we are like the sun, not the moon. The Self, the Witness, the General, is the sun. He is self-illuminative, Pure Subject with no object. The foot soldier, the individual, is the moon. Remember, the moon has no light of its own. Without the sun, there is no light. Without the Witness, there is no Consciousness, no light of awareness, no Love. To be in right relation with the General and with the world, the foot soldier must relinquish its sense of itself as the center of the universe.

The responsibility of the General is to emit Pure Consciousness. The responsibility of the foot soldier is to clean and clarify himself, moving from *tamas* to *rajas* to *sattva* and beyond so as to reflect that Consciousness perfectly. Our capacity, capability and will must work clearly for the General. Not until the foot soldier is purified will he fully express the General's purpose.

On Board with the Mission....

What is the mission? This question is rarely asked, yet it is assumed we are all on board with the mission. We assume we are all on the same mission. In the Absolute sense, we are, but from relative reality, most of the time we are not.

Our sense of how to function on a mission arises from our understanding of community, groups, and teams, which ultimately comes from our family of origin. We will relate in groups based on that understanding. That can be a good thing or not. How each of us approaches a mission hinges on that understanding. When our response to a group environment is dictated by our family of origin, we may contribute appropriately, or we may stray from or even undermine the mission. This will not be a good thing for the team.

How many times as a young student were you in a group project? The mission was clear: one person does all the work and everyone else sits back. They get the grade the one person accomplished, and everyone is on the same page—even the teacher. Mission accomplished. I was that one person, and always wondered what the mission was for the other kids. They seemed so sure of how it worked and were willing to have it the way it was.

Teachers themselves lose sight of their true mission. How many teachers want to be liked rather than to teach their subject? And the outcome is always the same: students learn nothing and resent the teacher. It is the same with parenting. Parents who strive to have only "positive" experiences with their children will ultimately reap resentment.

When there is a clear mission and every individual involved is on board with that mission, it can be accomplished.

But when every individual has his own mission, the team or community will not be able to work together effectively no matter how clear the overall mission might be. The truth is, every individual has his own mission— preserving himself. If the goal is to preserve the individual, the real mission fails. No matter how much you may think everyone is together, the dialectic of selfish/doormat prevails. The leader who wants to be liked will be selfish and miss the mission. And when team members have their own missions which go against the leader, the one in charge feels like a doormat: not only is he trying to fulfill the mission, he is also trying to keep the ones not on board "happy and okay." Sometimes we just have to let others go.

We have to agree with the mission not just superficially, but in the very core of our being. All our vehicles must be in line with the mission: our intellects, our emotions, our personalities, our bodies, our senses, our minds and our hearts. This means letting go of our individuality, so we can discern where real community lies and contribute appropriately.

Fulfilling the Mission….

In order to fulfill a mission, we have to know the mission. We mustn't fool ourselves or others with a misguided sense of mission. And if we are going to take on a mission, we must be willing to see it through. If at some point we decide to abandon the mission, we must also be responsible for that decision. Again, we must not fool ourselves.

In an elite military force, the mission will take precedence over the individual. Every member of that force must accept this principle; had they not accepted it, they wouldn't have made it through the necessary training. Individual cares and desires are left out of the equation; everyone has to have signed on to this code and proven it in the selection process. If they care about other soldiers more than the mission, they may be seen as good or nice human beings, but they will have failed in their purpose. They would not be fit for the force, because they could not be trusted to fulfill the mission.

In spiritual practice, the same principle applies. If the individual is encouraged to thrive, then no one grows, no one changes, the mission fails, and the shrunken self is alive and well. We will not get to who we really are. Instead of letting go of wrong identification with the individual and being who we are—Love—the mission will become the propping up of that very individual, the perpetuation of separateness.

If we are not in line with the true mission, then either we must realize that and excuse ourselves, or the leader/teacher needs to inform us so we have the opportunity to either commit to the mission or leave. It is okay if we leave, it is okay if we stay. We need to call everything what it is, not what we may prefer to call it. After all, no one does anything because they think it is bad; they rationalize it as good.

For instance, I may think I am fighting or standing up for myself appropriately when in fact I am being selfish. I may think I am fighting for others and being a team player when in fact I am being a doormat. If I operate this way, I will not be able to fulfill the mission appropriately. Instead, I will be pursuing my own, hidden mission of individual self-preservation.

Here is a fourchotomy that allows us to work with this dynamic:

Fight for self / self-care	Doormat
Selfish	Fight for others / selfless

In spiritual practice, many people abandon the real mission out of fear. The Zen Master Nan Huai-Chin addresses this issue in his commentary on the *Diamond Sūtra*:

Are there actually people who have fright, terror or dread over these teachings? Among practicing cultivators one will see this. In their practice, many people are seeking the alambana [foundation] of emptiness but when this alambana actually appears, they take fright or are terrified. People say they are scared out of their wits and sweat bullets because they've "disappeared." I say to them, Aren't we seeking to be selfless? How can you be frightened? Wisdom needs strength behind it.

At times, our strength may free us to abandon an inappropriate mission. Many years ago, someone told me they were not a quitter. What I then said was to imagine that it is 1935 and you are a member of the Hitler Youth. You have now seen what the mission is, how destructive it is, but you are not a quitter. The truth is you should quit, but because of your idea of yourself, you will not quit. You are in fact selfish in the maintenance of your individual identity.

So we all have to face up to the mission we are actually on. If we are on a secret mission to preserve our separateness or specialness, we have to recognize and own that. Otherwise, we will defer joining the true mission of Love and Liberation. But join it we will, sooner or later—because Love is our True Nature.

Safety Comes from Within….

The Indian translator and commentator I. K. Taimni speaks of two paths: one outward, which involutes deeper and deeper into the chaos of the world and away from Love; and one inward, which evolves back to God.

We do have choice, but most of us are unaware of that choice. Because there is a force that continually is moving outward into manifestation, we tend to ride that force and easily, unconsciously, choose the path of involution. The path of return has to be taken consciously. This path appears to be going against the flow, but in truth each step on it frees us a little bit more from the vibrations that cloud and delude us.

Involuting into matter makes us dangerous to ourselves. Here are some of the qualities and states that arise when we involute: nervous wreck, stressed, careless, unconscious, lost in others, guilty, unreflective, impulsive, overconfident, indulgent, violent, disrespectful, stirring up hostility, depressive, in denial, defending, rigid, "good," numb, obtuse, risky, sloppy, defiant, rebellious, oppositional, grandiose, insecure, no core, humorless, resonating, wounded, victim, isolated, envious, fearful, angry, confused, enabling, prideful, judging, griping and complaining, greedy, vicious, malevolent, false, deluded, passionate, craving, wrathful, sunk in folly, controlling, unprepared.

When we involute deeper into matter, we create vibrations that perpetuate our unhappiness. We are not being kind to ourselves. But once we are committed to this, we will continue to look further and further outside ourselves for our solutions. The cause must certainly be this person or that thing or this situation. Because we are only turned outward, we believe the cause is never ourselves. In truth, nothing is ever solved this way. We may have moments of calm, but we had nothing to do with making that calm happen; something just got exhausted and stopped for a time. Not to worry: the problem will return and our focus and blame will again be on something outside ourselves.

When we evolve back toward God, the vibrations begin to quiet, and we learn to still them further, moving us closer and closer to God. Evolving back to God means being truly safe to ourselves. Here are some of the qualities and states that arise when we evolve toward God: healthy, inward-turned, conscious, reflective, responsible, respectful, modest, still, self-contained, accepting, restrained, nonattached, flexible, careful, kind, compassionate, empathetic, nonviolent, rigorous, disciplined, surrendered, good-humored, discerning, comfortable in your own skin, transparent, honest, seamless, confessing, compassionate, joyful, dispassionate, competent, pure, impartial, direct.

Turning in will aid us in experiencing the reality that safety is not about anyone else; it is really about us. Then, as we inwardly reflect, we ask questions. Are we willing to be safe only in juxtaposition to unsafe? Are we unsafe? Are we resonating with the unsafe, or are we still? Are we willing to see that resonating with the unsafe shows us where we still have work to do stilling?

There is no need to blame the people we resonate with; they are our teachers in a given situation. And if everyone in the room is resonating with the unsafe, how are we supposed to tell the safe from the unsafe? We can't. Everyone is unsafe. When the safe people stop resonating and still, the unsafe are exposed; they stand in stark contrast. Recently at the airport, I watched a very skilled TSA officer work the crowd. He played the part of the friendly puppy and jester. As he interacted with people, they tended to relax and quiet their apprehension. Anyone that did not quiet he engaged. He changed the atmosphere to allow for anyone unsafe to be exposed. Very adept.

In order to be and remain safe, you have to know what you bring to the table. This means you have to know your vibrations by their true names in order to still them. The literary scholar Nathan Scott put it this way: "Not to know how to feel is to be at the mercy of dreams and fantasies and fears by which we may well be undone."

Know your narrative. Know that your narrative is unsafe. Your narrative is unsafe because you never truthfully name what it's really doing; you only call it by its positive term. Everyone's narrative has to be exposed for what it is. Knowing you are not your narrative is not enough; you have to know how it works and what part you play. If you are always defending yourself, you are not safe. You are defending something not to be defended. Therefore, you are not safe for yourself or anyone else.

This means that for you to be safe, you have to be unsafe for your shrunken self. The delusion is that we are safe as shrunken selves. The challenging transition between knowing your narrative and then realizing that it isn't such a great idea is why so few people do *sadhana*. It is unsafe for the shrunken self. It throws everything up in the air.

If you want to be safe, be your own janitor: clean yourself up. There is not a spot you can leave; every nook and cranny needs to be cleaned. Every corner contains all the components of what's not safe. True *sadhana* brings all to safety.

The Real War To Be Fought, Part One....

Be with your experience. Let everything that comes up from that experience come up. Function appropriately on the physical plane. Seems so simple, yet it is so difficult to practice. Simple, but not easy. This is the war to be fought.

Every worthy religious and even martial tradition speaks of this war. But because of our wrong vision and understanding, we do not walk onto the battlefield. We tend to believe that aliveness happens outside of us, and the world within us is empty. With that understanding, we pursue the activities we should actually be avoiding. We will seek the excitement of violence and destruction rather than turn inward to true life and joy.

We live in a world that pursues violence and destruction in this way, consciously or unconsciously. As I. K. Taimni has said, "Even the excitement of war which brings so much pain and suffering is preferable to the intolerable monotony of everyday life which results when we are deprived of excitement in our ordinary life. Absurd though it may sound, I think a large number of people in their heart of hearts like war in a perverted way for its excitement, in spite of the terrible pain and suffering which it brings" (*Glimpses into the Psychology of Yoga* 130).

Even scripture can be misread as counseling us to turn outward and seek violence. By missing the inner fight, we misinterpret scripture as an encouragement or even an incitement to outward war. Psalm 18 reads, "He teacheth my hands to war, so that a bow of steel is broken by mine arms" (KJV). The verse could easily be read as a declaration of external power, but it is really telling us that if we arm ourselves by fighting the interior war, no external weapon can harm us.

With this in mind, we can see that discernment in external action is crucial. We truly should not think of acting externally without having first fought the internal war. When my sons were young, I taught them, "Do not shoot until you see the whites of their eyes." They learned that in order to be ready to act, they had to wait until they were completely clear, and then in many cases the appropriate action was something they hadn't imagined. Sun Tzu is right: in order to be clear and safe, you have to know yourself, know the terrain, and know who you're playing with.

This means knowing our own lurking motivations, so that we can master and transcend them. Once we have done this, our actions in the world will be clean and clear. "It may happen that myriad people suffer because of the evil of one man," said the great swordsman Miyamoto

Musashi. "In such a case, myriad people are saved by killing one man. Would this not be a true example of 'the sword that kills is the sword that gives life'?" (*The Book of Five Rings*, transl. Cleary, 96). We should always be checking our motives, which we can only assess by turning in and listening to our Hearts. Outward-turned people aren't safe. Cowards are often outward-turned people who are sure they see clearly.

But Sun Tzu is also right that the greatest strategists and warriors are wise enough to win without fighting. As my Tai Chi Chuan teacher, T. R. Chung, used to say, the true master of martial arts will be two to ten miles away from a fight when it starts. If you are inwardly still—empty, no vibration—you can be present but not be there. When fraught with vibrations, we are not awake. We're more interested in numbing our vibrations than in the alertness we need. This fourchotomy shows how the dynamic works:

Stressed (agitated, anxious, pressed upon)	Tranquil (at peace with self and world)
Vigilant / challenged (awake and aware / encouraged to tap inner resources)	Asleep / numb (not paying attention inwardly and outwardly)

In a situation where we have to act, we need to understand how to de-escalate, neutralize, and not be there. This means being present, and de-escalating within ourselves. Only the inner war teaches us how to do these things.

The paradox is that in order to fight the war that has to be fought, acceptance and surrender are the greatest weapons. In the *Bhagavadgita*, Arjuna has to surrender inwardly to God and accept his destiny before he is able to triumph. It is not about the outward battle; the inward battle is all that matters, and then everything else is in its place.

Surrendered (having let go)	Resistant (pushing against)
Beaten (crushed, caved in, folded, demoralized, abject, need to be healed)	Resilient (bounces back)

Whether we are generals or street sweepers, our job is to fight the inner war. Then we can appropriately function on the physical plane.

In Matthew 15:10-20, Jesus makes absolutely clear where the true war is to be fought: "And he called the multitude, and said unto them, Hear, and understand: Not that which goeth into the mouth defileth a man; but that which cometh out of the mouth, this defileth a man. Then came his disciples, and said unto him, Knowest thou that the Pharisees were offended, after they heard this saying? But he answered and said, Every plant, which my heavenly Father hath not planted, shall be rooted up. Let them alone: they be blind leaders of the blind. And if the blind lead the blind, both shall fall into the ditch. Then answered Peter and said unto him, Declare unto us this parable. And Jesus said, Are ye also yet without understanding? Do not ye yet understand, that whatsoever entereth in at the mouth goeth into the belly, and is cast out into the draught? But those things which proceed out of the mouth come forth from the heart; and they defile the man. For out of the heart proceed evil thoughts, murders, adulteries, fornications, thefts, false witness, blasphemies: These are the things which defile a man: but to eat with unwashen hands defileth not a man." (KJV)

It is not what comes to us from without but what we bring forth from within ourselves that dictates our relationship with the world.

The Real War To Be Fought, Part Two….

Once we have realized that the outer world is not the real battleground, we then must turn to the place where the real war is to be fought. We turn in, within our own territory, and do battle with ourselves. If we do not do this inner work, the work we do outside will not be clear and clean. By our very manner, we will cause disruption. Our job, then, is to surrender to God and have God direct the actions we perform.

As Ezekiel says, "And he shall set engines of war against thy walls, and with his axes he shall break down thy towers" (26:9). We can either resist God's will or be in right relation with God and help dismantle the fortifications of the shrunken self.

We accomplish this dismantling by doing the work of being with our experience, letting whatever comes up come up, and functioning appropriately on the physical plane. By practicing this, we are moving towards *sahaj samadhi*, walking bliss. Every time we manage to *be* with our experience and function appropriately, we are grinding down the ego's wrong identification. We are facing the battle that needs to be fought.

The Sufi teacher Muhammad Raheem Bawa Muhaiyaddeen understood this:

Do not wave your religion like a banner and go out to capture others. Only one kind of war is permissible in the eyes of God: the war you wage within yourself to defeat the demonic forces of lust, anger, jealousy, desire for revenge, and other evil feelings and attributes that may exist within your heart.

The irony here is that we believe that asserting our individual will brings us freedom, and that surrendering to God limits us. But the truth is, the more we pursue our individual "freedoms," the more we are imprisoned. Only through the right internal action of surrender to God do we win the war to attain true freedom.

As we face ourselves inwardly, we find that our interior space expands.

More space is within than without. The universe for us becomes deeper and deeper. Like that vastness, our understanding expands. What made sense before now seems young and superficial; what seemed incomprehensible before now becomes clear.

Few saints and teachers have written about the interior war with more authority than St. Symeon the New Theologian. In the *Philokalia*, he instructs us in how to do battle:

Attention should go on ahead, spying out the enemy, like a scout. It should be the first to engage sin in combat, and to oppose evil thoughts entering the soul…. On this warfare against thoughts by attention and prayer hangs the life and death of the soul. If by means of attention we keep prayer pure, we make progress; if we have no attention to keep it pure but leave it unprotected, it becomes soiled with bad thoughts and we remain futile failures.

Symeon goes on to explain the three levels of attention and prayer. Not until we reach the third level, which is called *shambavopaya* in the Kashmir Shaiva Tradition, do we have any success in this war:

[T]he mind should be in the heart—a distinctive feature of the third method of prayer. It should guard the heart while it prays, revolve, remaining always within, and thence, from the depths of the heart, offer up prayers to God…. To those who have no knowledge of this work and no experience of it, it mostly appears difficult and oppressive. But those who have tasted its sweetness and have enjoyed it in the depths of their heart, cry with the divine Paul: "Who shall separate us from the love of Christ?"

As we delve deeper within, we use different weapons to proceed. We began the battle by using our five senses, constantly redirecting them away from indulgence and towards the pure. We have fought for the stillness now achieved in our morals and behavior. We have quieted our bodies. The breath has stilled, and our senses no longer run out after any attraction or repulsion.

The danger is, we can get lost in either direction. Even turning inward can result in wrong understanding. The great Zen patriarch Hui-neng explains how this can happen:

The people of the world, lost in externals, get fixated on appearances; lost inwardly, they get fixated on emptiness. If you can be detached from appearances while in the midst of appearances, and be detached from emptiness while in the midst of emptiness, then you will not be lost inwardly or outwardly. If you realize this truth, your mind opens up in an instant; this is called opening up the knowledge and vision of buddhahood.

No longer are we fooled by the delusion that within ourselves we will find only emptiness. We have faced this battle and now forge on, using our will as the weapon of choice. With our will, we move our attention deeper inward towards the Heart.

Only by continual surrender can we keep moving deeper into our true nature. The irony is that in order to win the real war, we must surrender in this way. As we approach the Heart, we will know what Baba has described for us:

Keep observing carefully where the inner fivefold actions continue to arise and where they dissolve. Keep watching the petals of the heart lotus; observe how desire, greed, delusion, jealousy, enmity, arrogance, and envy form and dissolve in each petal. Where do they arise and subside? Why does this happen?

If we persevere in the interior war, our outward manifestation will be increasingly informed by the Truth. We will cease to create conflict outside ourselves, because we will have resolved it at its true, inner root.

Speak the Truth, Don't Get Angry, Part One….

Baba used to tell the story of Dronacharya and Yudhisthira. Dronacharya was the teacher to the Pandavas. One day, Dronacharya told his students, "Speak the truth, don't get angry. I want you to go home, learn this, and come back."

The next day, everyone came back, and each one could recite the statement except for Yudhisthira, who said, "I understand the first part, 'speak the truth'; I don't have the second part."

Dronacharya repeated, "Speak the truth, don't get angry. Now go home and learn it."

This went on for days, until finally, after Yudhisthira said yet again, "I can't get the second part," Dronacharya took a stick and hit him. At that moment, Yudhisthira said, "I got it! Speak the truth, don't get angry."

"How is it that you understand it now?" said Dronacharya.

Yudisthira replied, "I got the first part, 'speak the truth," but until I was tested, I didn't know about the second part, 'don't get angry.'"

Baba used to tell this story over and over again, and every time I heard it, I'd understand it a bit differently, a little more deeply. Even now, my understanding continues to deepen.

When we are dispassionate, free of attachment, we have the ability to speak the truth and not get angry. If I have any kind of attachment, I will protect the one who is attached and not speak the truth, and I will get angry. I will be selfish, and not serve the situation.

This does not mean we don't use anger. Baba expressed anger. But it was always clear that under his anger was nonattachment, because everything came from Love.

Baba used to yell at me. He yelled at me a lot. He yelled at me in front of thousands of people, and he yelled at me with only a couple of people in the room. It was always for my good. He always spoke the truth and didn't get angry.

When we are attached and get angry, we are that anger; our truth is clouded by anger, so it really isn't truth. Our sureness that we see clearly is itself clouded. If we are nonattached, we will not be attached to our sureness—we will serve the situation. When Baba expressed anger, he was always serving the situation. He was using anger; anger wasn't using or clouding him.

A parent who loves her children will use anger as a way of teaching and directing them. How many times these days, when so many parents want their children's approval, do they fail to love their children appropriately by expressing anger when it is called for?

Not speaking the truth and not getting angry is selfish. In order to speak the truth, we have to be willing to be with our experience, let whatever comes up come up from that experience, and function appropriately. The more deeply we are able to be with our experience, the closer the truth is to the Truth. We can only move toward resolution, toward God, if we speak the truth and don't get angry.

In today's climate, anger is everywhere, but truth is in short supply. Everyone is speaking out, but almost exclusively from a place of attachment—which means their anger is using them, not the other way around. And part of the problem is that when we speak in rage, what we are saying can't get through. If we speak the truth and don't get angry, there's a chance that we will be heard.

But the prevailing belief is that anger is the only way to have agency. In this mindset, to give up hate is to give up agency. People who are nonattached find themselves accused of being apathetic, and people who are enmeshed and clouded are applauded as engaged.

Nonattached	Enmeshed
Apathetic	Appropriately engaged

There's a difference between nonattached and passive. To be passive is to evade responsibility by choosing inaction; to be nonattached is to act always from a place of Love, so that we act appropriately in any situation—even when non-action is called for.

When you speak and act in anger, you remain trapped in the problem you are trying to address. If you speak the truth and don't be angry, you free yourself and others.

Speak the Truth, Don't Get Angry, Part Two....

"What we bring to the table" is a phrase I use often. It means what and how we feel, think, express, and act in any given situation. In *The Art of War*, Sun Tzu instructs us to:

Know yourself. Know the terrain. Know your opponent.

But most of us only know and can speak to the terrain and the opponent. We will know the ins and outs of what our opponent brings to the table, but we will not know what we ourselves actually bring to the table. We will, however, label ourselves in most cases as the one not causing any trouble. We can call ourselves victim, sensitive, right, good, true, even wretched, but we will seldom call ourselves the cause or instigator. We are just looking out at the world. We have forgotten and have missed ourselves.

Just after the Second World War, Albert Camus wrote about the danger of not knowing what we bring to the table: "[W]hile there are many people nowadays who condemn violence and murder in their heart of hearts, there aren't many willing to recognize that this obliges them to reconsider the way they think and act." It is all too easy to stake out a high-principled position without recognizing your piece in it.

As I have learned from experience, living in unsafe environments doesn't necessarily cause us to choose the safest course of action. It's not automatic that we will choose safely; we have to know what we bring to the table and discern whether it is truly safe or not.

When I was in such an environment, I had to look at what I did, what happened for me, what I brought to the table. And what I brought to the table many times was fear, cringing, bracing for the blow. Also anger. Bringing these things to the table never brought safety. I had to learn to still what I brought to the table.

Most unsafe environments revolve around someone who must not be displeased. That person becomes a dark backdrop to everything in the environment. Displeasing the unsafe person is not an option. We have to find safe people if we want to express our feelings. But our feelings themselves can be unsafe. We end up calling our unsafeness our truth.

As a result, we take out our feelings on a safe person like a child beating a pillow. But beating a pillow is not what we need to be doing; though it may provide momentary relief, it actually perpetuates and even escalates the unsafeness we think we are resolving.

What we need to be doing is minding our own business—not in an isolationist sense, but by minding God's business, which should be our own. That would require us to know what we bring to the table and be able to adjust it. If we are minding God's business, we will do what is appropriate. We will speak the truth and not get angry.

When we are nonattached enough to speak the truth and not get angry, we will find that openings appear that allow us to bypass the unsafe person we are facing. We have to withdraw our energy from them; they cannot be our focus. This is what Patanjali means when he refers to indifference to vice. If we do not know what we bring to the table, we cannot achieve this nonattachment, and we remain accomplices.

A great example of speaking the truth and not getting angry is Joseph Welch, the Chief Counsel to the U.S. Army during the McCarthy hearings. It was his measured, nonattached question—"Have you no decency?"—that removed the scales from so many people's eyes, reminding them of their own decency and revealing Joe McCarthy for the malevolent force he was. Had Welch spoken in rage, no one would have been able to hear him, and McCarthy could have exploited that rage to make himself look judicious. Welch knew himself, the terrain, and his opponent, and he won the battle in one swift blow.

Self-sufficient

Self-sufficient	Incapable
Isolated	Open to Help

mirror mirror....

    the little girl
        looks
     at her
          reflection
      sees
        the old
      bitter Chinese
        renunciate
      misses
        him
      holds onto
        him
      finally
        the Guru
                        frees her
      to love
        the renunciate
              smiles
        dissolves

ode to Sylvia....

where are you now

the house you clung to
   so proud of
       is
   gone

do you wonder
   wander

have you settled in
     to the job
   of learning kindness

so foreign so
   difficult
  for you

demanded from others
   exempt for you

committed to your story

as your house crumbled
   your strong will
     determined

to imagine yourself
       eternal   gorgeous

hold on you did

   even death defied

peace was boring love was weak

conflict pleasure
      fought for

applauded

o great teacher
    your house burned
        have you returned
to play

to learn your lessons

o Sylvia
     piece of work

you were the cautionary tale

   did you learn from you

  i did

so appreciative of the
   part you played so
      well

Hidden in Plain Sight

reflections….

two   birds
          meet
   at   the   window

their souls
           stunned
   different   degrees

          patience
  will   stirred
     with   shakti
      surrender
  God's   decision

       to breathe
       to blink
       to walk
   to   fly
     again
         actors
   play
     and   part

interruption….

    in   the first moments of
blissful   oblivion   as sleep drapes over
            reality
              rips   through
      the black sweetness
        to
        the   scream of
   death
as   battle   ends
    so   quickly
  for   the prey
        of mr fox

      fox   rabbit   sound
  vibration
        action
  all blend
          into
  out of
            me
nightmare
       sweetness
    that
        coddles
     us to
      death
  playing   the
    part   part
changes   in
  world   plane
of differentiation
     fox
  rabbit
      listener
witness   judger
  assessor

all
parts
of
play   for   the
All
who
watches   all
channels
at   once
manifests   at
once
for   All's
pleasure
joy
sat
chit

ananda

missing the boat...
we are all going
to drown
in God's Love
yet
we swim
to survive
treading dreading
in our ideas
do termine to
know no better
and gasping for
life
swallowing and
spitting out LOVE

Missing the Boat

Gethsemane....

   the moment
       the drama
the struggle

       the surrender
   to   God
     to the Real

leaving the part
      to play
  fully
and
      detached
  with God
at all times

the model
   acceptance
      to God
  and path
     God presents

to surrender
     must know
  God's will
to surrender
     not
     idea
     belief
     made up
      story

    God's will
       paves
   our road

  walk

Body Fourth

examination….

Baba asks me
shakti
that remains inside
shakti
that goes out
the same?

i say no

he looks at me
i continue

the inside circles
the heart

the outside drives
out
hands
feet
head

my body begins
to shake
full scream
rigid
levitates

i go

light and energy
the Witness is awake

i awaken

relay....

each teacher
    led
  to the next
    illustrious
one
                until
    the Guru
                showed
  the way
        to fulfill
  the desire
        for understanding
        for the bottom line
        for the truth of who
  we are
each teacher
    led
  to the same place
but   stopped
            long
before
                    the final
  Truth
        the baton was
                passed
until the final sprint
  so long   yet
        so short
Baba led me from
    being
            at the mercy
    of material
            no matter
                how subtle
Muktananda shared
        the Bliss of Freedom

    and
          modeled the external
   manifested
         informed
     by internal
  without being
      tainted
  by the exterior
freedom
     independent
        yet
  playing

who is the baker....

       half

                             baked

is   not

       baked   fully

                choosing

       what   baked

is   not

                 cooking

       only   maintaining

not   cooked   at

                all

       not   at

                All

the empathetic chair….

   it   feels

                for   me

   following   me

                     around

      the room

                    bringing

comfort

                  before

      lacking

              meeting

concrete

              view

    from   bottom

relief   now

   from   above

the care   the chair

  brings to the table

all places   all times

          every   wear

every where

          it bears

     my weight

  hour   wait

Autumn Spanda

CHAPTER SIX
TEACHING STORIES

My Second Morning Reflection....

My second morning reflection at Caux on 24 July 2012:

I want to share an experience that I had many years ago, which I wrote about in my book *Walking Home with Baba*. It contributed to directing me to where I am now.

During the monsoon of 1977, one of my tasks as head of security was to make sure mangy dogs didn't get into the ashram. I blocked the ashram gates with wire mesh, but the dogs were still getting in. Then I discovered that they were coming in through the drainage pipes in the upper garden. I had to wade into the dense vegetation there in order to block those passages. Afterward, I began to feel ill. I thought it was the flu. A homeopath in the ashram agreed, but every two days, in the early afternoon, I got worse.

Baba sent the head of Kaliyan Hospital and a couple of other doctors to my room to examine me. The doctors concluded that I had an amoebic abscess. They wanted to take me to Kaliyan Hospital, a crowded, fly-infested facility nearby. Not knowing that one of them was the chief of Kaliyan, I said, "I'd rather die than go to Kaliyan Hospital." They reported their diagnosis to Baba. Though I had been taking chloroquine, he advised them to treat me for malaria.

The next day, I was sicker than ever. I felt as though an elephant was standing on my chest. In the hundred-degree heat, I couldn't stay warm. When I wasn't freezing, I was burning up. My temperature hit 106°F. I lay on my bed wrapped in six blankets, and still my teeth chattered.

Suddenly, I was out of my body, looking down from near the ceiling. I was no longer an individual. Everything was still, and everything was perfect. I could see my body on the bed, but it was as if my seeing was everywhere, and I was everything. Then a decision was made—simply made, not by me—that I would return to my body. Back in my body, I opened my eyes and looked through them.

What I learned from this is that Everything IS perfect; we just don't always see it. When we are STILL and are surrendered to God, we can see that "whatever God does He does for good." There is no situation, in truth, that isn't perfect. Grace IS always present, and if we are surrendered, we can receive it. Our job is to return to the Heart, rest there in stillness and God will then come forth.

It is as Theophan the Recluse said:

Congratulations on your safe return! Your own home is paradise after an absence. Everyone feels alike about this. Exactly the same feeling comes to us when, after distraction, we return to attention and to inner life. When we are in the heart, we are at home; when we are not in the heart, we are homeless. And it is about this above all that we must take trouble.

(Quoted in *The Art of Prayer*, p.192)

Now let us practice. Be still and feel the peace and love within our Hearts. Then we will know that everything IS perfect.

It is 1:45 and....

It is 1:45 and we have been queued since noon with still another hour ahead. We are waiting for the opportunity to vote early. There are hundreds of us, all waiting to vote. When we got here, we thought the line wasn't too long to get into the building, so we waited an hour and a half. But when we got into the building, we learned we had another hour and half. Once in, the line wound around the halls of the building. So we were committed, or at least I was.

We are getting there. People are on their phones. One woman is knitting. Some are reading. People are meeting and talking with each other. All are sharing the one purpose of voting early. None of us will meet again, yet we are here today. The goal and the circumstance have contributed to a bond.

Presently, we are in a long hallway with people on both sides. We are sharing a rather close space. We are all so different and yet each of us is here to vote. And each of us has a voice and is here to contribute that voice. We are able to participate in a collective voice that is able to move the country in which we live. No one voice is more important than another; together we have a great impact.

We are on a pilgrimage, we hundreds of people. And there are milestones we must pass through. The first milestone was to get inside the building out of the cold. Then we faced the disappointment of yet a longer wait. We had to then decide, do we leave or face the challenge ahead? Once that decision was made, we quickly, or rather not so quickly, headed toward an unexpected long narrow hallway. We were encouraged by people not to lose hope. And so the next milestone arrived after moving down the hallway; we were able to turn the corner and return down the hallway toward the entrance. On this other side of the hallway, the next milestone was a light in the distance before we turned and reached the final approach to the voting room. During that last stretch of hallway, most of us were tired, our backs ached, and we wondered if this was worth it. Just like any pilgrimage, we had all the trials and tribulations.

Finally, the end is in sight. And we have reached our destination. As we wait to go into the voting room, we see people just coming into the building, and they have all the feelings we had an hour and a half ago. We want to assure them, we feel sorry for them, we sympathize, and yet we are not going to discourage them from going through this journey.

Once in the room voting only takes a few minutes. I had already prepared my answers and knew which way I was voting. The whole process took three hours. So was it worth it? Absolutely. Every day we go on a pilgrimage. Sometimes it's rough, sometimes it's easy and in the end hopefully we reach our goal. Today we did. And why was this so important to me? So many of us see the right to vote as no big deal, but as humans we are directing what lies ahead and contributing to the directing of what lies ahead.

Everything we do is and can be spiritual practice. Yesterday, while going to vote, I practiced internally. Today in the midst of a hurricane, I practice. Tonight as we celebrate Baba's *mahasamadhi,* I will practice. At all times, in all places and in all actions, we should turn to God. Go into the Heart and love your life, your pilgrimage.

Correct or Right....

There is a difference between being correct—following protocol—and actually being right.

Baba taught me to be okay even if no one talked to me or liked me. Yes, Baba taught me to be okay no matter what. How did he do that? In 1979, when Baba took the appointments secretary position away from me, people stopped talking to me. They believed I had committed some terrible sin and so did not want to be seen with me; they distanced themselves from me. So I got to see who had only talked to me because of my position and who still talked to me after that position was taken away. When there was just me, nobody got anything; nobody got any prestige or value from being with me. In this kind of situation, we get to see people's motives. When there is difficulty, we see where people are. I remember learning how few true friends I had. Even if you are just asking for help and you think people will be there, you may be surprised. Baba wanted me to be human and free, and in order for that to occur, I had to see clearly. He made me see what I was attached to and then let it go. Baba was no fool. When Baba said, "Love everyone, trust no one," he was speaking from experience. He was a realist. He was a saint. He saw things the way they really were. He wasn't going to pretend things were nice; he knew how things are.

It came to me recently that there is a big difference between being correct, as in following protocol, and actually being true, as in being human. If there is anything that Baba taught me, it is how to be human first. Don't get me wrong, I love structure; I always loved being in a situation where I knew exactly what was expected and knew the protocol and could easily follow it. Baba tortured me with that. He made me keep letting go so that I could see what was truly human as opposed to what looked appropriate and correct but was really rigid and cold. And tested I was. Most people found me tactless, and from a certain perspective, I was. But they did not understand that Baba was directing everything I was doing. He used my willingness to be out there to place me in situations to teach me. Baba wanted us to be free; he taught in ways that were appropriate for each individual.

I remember a time at the DeVille in 1976 when the head of SYDA was to tell somebody something Baba had told him to say. It was not the nicest thing to say. And this man was a nice man, truly a nice man. So when he told this person, he softened it. Of course, Baba found out. And Baba's response was, "Everyone's going to like you but me." This stung the man to the quick and he knew what he had done. I'm sure he never did that again to Baba. So is the lesson here just to follow the Guru without thinking? No. This is about discernment. This is about being human; being appropriate. This is about having the guts to say what needs to be said even if it is uncomfortable.

Baba, for me, was always appropriate. He was neither tactless nor correct. He was right and human. And he was not rigid. To be human, we must be fluid; we must be able to assess what is actually needed and then act appropriately. This is not about following a formula. This is not about self-interest. For many people, taking care of themselves means taking care of their shrunken selves and this is their motivating force. And that is what ends up being correct and following protocol. We will say the same lines again and again, believing we are kind and good and following the appropriate path. Only later, if we are lucky, do we find out how inappropriate and tactless we actually were.

At Yale Divinity School, the spouses of future priests started a support group. I went the first night. We were to go around and share our backgrounds. When it came to me, I was honest, which brought an awkward silence. Afterwards my neighbor said, "You didn't offend anyone." I never thought that I was offensive, so why would she use that word? This was my history; there were no crimes or offenses of which I was aware. After that, the women were in fact distant and one little girl said to my then two year old that she was not allowed to play with him. Human? I think not—rather, correct and definitely safe. My then-husband had already told me I could not display pictures of Baba in the living room and not to tell anyone I came from a Jewish family. I had been tactless by telling simple truths about myself. Wow.

So here comes the reason for correctness and protocol: the avoidance of discomfort for all the players. When we are human and right, things can get messy. There can be awkwardness; we can feel wronged by the messenger. Or, as the messenger, we want people to like us so we cloak the honest answer and deceive them and ourselves. Protocol looks safe, but if it is not appropriate, it causes injury and is tactless. Being human brings us to resolution. There is resolution with protocol and correctness when they are right, human and appropriate.

We have to discern when to speak up and when to be quiet. This decision needs to come from deep within the Heart. Depending on the situation, we may open our mouths, following protocol and believing we are being appropriate, and cause terrible injury, because keeping quiet would have been the human and appropriate action. In a movie from many years ago called *Absence of Malice*, a journalist reports something that is correct but inhuman, and it causes terrible injury. You can feel that your intention was good and clear, but then what do you do with the injured person in front of you? Do you say that it is theirs to deal with and you did nothing wrong? You followed the "correct" path. Was it correct? Were we human? Did we have empathy? Did we see from their side or do we not have to because we are "correct" at all times?

Where is seeing the other as ourselves? If we knew we were standing on the other side would we be so "correct," or would we be human and appropriate, and express love in a way that Truth shone through and resolution was available for all the players?

Work Is Fun....

As a child I was active; I had "productive" and "work ethic" written all over me. My girl classmates in the sixth grade would say, "We like boys, we carry pocketbooks, we cut our hair. You are so different than us." They were right, I was different. I was boring, in that I danced every day after school with a prominent dance teacher in Boston, taking a bus downtown and coming home late. I loved those classes; I loved dancing, the discipline, all of us together working for the same purpose. That was where I lived. That was my fun.

In the eighth grade, my one year at Fort Lee, NJ, I was in a class for gifted kids. The lessons were stimulating, and I so enjoyed school. The kids in my class worked hard and were good kids. We were not, however, part of the popular crowd, the crowd that partied and did no work but appeared infinitely more fun than my classmates and me. At graduation, for some reason, I was included by this crowd. So excited to be "in," I was embarrassed about my other classmates. I played a part with the popular kids in order to fit in. This play luckily only lasted for a couple of days. Boredom set in; they thought of nothing but instant pleasure with no discernment. Done.

High school brought me back to Boston, where I kept more to myself. Sports occupied much of my after-school time. I participated on a varsity team every season. I did not hang out with kids that went to parties or were "fun." I did not know whether I was experiencing sour grapes about not being a popular girl or it was just not "me." Because of this, when I got to Washington University in St. Louis, I went out for cheerleading and a sorority. I went full out, and became the president of my pledge class and a Washington U cheerleader. The next year, as a varsity cheerleader, I became a cheerleader for the St. Louis Cardinals Football team. I now knew I could do it. I also knew it was not "me." This was not where I wanted to live forever. Fun, yes, but for only a short time. I definitely grew bored. There was nothing wrong with the people or the activity, I knew that from experience. I was neither repulsed nor attracted. It just was not my path.

I wanted to return to the discipline of dance. This is where I started heading more and more inward. Dance took center stage at Washington U and then Mills College. I built my life around hard work, focus, and people who shared the same vision. But life is a treasure hunt, and with a hundred percent commitment, we can move quickly from clue to clue. By putting all the effort into dance, I seemed to complete my relationship with it, and the next step showed up. I moved from dance to Tai Chi Chuan, where I applied the same commitment in a different venue. I delved deeper inwardly than I had with dance. Again, I deeply enjoyed the work.

Each of my teachers, whether they knew it or not, handed me off to the next teacher. Looking back, it makes sense, but in the midst of it, there were times of confusion when I questioned where I was going. Tai Chi Chuan led me yet again to a point where I knew I needed something more. There was a sense I could not get to the bottom of understanding. Tai Chi Chuan made way for Swami Muktananda, and that is where I have stayed. The outside may have changed, but the focus remains the same: looking inward to God. Does this mean I have no fun? Not at all. I love to play, but my focus is on the goal of life; moving from hell through purgatory to paradise.

Love is our birthright. I know this cannot be achieved by living only on the surface and fitting in. We each have to follow our *dharma* and accept it. I love to work and share in that work with others. If we look back at all the different events in our lives, we can see that we have always been directed toward what will bring us to God. The problem is discerning correctly and then persevering. No matter what we are doing on the outside, inwardly we must be boring into the deeps. That is where the real fun is.

Low and Behold....

Around our cottage in Orkney, there are fields filled with cattle, sheep, wheat, grass pasture, or wild growth. The ocean, with cliffs rising from it, is within walking distance. Spotted around are farm compounds. No stores. Virtually no people for us to see or hear. The main landmark, high on the ridge two miles away, is Marwick Head. Entertainment is quiet.

So when a farmer arrived with two women right outside our cottage, we went to see what they were doing. I watched the man attempt to herd cattle using a truck. The purpose was to get the twenty cattle, each worth around £1500, through a gate across the narrow road, down the road for ten yards and into a field adjacent to our cottage.

For forty minutes, the man used his truck, driving back and forth, back and forth in the field. Rather than working with the cows, he was fighting them. And the cows won. He kept pushing them one way, and they kept moving any way but the way he wanted. The man even hit the cattle with his truck. Frustrated and angry, he seemed sure that if he continued the way he was going, he would force the cattle through the space down the road and into the designated field. The women stood in the road on either side of the gate, ready to direct the herd.

We watched this battle between animal and man with truck. I was sure there was a better way. Aaron, who has worked on a cattle farm, could name three better ways, all of which would not have entailed a fight. There was no question both parties wanted to fight. Finally, the cows looked like they had conceded when they went through the space onto the road—and then smashed through a barbed wire fence as if it were nothing and into the wrong field. They won. There was nothing more to do, except the man now had to at least fix the fence before the darkness settled in.

How many teachers and students have we all seen who work this way? What a great lesson.

And "low" and behold, today, the cattle are back in the original field. The farmer opened the gate between the two fields and the cattle went back to where this present dance started. In the meantime, the field he wanted them to go to is empty and covered with lush green grass. The cattle never even saw that field. So everyone wins. The cows are back at their original place and feel smart. The farmer knows he is smarter than the cattle because he thinks he has now manipulated them. Nothing has changed.

Both have a poor sense of agency, though they each believe they are in charge. Neither made a conscious choice. Consciousness was in neither the farmer nor the cattle. Both were being instinctive, impulsive, and of course animal. No consciousness, no agency, no choice. All decisions and actions were based on reaction.

Yet we believe we are controlling the situation, don't we?

If we are focused on God completely, then we know that we are not the "doer." God is. We should just focus on God and be still; then, even if we are moving forward one inch, we are not the doer and movement is happening. We are moving forward. We are riding the cow in the direction it is going.

Neither the cattle nor the farmer moved forward. They danced the same dance and landed in the same spot. They were the doers. When we are the doers, this is what happens to us.

Stop the fight. The farmer did not ride the cow in the direction it was going. What could he have done? He could have coaxed the cattle with apples. Using instinct, they go for food. He could have gently herded the lead cow instead of chasing with the truck. We do not need to fight. And if fight is all the other person wants, then we can quietly walk away. The cattle wanted and were trained to fight with the farmer.

The *Shiva Sutras* say that the three impurities are "we are separate," "we are imperfect," and "we are the doers." The truth is "we are not separate," "we are perfect" and "we are not the doers." If we stop our shrunken selves, our characters, from dancing the same steps, saying the same lines, feeling the same feelings, and let God be in charge, we will witness moving forward the way God wants for us, which is Love.

Grow up by Giving up....

One day in late summer, in the heat and humidity of Maryland, I was out on the deck when I heard a horrible whine. I could not figure out what animal was making the sound. The animal sounded injured. Finally, I saw a hawk, a male hawk, screaming. A female hawk flew into the area and the young hawk went crazy flying after her. The female turned around and left as fast as she could.

Searching on the Internet, I uncovered that this was not a fluke event. The female was the mother of the young male. The mother hawk had waited too long to kick her young one out of the nest and encourage him to learn how to survive. So when she finally threw him out, he had no tools to survive on his own. His cry was the cry of juvenile hawks when they are in this condition. Now he would either figure it out or die. For the next couple of weeks, I watched this apex predator pecking around in the dirt looking for worms, bugs and anything he could possibly eat. The season was at a point when all the easy prey had already been taken.

Obviously, this hawk struggled. He would walk in the field looking for food. He even would crawl along the fence looking more like a sparrow than a hawk. The mother would occasionally show up, and he would fly after her as she evaded pursuit. And the cries were pathetic. When I told some people, they would say, "Oh, the poor thing." No: the mother crippled him and abandoned him, but he certainly did not need sympathy. He needed guts and perseverance. I waited to either hear a change or silence. Finally, one day, I heard him make the familiar call of an adult male hawk.

How many children are in that hawk's dire situation? How many of us are crippling through life, unwilling to "be" alive and "live" to our fullest? We win by losing, believing that is the only way to get love. We may have gotten attention that way, but we did not get love. When my children were young, I had a sign on the wall: "Get attention by doing things right, not by drama."

The culture of self-esteem produces young hawks unable to survive. We are bringing up children who win by losing. The winner is the victim, the most crippled. As Radhakrishnan put it in his translation and commentary on the *Bhagavadgita*, "The *tamasa* nature is dull and inert; its mind is dark and confused and its whole life is one continuous submission to environment" (319).

Here is a fourchotomy that might illuminate our understanding:

Codependent	Independent
Connected	Isolated

Through this culture, we create a narrative that poisons us. We buy our narrative of victimhood and goodness and innocence. And when we buy it, we then contribute to our own poisoning. In seeing ourselves as victims, we submit to environment. We then have no choice and are determined to be mired in this Hell. We aspire to be and remain in our childhood experiences.

In the introduction to his translation of Sun Tzu's *The Art of War*, Thomas Cleary quotes Master Sun: "Look upon your soldiers as beloved children, and they willingly die with you." But he also points out that Master Sun counsels against being indulgent, so that your soldiers become like spoiled children (24-25).

Sadhana is about letting go of our cherished narrative and realigning ourselves to God. The Guru is the parent that is constantly supporting the *sadhaka* in this process. It is not a one-time event. It is an ongoing process, so that when the disciple stops fighting the Guru, everything goes easily and joyously and with great humor back to God. Who we truly are is "perfect just the way we are." But as long as we believe we are the narrative we perpetuate, the joke is on us. And this is so sad, because we look and act like that apex predator pecking for worms.

For God's Sake Live Your Life....

The most clear resistance I meet with is the push against living our lives to the fullest. So sad. Baba wanted me to be independent and free to experience the Bliss of the world, which in fact is the bliss of God. Granted, there were times when I fought him, not out of thinking he was wrong but out of my own deficiency. I was afraid to stretch. Ultimately, and luckily for me, I loved Baba more than I loved my shrunkenness. He pushed me, stretched me, prodded me, encouraged me, punished me; he did at any given moment the appropriate action to move me to God.

How do we move toward God? By accepting that we are alive and living our life to the fullest. Not by being selfish and boxed into our personal narratives, thinking we are safe. Remember, if you are boxing yourself in, you are also boxing everyone else in. The boxes in which you put people may be smaller or larger, but they are boxes nonetheless.

"But I wish…," people say. This is wrong understanding; it is just a comfortable kind of hopelessness, a refusal of life. And if you really want and wish, then go for it and see whether the direction is appropriate or not. I always say I would rather make my own mistakes than someone else's. Taking responsibility in this way is living your own life. If we look outside for our motivation, then we can tell ourselves we are not responsible; whatever or whoever is out there is to be blamed when things do not go according to our plans.

Living to the fullest is riding the horse in the direction it is going and accepting where we are going in harmony with God's will.

In 1979, when I was Baba's appointments secretary, I hit a wall. I was seeing too much around me that I did not feel comfortable with. This was never about Baba, but some of the people around him. A person I worked closely with was more interested in personal power than in God. I could not at the time resolve it within myself and be okay. So I was in conflict with the environment around me. I loved working and being close to Baba and did not see that there was a way out if I wanted to remain close to him. Little did I know, Baba knew everything, including all the power plays and politics. He knew how I felt. He knew it all. I was in fact limited in my understanding; I still equated physical closeness with internal closeness. I also loved Baba as an amazing expression of humanity. So I wanted to remain "close."

Baba wanted me to be free and independent. He did not want me to be small. He did not want me to be afraid. He did not want me to settle and not live my life. Baba wanted me to fully express God's greatness. This is what he wanted for each of us. He was fighting for my Life. And in his love for me, Baba destroyed my narrative. Not what I would have expected. He did not care about the organization. He cared about each of us in the truest sense of the word. He cared that we live in our Hearts, and express and be the Bliss of God.

So for the sake of the Self, one day Baba turned my world upside down. I thank him every day for that gift. Baba quietly spoke to me for over an hour. Without so much as raising his voice, he told me how disappointed he was in me for not having been true to myself and spoken up. Then he removed me from my position as appointments secretary. As he made clear later, he did it out of Love, so that I could be free.

As the days, weeks, and months moved on I kept my mouth shut. I did not complain to people close to me or to myself. I did not blame. I was responsible for what happened to me. My job was to learn from it, not wallow in it. I kept quiet internally so as not to support a narrative that had no reality, such as victim, unjust, mean, or anything else I could have come up with. By keeping quiet inside and out, I knew I was burning up the karma. This was not easy, but I wanted freedom and Baba was helping me attain this. He was making sure anything that was in the way, whether I was aware of it or not, was removed.

If we want to live our lives fully, we first have to recognize and accept that our shrunken selves are not self-illuminative. We have to realize that the only source of light is the Self of All. Until we make that leap, we are merely like the moon, deluding ourselves into believing that we are the source of the Light we only reflect.

Watching and Waiting....

Is God everywhere or only where we want Him to be?

Our flight back to Baltimore was supposed to leave at 4:30, getting us back to Baltimore by 7:30. Here it is 7:00, and we have not moved other than from gate B1 to gate B9. We have been texted that the flight was leaving at 7:40, then 6:30, then 6:10, then 7:30. Now we are waiting until 7:30, when they will update us as to when or whether we are leaving this evening.

There is chaos here with so many people not knowing what is happening. Waiting. Waiting. Waiting. We are all waiting for the Groom, yet He does not arrive.

Are we ready? When He comes, will we be vigilant and not lose our focus? Will we hear when He comes or will we be distracted and miss our flight? There have been many last calls for this person or that person because their flight is about to leave without them.

So we sit here. God Is here. Can we see Him? People tap on phones and iPads, distracted. People in their heads, wandering in all the stories that a novelist comes up with on an average day. There is nothing any of us can do. We are all practicing surrender. No choice.

Then the announcement that we are going to board. Cheers resound.

Once on the plane, we are seated and waiting again. Everyone anticipates takeoff. All looks good. There is sun. Still daylight. The captain tells us there are no problems. We wait. We wait. Then we get another announcement from the captain. Our flight has been assigned a different route. We do not have enough fuel to travel that route, so we are turning around and going back to the gate to get more. Now it is close to nine. It is hot on the plane, and we are all just waiting again. Will the Groom come? Did we miss Him?

Not yet. We are loading more fuel. When the bridesmaids left for fuel, they missed the Groom's arrival. Will we miss our chance? Are we willing to be patient and move toward the goal no matter what? The weather has finally cleared out. We are hot and waiting. Children. Men. Women. Life.

All waiting. New announcements. Time moves and we stand still. Patience. How will this play out? Will the Groom come and we, as bridesmaids, all be awake? Will some of us know? Will any of us know? Distractions accumulate, and we still wait.

What is the lesson? What is each of us to learn? What do we share? Humanity. God. Life. Love. Relative Reality and Absolute Reality. We all share whether we are aware of it or not.

Finally, so many hours later, we take flight. Tired and worn, we all make it home.

The Groom is always here, and the wedding is always ready to happen, no matter where we are.

My Neighbor Elvis….

A beautiful autumn day with shifting light, and the wind speaks of the cold and sleep ahead. The leaves are turning, and caught in the waves traversing the garden. Beautiful and sad. A melancholy settles on the ground as everyone and everything scurries in preparation for what is coming. All this is very familiar.

What is new is the disappearance of Elvis and all his friends and co-actors. About three weeks ago, when the weather was deciding whether to change or not, our neighbors left. What a summer sharing the garden with them.

Elvis, with his red cravat, was in charge of the feeder. He took his job seriously and did not fail to make sure everyone knew what was allowed. When Elvis was not drinking the nectar himself, he was guarding it and regulating its use. Others, mainly females, were allowed to imbibe or chased away at incredible speed.

The dance was amazing. Always coming and going, weaving in and out of the branches in patterns that no one could think up. Witnessing this, it was clear that thought could not even be ascribed to any of them. They were with their experience. They let whatever came up come up, and for them there was no question that they were all functioning appropriately and efficiently.

The darting and diving were amazing to watch. So fast and able, so clear and decisive. But that was not the greatest part: seeing the action so clean and direct, all of the birds passionate and disentangled participants.

Elvis's stillness was gloriously aware. Though I loved to watch him dive and chase others from the feeder, when he stood totally ready without attacking or retreating was the time to really watch and learn. Elvis was one-pointed without being rigid. He could move in a heartbeat without forsaking stillness. When most of us think of hummingbirds, we have in mind a constant movement. The wings never stop. Elvis commanded through his still awareness.

Elvis was the king. One day, a large hawk came and settled on one of Elvis's boughs. Elvis was not far away. The hawk never went for Elvis. He wouldn't, probably because the hummingbird is too small. But we knew it was because Elvis was the king of the garden, and when he stood at attention, he was bigger than any other bird entering this terrain.

Elvis knew who he was, knew who the other hummingbirds were, knew the other birds and thoroughly knew the terrain. There was no movement, no going forward, unless appropriate. No retreat occurred without the utmost of strategy. Elvis did not think: he knew.

Birds like Elvis are teachers of stillness. They may not have our level of consciousness and sophistication, but they are committed and decisive, both in stillness and in action. And even in action, they remain still. Elvis was, in his limited way, one-pointed. And it was brilliant to see. Though I attributed individuality to him, he had none, nor was he looking for any.

My summer was spent sharing the stage with Elvis. Whether I was inside or on the deck, every day was interspersed with sitting and sharing the stillness and life with Elvis. Such a large being within a small body, his presence was always felt. So alive.

Looking forward to next summer when Elvis returns—or at least an Elvis impersonator.

Removing a Shell....

The six-year-old girl looked intently at her image in the mirror. She saw an old Chinese man with high cheekbones, gray hair knotted on the top of his head, sharply slanted eyes, and a long thin beard. His expression was serious, his eyes intense. "I'm in the wrong body," she thought. "How did I get here?"

This old Chinese man has been with me all my life. My relationship with him has changed, from yearning to be him once more to learning from his presence and realizing the need to let go of him.

As a young girl, I longed to be back "there." My preferred gifts were always of an Asian character. These requests were minimally indulged, with no grasp of where all this was coming from. My parents did not understand, and I had trouble understanding them. Out of place internally, I never fit in. There was always a nostalgia for Asia, for what I thought was my real life. The Chinese man was always just under my skin.

The truth is, I did not understand what I was doing here in a little girl's body living in a house outside Boston. Neither did I really understand the Chinese man always so close by. But I felt that affinity with him, and it seemed normal despite the confusion.

As I grew, my attraction to Asia continued with art, movies and finally Tai Chi Chuan. Diving deep into the world of the five excellences, I found Mandarin came easily to me, as did calligraphy. I surrounded myself with green tea, Chinese art, and Asian music. I even got a degree in acupuncture and worked in a clinic under the great Dr. James Tin Yao So. My dress became that of a martial artist, with shoes and jackets right out of a Bruce Lee movie. Outside my Tai Chi Chuan school hung a sign with Chinese letters signifying the authenticity of what occurred within.

The problem was, the Chinese man was stern and unyielding. Everything was serious. Discipline. Toughness. Work. Asceticism. Nothing was ever easy with him around. Though I had a weird sense of pride about the Chinese man, he seemed to encourage a coldness in me.

Then I met Baba, and the Chinese man was allowed to manifest fully. By allowing him the freedom to act, I was able to see that I did not like him or what he represented. He was rigid and unhappy. Something had happened to him, and there was no love.

So I watched as my relationship with the Chinese man evolved. The nostalgia evaporated. No longer did I long for the good old days; those days had never been. I had romanticized him and therefore myself, so my life had not been so good. Baba helped me see this. The ascetic in the mountains had been disciplined, but stuck and attached to the goodness of an austere life without love and joy. I came to understand that the life of intense discipline has its place; but, at a certain point, attachment to it has to be let go. Baba brought me into the light of love and laughter.

The link to the Chinese man manifested physically as well. When I was eleven, someone came from behind while I was standing by the kitchen counter and startled me. In reaction, I brought my head down and knocked my teeth on the formica. My front tooth broke, beginning decades of caps and trepidation. This culminated last winter with two root canals. The year since those procedures has slowly brought the death of the Chinese man. In his lifetime, he had been attacked and struck in the mouth with a blunt weapon. The pain I suffered prior to the root canals triggered the experience of his anger and hate. There was no compassion or acceptance. No need. He was a warrior ascetic, a tough hermit who could put up with the worst of anything.

For the Chinese man, there was no Grace, only self-effort; the kind of self-effort that brings power and pride. Receiving the Grace and Love that come from God was not for him. My openness to Grace and Love meant that the Chinese man could finally die. Baba's Grace had been working toward this from the very beginning.

The truth about the Chinese man took a long time to see, but Baba is patient. Once in Ganeshpuri, my teeth were bothering me. I asked if I could go into Bombay to see a dentist. The day-long trip proved that my teeth were fine. Baba said that next time he would just use a hammer. He knew.

With the demise of the Chinese man, the husk of that identity fell away. I am now like a hermit crab between shells—raw, vulnerable, caught up in a transformation. While I feel a sense of loss, I am thrilled to see how my understanding has evolved to reach the final surrender of this *samskara*. Whether what we lose is positive or negative, we always feel the loss. The transition will take time, and I must not try to enliven what is gone.

The new shell, the new life, will manifest in due course. I am not sure how it will be, but I do know that removing that old shell has already created more room for Baba and God, which means much more Love and laughter.

Conscious Non-resistance....

As a teenager in Boston, I participated in civil rights marches. These marches were silent and orderly, with large numbers of people coming together. Later, at Washington University, there had been protests, but these were more about venting anger than reaching resolution. After being present for some of those demonstrations, I realized what was going on and withdrew. Eventually, there was a shift, and we all came together to express our anger and desire for peace in the university chapel.

Protesting in the streets was not new to me in 1972 when I came across it in Berkeley. While working on my Master's degree at Mills College in Oakland, I was intensely studying Tai Chi Chuan with T.R. Chung on University Avenue in Berkeley. I would take a bus daily from Oakland to Shattuck Avenue or Telegraph Avenue and then walk to Chung's storefront. One day, I finished at Chung's as it was getting dark. I had not seen the news and was not expecting anything as I began my walk to the bus stop a few blocks down Shattuck. Apparently, things had really blown, and people were angry and beginning to gather in the streets. I continued to walk, minding my own business, just heading to the bus.

Out of nowhere, a four-door sedan stopped in the middle of the intersection near where I was. The four doors opened and four large men in the blue riot gear of the day charged out. One of them was running right toward me, with his menacing baton up in the air, ready to come down. I watched, curious but uninvolved because I "knew" I was not part of this play. It never occurred to me that the policeman did not know I wanted no part of the conflict. I just stared and did not move. This happened so quickly, yet for me it was quiet and timeless. When the man was just about to reach me, he tripped on the curb and landed face down with his head at my feet. My response was to bend down and ask him "Are you OK?" I still had not grasped that he had been heading toward me. Someone from behind grabbed me and pushed me down the street. "They'll think you want to hurt him. Run." I left the man still lying on the ground, and escaped a couple of blocks away where there were no people.

For me there had been no anger, no conflict. I was detached and had no resistance. I was not a doormat; I felt that policeman was a human being like me, and though he was in the role of riot policeman, he was still me.

The riot police in Berkeley were called "Blue Meanies" because of their one-piece blue suits. Years later, when I was head of security in Baba's ashram, I was "Rohini the Meanie." I enforced the rules of the ashram. There were many who did not like the role I acted out, especially people who were rebellious. But I came to understand conflict from all sides, and, with Baba's guidance, learned how to let it go.

Non-resistance	Resistance
Doormat	Standing up for self

When we accept what is in our world, we are then able to choose how to act appropriately. We are not doormats; we are able to stand up for ourselves and yet not be resistant. Non-resistance means we can hear what someone is saying to us. The more clear I am, the more I see others' points of view and understand where they are coming from. We are not fighting. We are not in conflict. This is where "other" disappears. It is just us.

If I hurt you, I hurt myself. This is the understanding into which each of us must grow.

If you love, then I love. Conflict and resistance disappear, and even when we are angry, we are yelling at ourselves. This is what I call healthy narcissism. When we come to this as our living experience, then no matter what happens, it is only us. There is only the pure Subject. Love permeates everyone and everything.

Belonging....

We are in this together. Who is in it? All of us. Who? All. In order for me to be special, I have to be separate. In Truth, I have to be together. When we separate, we believe there are places we do not belong. When we unite, We belong everywhere.

"I am uncomfortable here because of them." "I am uncomfortable there because of the environment." In truth, it is because of me. That is the reality, and I have to work to be ME everywhere. Then everyone gets to be themselves. The risk of being excluded is always there, based on our karma. Not everyone in our midst wants us to be included. The more limited we are, the more narrow and superficial the criteria for membership.

When I went to Washington University in St. Louis, I was not sure how I was going to navigate the environment. In high school, I had played a varsity sport every season. Now in university, that was not an option since Title IX was not yet in place. So I went out for cheerleading and pledged a sorority because those were two kinds of activities I had shunned in the past. I wanted to see if my dislike of them was because of sour grapes or they really were not me. I became president of my pledge class and cheered as a varsity cheerleader then as a professional cheerleader for the St. Louis Cardinals. Because I belonged to particular groups, other groups tried to exclude me. I would have none of that, and found myself going back and forth across borders. There was a sense that I was testing to see if I could do it all. I was unwilling to be forced into limitation.

Years later, I had lost this understanding and willingly limited myself. At the time I first was introduced to Baba and his teachings, I was not interested at all because the tradition Baba came from was Indian. The trappings turned me off. This was not where I came from; I came from a Chinese Taoist and Zen tradition and culture. I believed there was nothing in common between what I was studying and what Baba taught. Of course, I was completely ignorant. Surrender to the truth of my own stupidity came when I saw I was approaching the teachings as if they were glued to culture and not to the essence.

Of course, there were others who divided rather than included. One woman in the ashram told me that Baba did not like women with suntans or with short hair. At the time, I had both. Then there was, "Baba does not like Tai Chi Chuan." When I finally allowed myself to do the form even if Baba did not like it, one of the trustees said that it was beautiful and there was no way Baba would be against it.

Baba taught me that the physical trappings were not what any true tradition is about. He made sure I was not attached to anything temporal. What Baba taught was universal, eternal, and internal. We are truly One. What divides us can and must be let go of.

Coming back to America after Baba had left his body and my first son had been born tested me to see if I could really live being inclusive. After three years at Yale Divinity School we moved to Wilton, Connecticut, the town that inspired *The Stepford Wives*. These people prided themselves on belonging and fitting in. No one who did not fit in could easily survive. My then husband was the curate of the Episcopal church. It was expected that I attend services weekly. I now had a second son whom I was nursing discreetly in the back of the church. After nine months in Wilton, I was told I could not nurse my baby there. A prominent woman in the parish said, "They may do that in India, but we don't do it here. We have put up with you; now you have to toe the line." Someone from the diocese came to help and told us about an Eccentricity Quotient. This meant that groups can handle just so much difference. To fit in, we could not have too many elements outside the norm. We would have to decide which things we could give up in order to belong. The irony was, I now had long hair. This was unacceptable. Rather than cut my hair, I began to wear it up. Friends sent fancy clothes that were not me, but I did not care. I stopped nursing in the church. Though I now fit in externally, I never fit in internally. Thank God.

Skin. Clothes. Hair. Language. Accent. Food. Style. Education. Money. Race. Profession. Nationality. Gender. Age. Sexual orientation. Body type. Sports affiliation. Ethnicity. Religion. Politics. Music. And all other element we can use to try to separate ourselves from each other. Even if we had all the same attributes, none of them would be what keeps us together or separates us. We all belong to each other. We all belong to God.

Avian *Samadhi....*

The winter was brutally cold. Weeks on end below zero degrees Fahrenheit, with wind chill minus 20 to 30. Even when the sun came out, it was bitter cold and dangerous to go outside. Our acre garden spent the winter covered in snow. No hellebores blooming through February for us. A couple of years ago, we began feeding the birds that wintered with us. Word has gotten out in the neighborhood. We now are feeding a large group of birds that, on most days, function politely at the various feeders.

There are always moments, though, when all the birds disappear. That is when a hawk comes through looking for a meal. If a bird remains in the branches of a tree, he is usually safe. The hawk cannot maneuver through the tangle to reach its prey. Only when a bird makes a run for safety is it lost. The hawk will appear nonchalant until a bird dashes from its out-in-the-open hiding spot. Then the hawk will strike like a laser.

The irony is that hiding in plain sight in the tangle of the branches is actually the safest choice. Yet the birds tend to feel exposed, or they feel the hawk's dangerous vibration of no vibration. Even instinct will not save a bird fearing death.

On one of those below-zero days in February, we were remaining warm in the comfort of the house, congregating close to the fire, when one of us noticed the hawk on an ash tree branch ten feet from the house. In the downstairs rooms there is a great view, so we all scurried down the stairs to the window.

The drama was unfolding. The hawk was cold, so he would only stand on one leg at a time. The other he would tuck under him in the warmth of his feathers. Shifting side to side, side to side. We were so engrossed in watching the hawk's regal and martial stance and dance that we were missing the real drama playing out before our eyes. As if the curtain had opened and we were entranced by the star, we needed to expand our awareness to see the whole stage. As we each adjusted to the hawk, one by one we noticed an equally compelling actor, a blue jay.

The blue jay was clinging with both feet to a branch of the snowbell tree not ten feet away from the hawk. He was staring at the hawk. The blue jay was mesmerized, unable to move, even in the extreme cold. He never blinked, and no matter how cold he was, he did not even shiver. He was one-pointed on the hawk. Even while the hawk appeared nonchalant, the blue jay was riveted and lost in the hawk. Minutes went by, which seemed like hours of intense drama. Everything was on high alert, with life and death in the balance.

We, the audience, were in awe of the performance; we barely moved ourselves. Each of us now moved our focus from the hawk to the blue jay and back to the hawk. What was each going to do? Who would make the first move? Could the blue jay in its terror not be able to stand it one more minute and make a run for it? What was going to happen? In the bare, relaxed movement of the hawk and the frozen one-pointedness of the blue jay, the externals were minimal, yet internally all was vibrantly alive, so utterly important. Life and death was playing out before our eyes. The actors were magnificent.

Then, offstage, there was a sound and apparent movement. The hawk exited stage right. In an instant, the drama was over, but the other actor remained onstage, so caught in the moment that he could not move. The blue jay was still frozen, unable to free himself from his one-pointedness. We were now rooting for him and wanted him to leave. We called out and banged to get him out of his *samadhi*. He became aware of the mundane once more and flew away.

The Oncology Lesson....

I have always approached my yearly meeting with my oncologist with great trepidation. It means returning to the scene where I played the part of the patient. My oncologist had always engaged willingly and graciously with my dialogue of facing my fear, of wanting to conquer both fear and my desire to remain in this body. Looking back, as the chemo proceeded and my body disintegrated, I would openly say I wanted to remain in the world. And yet I did look for a back door out in case it all got too much for me.

Even after the powerful experience I had in Ganeshpuri while stricken with malaria, when I left my body and was no longer "Rohini" and everything was perfect just the way it was and is, there was fear, pain, and of course terrible nausea.

It was not until today, at an annual check-up twelve years out from my diagnosis, that I finally got something I had been unable and unwilling to face. My body had had cancer; I had not, nor could I ever have cancer in truth. It was never personal. I had taken it so personally, which then did not allow me to fully get the lesson I was to learn from all of this and move beyond it.

When I walked into the waiting room today, as with any time I have gone to the Oncology Center, my blood pressure went through the roof, and I felt a tremendous sadness and fear permeate the area. No one is acting inappropriately or even giving away that this vibration is just under the surface. But the vibration is still there. No tool, technique, or approach has been able to lower my blood pressure. It has been just so personal. My body remembers the place and goes into flight mode. The seat where my blood pressure is taken looks directly at the doorway to the room where the chemo is given. Sitting in that seat, I would try not to care about what happens there, and intellectually I did not—but deep within, there was always something, whether I felt it or not, that would send my blood pressure soaring.

Actually, maybe today was a little worse, fraught with the fear of something. Each year I have been fine and my MRI was in November, so there should not have been any surprises. And yet why not? Why not a surprise that would signal the return of the cancer? Why not? Intellectually, I knew better, but in the spot where the unknown is unknown, why not? Of course the cancer could come back.

So when I was called to have my vitals taken, I was surprised to be escorted down a hall and into a side room that does not look at the chemo room. A change. But no change with my blood pressure. No change internally facing death, and more importantly facing the fear of death.

Back at my seat in the waiting room, I saw a man whose body was having a difficult time, and yet inside him there was strength. People were speaking about their different kinds of cancer and treatment. Sitting there, after twelve years, I felt the same feeling inside and out. My name was called and I went into the exam room I had been in so many times. I waited for the doctor. I closed my eyes and worked to let go. And then finally, for the first time ever, it was not personal. Never, after the intense experience I had been through, would I have allowed "it is not personal" to come forward. But it is not about me, and it never was. It is not personal. A relief.

Sitting down in the examination room, my oncologist asked the usual questions as to my health, which has been fine. The exam, fine. I brought up the sadness and fear that fill the Oncology Center: how does he handle them? Empathy, he said. Yes, he has empathy.

Then I brought up the one piece that I had failed to see and therefore failed to detach from: that it is not personal. It was hard to get clean of this one, hard to see that it was not about me when I believed I suffered so. But how attached am I to my vehicles, how much more do I have to clean out? The doctor and I agreed that in order not to take it personally, one has to get to the essential self. My body had cancer; I did not have cancer.

This is what I was meant to learn. Now I could and would take the time and learn it. Then my oncologist said we could suspend the regular visits and come only as needed. Really, is it true? Are you sure? Twelve years. My doctor visits are safety nets. No net now. Really? I graduated? I feel deep gratitude for the team of doctors who saved my life: Michael Schultz, who caught the disease early and cut it out of me; my oncologist, who shepherded me through the dark night of chemo; Mark Brenner, who figured out how to attack nothing but the diseased area with radiation. Along with all the other nurses, technicians, and administrators. Thank you all. And I now know it was not personal. We were together in an intense drama that came to a happy ending. Many such stories do and many do not. It is not personal. And yet here I am tonight, sitting in this body and not some other one. The family I love dearly, people who worked so hard to keep me here. It is not personal; it is Love that is universal.

The Great Stories….

It isn't that we don't know the stories. But the important thing is that the great stories are always teaching us. There are many great stories. Within them, at every moment, the great beings choose to live completely—not to settle for a mediocre, unconscious life that depends on emotion for its heights. The stories teach us the great lessons of life. They teach us how to live and what to work toward. They are not personal, and the characters always know it is never about them. The greater good is always working.

We listen to the Passion narrative again and again. The results remain the same. The Passover story, too, is repeated every year—the same story. The results remain the same.

Jesus played his part fully, as did the other actors in the Passion play. Jesus could have left Jerusalem; the story would have been very different, and we would not be listening. So what happened? At Gethsemane, Jesus faced what was to come. If he had said "no" and had not surrendered to God, then we would not be looking to the Passion for how to model our lives. He lived each moment fully; he did not run away. And yes, he questioned: he asked if some other outcome was possible. But God was clear: this was the way it was going to be played, and Jesus was to fulfill his role.

Jesus surrendered to God's will and did the unthinkable: he submitted to the cross and attained the highest. He is Christ. And Christ does not die; only Jesus did. The story reveals that true life comes through surrender to God's will. Even in the horror of being killed on the cross, he revealed the greatness of character, strength, and will, all in alignment with God. That is how we are to live, no matter what actions we perform. We are to surrender and live fully in God.

The Passover story brings us to the same place: exalted awareness of God's play and our roles as actors who are only here to express His greatness. One part of the story that has always been important for me is God's direction of Pharaoh. When the plagues and pestilences get to be too much for Pharaoh, he agrees to let Moses and the Israelites go. But each time, God hardens Pharaoh's heart. It is as if God is saying, "No, Pharaoh, you have forgotten your lines. It is not the time yet, and I will decide, not you." God directs all: it makes no difference whether we believe or not.

Moses surrendered to God and, as Jesus did, he questioned. God used Moses as the example for all to see: if we obey in every fiber of our souls, all will be fine. Moses is also used as a negative example when he disobeys and takes credit for what God has done. As a consequence, Moses is barred from entering the Promised Land. Isn't this also God using Moses to teach us that if we are prideful and disobey God, we will not attain what we think we are entitled to?

The stories of Jesus and Moses teach us that we must overcome our flawed character and surrender to God's will. It was not personal for them, and it is not personal for us. The way we relate with the world is based on how clearly we see this truth. Jesus and Moses both lived fully through their commitment to God. We are called to do the same.

So as we listen to these stories, do not assume that they are just stories. Every person who hears them is being exhorted to live fully with the Love and awareness that God is the director of our play. Surrender to His script, and you will be with God at all times, in all places. We are to Love God with all our heart, mind, and soul. Then our lives, no matter what mistakes we make, are not for naught.

Who We Think We Are….

The life of self-esteem is the death of the soul.

Self-esteem is one's overall assessment of oneself as an individual. The assessment can be backed by actual internal experience or it can be decided by phrases we repeat to ourselves. When the self-esteem becomes more important than the soul, we are lost.

Our job is to reassess the assessment. The truth is, no matter how low or high our self-esteem is, it is still just an idea we have about our character. Not until we actually experience the differences between self-esteem, our character, and who we really are can we understand them any way other than intellectually.

Spiritual practice brings us from who we think we are to who we really are. This allows us to set our inner and outer lives in order. As I wrote years ago, "Bring into harmony how you feel about yourself, how you think you come across, and how others perceive you."

Last week, I spent three days in jury duty. I admit that when I learned the trial might be five days long, I tried to be excused. "Whatever God does, He does for good," I said at lunch on Monday. "I know it, but I sure cannot understand it. I will be missing work. I have writing I need to do. My son is only home for a couple of days; there is work we need to do." No. Whatever God does, He does for good. There has to be a reason for this; I just do not know what it is. And so I began my lesson. There were eight of us on the jury and we each had lives that were being disrupted. We each needed to surrender; we had no choice.

I was the last person to be added to the jury. When we returned after lunch, we each had a notebook and pen we could use while in the courtroom to take notes. On the cover of each was a number. My notebook said Alt #2. I was second alternate; unless two other jurors dropped out, I would not participate in deliberations.

Why, karmically, did Rohini have jury duty as second alternate? Rohini was there to witness a system built by and for shrunken selves, as a drama of shrunken selves. She was not to get involved in that drama.

This was an important clue and help for me. Baba was moving me toward the understanding of the witness on all levels. All my years with Baba, he would have me witness different situations and then tell him what I saw. Here, too, I was only to be a witness. What was I to see?

This was a discrimination case; an African American woman against the Board of Education. She felt the Board had not taken sufficient measures to ensure her well-being while working in an alternative school. She had taken the job knowing full well the population of the school, and yet when they began ridiculing her skin color, she wanted the school to stop these children. The students she worked with in this middle school were ages 12-14. The complaints were only about boys, and those boys were mostly African American.

As the African American lawyer for the Board of Education said, "This is about words, only words. Words spoken by children 12 to 14." From the names she was called, this para-educator felt humiliated and her self-esteem was damaged. Her idea of herself was being attacked—by children she knew were a problem. And even though the Board used various measures to shift these boys from their behavior, she was intractably upset. The one thing the

Board did not do was expel them because they were under the age of 16. And yet this woman was not satisfied; nothing was going to quell her pain unless the boys stopped ridiculing her or they were expelled. Never did she see that she needed to do some adjusting. There was no clue for her. No lesson for her. No reassessing of her ideas about herself.

As for me, I witnessed. I watched everyone. The jury, the judge, the clerks, the lawyers, the witnesses, the plaintiff. My job was to see it all and understand what was happening. I was to witness, the way I did with Baba, knowing I would not be deciding, deliberating, coming to a verdict. And yet as a witness, I was a full participant. Though detached, I was participating by being present to the entire event. On both levels—as an alternate juror present at a trial, and as the Self enlivening the manifested universe—the witness was contributing consciousness. My fellow jurors clearly were seeing through any ruse there was. Everyone was, in the end, on the same page, not swayed by posturing or political correctness. The assessment was to be straight, without bias of any kind. And so justice was served, and I so appreciated each of the actors who came together to provide the opportunity to learn and shed a layer of the individual.

Baba used to say we as individuals are wrongly identified with our bodies. For the psychiatric and pharmaceutical communities, the body is a machine; all we are is a soulless set of chemical reactions. For them, by changing our thoughts and using the right medication, we will be who we truly are; happy, pleasured, shrunken selves.

The belief is that what makes us human is our physical body. That was why the plaintiff could not resolve the situation. She saw herself solely as an African American woman; a human body with black skin. And because her self-esteem and identity were attached to the color of her skin, the calling of names about the color of her skin brought her great pain. For this, I was sorry for her, but that was not what was to decide the trial's outcome.

Our shrunken selves are of service to us. They are not us; they are vehicles. When we detach and disentangle from our vehicles, it does not mean the vehicles then don't function. They function under our guidance, but we no longer believe them to be us. They are serving us, not the other way around. When it is the other way around, we feel imprisoned. If we believe we are our bodies, then money, food, substances, power, and sex are to be pursued and worshiped as the sources of our happiness. God is no longer in the equation. We are worshipping false idols. And the greatest false idol is our self-esteem.

The Guru Stone....

Many people have read my story of being given the Guru stone in my book *Walking Home with Baba*. For those who have not, I will give a short summary and continue from there.

During my years with Baba, he gave me various semiprecious stones. There were several citrines; they are lovely but only resemble the Guru stone, which in Indic traditions is a yellow sapphire. At Christmastime in 1980, we were in Los Angeles. One day, after I had reached a place where I was no longer willing to waste my time and energy on someone who was not on the same path as me, Baba called me to his room and, in that person's presence, gave me an 11-carat yellow sapphire. The Guru stone. As he handed it to me, he said, "Now you have the real Guru."

He later directed me to have it mounted in a ring to be worn on my right index finger, set so that the stone touched my skin. I felt the ring was very intense, so to soften it I had two small diamonds placed on either side of the sapphire. When I showed it to Baba in the *darshan* line, he said, "No. Take the diamonds away." He was not pleased with what I had done. I had the diamonds removed, and wore the ring without them. Baba was happy.

After I came back to America from India with a newborn son in late January 1983, my life completely changed. No Baba, no ashram, no sharing *sadhana.* The environment was hostile to where I had lived and what I practiced. I removed all the trappings of my prior life and, as Baba had taught me, took my practice completely inward. Wearing the Guru stone as a ring on my index finger did not quite fit the lifestyle of a new mother living what felt like an alien life.

Part of the change was transforming the ring into a necklace. Simple, with a strong chain, it remained around my neck every day. Several years ago, I switched to a stronger chain with an extremely secure clasp. Every day, from simple living and teaching to traveling abroad several times, I wore the stone.

On the morning of May 20th, I finished teaching and went outside to talk to my student Fraz and his landscaping crew, who were clearing away a massive pile of yard waste. We spoke for a good long time. I walked around among the debris and in the parking area, which was layered with wood chips. The phone rang and David handed it to me. I talked and walked my way across the driveway and up the front walk into the house. While speaking, I went into my teaching room, and when I reached my pillow, I leaned over. Out of nowhere, the gold chain that had held the Guru stone slid from my neck and snaked down onto my seat. It appeared the chain had broken. The stone was gone. Without telling the caller why, I got off the phone abruptly and started the search.

I called to David, and we informed Fraz and the other two men outside. Everyone was one-pointed on finding the Guru stone. I patted down my body hoping it had fallen into a piece of my clothing. No luck.

Outside, we all scoured the large area. Knowing that the stone was large helped, but it was not large enough to find amongst the debris. I went in the house again. What did Baba want?

Surprisingly, I was calm. "Whatever God does, He does for good," I said to myself, and I felt it as well. The only thing was, I knew that later, at some point, I would be devastated. But for the moment, I was peaceful. Everything was as it should be. A half hour went by. Nothing.

Outside again, I walked along the front garden bed. At my feet were a couple of weeds beginning to wither on the asphalt. I vaguely remembered that I had pulled them out of the large area of sedum. Leaning over, I separated some of the plant. And there, just lying there as if the place were its home, as if it belonged there—was the Guru stone. Resting on the dirt under the sedum, of course it was there. "I found it," I called. Relief and quiet remained, as if everything was going according to the script. There was no excitement.

Now, I could take the time to look at the chain. What had happened to it? Nothing. It was fine. I had assumed the chain had broken, but it had not. There was no logical reason for the chain coming undone. What was I supposed to learn from this?

The answer was clear. The time when I had concealed the stone in plain sight was over. It was time to return the stone to what Baba had told me to do with it. No more necklace: time to make the Guru stone into a ring again.

Hummingbird Community....

We couldn't just have one hummingbird. Elvis, in his quiet imperial stance, was not enough. We wanted more Elvises. The Guru grants what the Heart desires. We now have seven hummingbirds dancing off and on the deck, causing mischief and chaos.

Going out on the deck in the summer morning light and coolness to have a quiet breakfast has been our ritual. Lately, we have been sharing our time with a few hummingbirds eating their endless series of meals. But today was filled with the chaos of seven hummingbirds clearly relating with each other—and showing no cooperation.

The seven daredevil, dive-bombing hummingbirds are more interested in attacking each other and whipping around than in serenely drinking nectar and quietly soaking in the day. They weave in and out, coming close to us, paying us no mind because they have important work to do: preventing any other hummingbird from going to a feeder. If a hummingbird gets the chance to drink, unbeknownst to him he is about to be crashed into by another. They plow into each other and pursue each other at ridiculous speeds.

Now we are reaching the end of summer. It soon will be time to fly south. These birds need to be eating and conserving their energy for a rather long journey. But that strategy would require consciousness. They would have to be aware. It appears that they are aware of each other. Are they, or is this just a focus born of instinct? Cooperation and coordination at the feeder would be so easy; there is plenty of nectar for all. And yet this does not occur. Ants coordinate and cooperate. Why don't these birds?

We tend to give animals too much credit. Life force is running through them. They have feelings—some of them. They form ties—some of them. But is this just the nature of the particular animal? Each having certain capacities? And when nurtured, those capacities shine forth? As humans, we have a gift and a curse: thinking. It will separate us from the rest of the world and bring us together with it. The Consciousness that feeds us brings us to an awareness of choice. We have options.

I am not so sure our hummingbird friends have options. Last summer, Elvis was such a monk, or rather an ascetic. But now, in community, the hummingbirds demonstrate individuality and warring just for warring, with no viable reason other than instinct.

I feel so lucky to have a human birth because I do have choice. I can consciously choose the Love running through every fiber of the world. I could, but do not have to, reject that which is Real and True. The hummingbirds have no choice. And though they look free and fun and amazing as they veer around and bang into each other, they can't help themselves. We can.

Deprogramming....

Recently, I heard that someone who once studied with me had to be "deprogrammed" because he had a hard time understanding why he stopped studying. I do not know if this information is even true. It is not my bent to go on hearsay, but I want to address the topic of deprogramming because over the years it has come up in conversation.

At the time this situation would have occurred, the Saturday group class was working on accepting our hate so that we could be able to get rid of it. We cannot get rid of something we have not acknowledged we have. If I will not acknowledge that I am holding something, then I cannot drop it. This gives a whole new meaning to "getting rid of what you haven't got."

In this series of classes, people were wrestling with accepting that we all actually hate. This went on for weeks. Finally, I told everyone they had permission to hate. Some were relieved, some were confused, and a couple resisted. The ones resisting were "good," so they could never accept that they hate. In the meantime, these people were definitely hating me.

Anyone who has studied with me can say that I am never one to hold onto a student, no matter who they are. You want to discontinue? Fine. And there will be no email or phone call asking you to come back. This is all up to the student. The only thing I cannot abide is willful negativity without any detachment or willingness to wrestle with that same negativity. You can be as willfully obtuse and negative as you like, just not in my class.

Along with his fellow students, this particular person was given an opportunity to distance himself from his experience of hate. Because he was unwilling to accept his own hate, the effort got to be futile. I offered the person the choice to stay or leave. If he left, he could return whenever he felt up to it. Silence. I then said there has to be a choice: "It is okay. You can do what you want." Now this person tended to be passive, and not make choices but be at the mercy of the situation. Others made choices; he went along with them. In this situation, I did not play his game; he had to decide what he wanted. So if he found me harsh, he now had a chance to take care of himself.

He finally chose to leave, and walked out of the room and out to his car. I have not heard from him since. I guess he does not want to come back. That is his choice, and it is perfectly okay. So why the "deprogramming"? Deprogramming from what?

When I hear the term "deprogramming," I think of groups where there is a closed system with closed rhetoric, closed communication with others and closed doors so you cannot leave. There is no real questioning, no voice for the members, no decisions made by members and no boundaries.

I know a group from which I needed to be deprogrammed: the family I was born into. The real process of growing up is a kind of deprogramming: we must become conscious of the pre-verbal belief system that has governed our life, and disentangle from it. Even when we rebel against family authority, we are just continuing our attachment to it, and keeping our anger is maintaining a repulsion relationship.

My time with Baba deprogrammed me. Baba taught me what Love is and how to relate with the world in all its aspects, including my family, as an adult human being. Most importantly, he deprogrammed me by showing me how to surrender the shrunken self and return to our true nature. Spiritual practice is the only real deprogramming.

The Life of Anastasia....

It's customary to deliver a eulogy when someone dies. Though the word generally means "praise," in the most literal sense it translates from the

Greek as "good word." Sharing my understanding of my mother's life and the part she played in her little corner of the world stage is itself a "good word," so I will offer this blog and the next as a kind of eulogy.

Everyone asks about how my mother died—not how she lived. Her death was easy. Death is easy. It is life that is so difficult. We have choices with each. Her life was long. Her death was swift. Her life was full of pleasure, but it was far from pleasant. It was full of fight and defiance to the end. She was active, and no one saw her leaving anytime soon, but she surprised everyone. Although she persisted in being combative and full of energy, her death was inevitable and quiet. Only in the last moment of life did her body relax.

My mother's nickname among the caregiving staff at her assisted living facility was Anastasia. The nickname was their gently mocking acknowledgement of her colossal sense of entitlement. She loved being called Anastasia, because she saw herself as royalty.

Regal	Servile
Tyrant	Dutiful

Smiling and lively with people she hardly knew—or with men—she would tell people she loved life. She would say she wanted to have fun, to be active, and to go places. But she was always complaining of being bored, having nothing to do. I called her every day for the last decade of her life and always heard that same lament. Rarely was there any contentment.

Nevertheless, my mother thought of herself to the end as young and beautiful. She was the most beautiful woman in the room. She was the most fun. The most attractive. The most independent. The most free. And the most thin. And yet she required so much care. Because of her own idea of herself as a completely independent person, she had no appreciation for her dedicated caregivers. She was consistent and never strayed from the course.

To the very end, she complained. Complained of quiet. Complained when she felt she was forced to do something she did not want to, like allowing herself to be cleaned.

She identified as a victim so she could be entitled. She had to make others into tyrants so she could be deserving. She believed no one ever did anything for her, so she never acknowledged others' care. She never felt any need to say thank you.

But "Anastasia" was also a term of endearment. Just as my mother's caregivers named her after a princess, in their own minds they transmuted her vices into virtues. They saw her as alive and the residents who were compliant as dead. With my mother, at least they were never bored.

They described her as expressive, unique, colorful, eccentric, strong-willed, willing to say what was on her mind, free. People thought her anger meant she was her own person. But as I listened and they grew more comfortable, I heard my mother described as crass, aggressive, mean, cruel, combative, having no filter. Her weapons were depression, lashing out, insults, and disdain.

The shrunken self mistakes getting what it wants for the good life. When everyone agrees and indulges that desire, we have made a tyrant. Others both envy that individual and enable it. My mother's mantra was "I want to do what I want to do when I want to do it. Why do I have to do what others want me to do?"

Through those eyes, she judged everyone. In July for her birthday, as we did every year, we spent time with my mother. One afternoon we sat outside her assisted living facility and she spoke about her life. She couldn't recall having any friends. She told mostly scornful stories of her parents and of the men she had known. Men were of two kinds: strong or weak. Women were of two kinds: warm or cold. She had always conveyed that she considered me cold. She believed that she knew how the world really is. She thought of herself as wise.

So my mother was not going to learn from the world. She defiantly maintained her worldview and refused to grow. She *knew* the world was about pleasure. She lived out the Seven Deadly Sins—sloth, envy, pride, gluttony, avarice, wrath, and lust—and thought they were worldly ideals, the good life.

Slothful	Productive / hardworking
Completely free	Burdened / exhausted

Prideful / vain	Humble
Great self-worth / great identity	Anonymous / self-loathing

Envious	Satisfied / at ease
Motivated / ambitious	Inert / no passion /boring

Wrathful	At peace / accepting
Just / right	Doormat / compliant

Gluttonous	Ascetic / disciplined
Full of Life / lively / enjoying	Starving / self-mortifying

Avaricious	Generous
Eager	Dissipated

Lustful	Chaste
Passionate	Cold / frigid

Life in the body is life in the world. We cannot escape the world. From the standpoint of the *Yoga Sutras,* the world is here for our experience and liberation. We are always having experiences; it is how we understand them and what we do with them that will decide whether we will just continue to experience or whether we are moving towards liberation. We all experience;

what we call our experiences is so important.

If we are not clearsighted but instead color our experiences with wrong understanding, then we will keep going further down the road away from liberation—the road my mother chose and modeled. Let her serve as a cautionary example for all of us.

Lessons from My Mother....

I could have learned to be just like my mother. Though as a child I did not want to be like her, we unconsciously pick up the qualities of our first caregivers and live them out even in our repulsions—and our repulsions can bind us even more than our attractions. If not for Baba, I may have ended up as she did. He saved me from that fate. Though my mother met Baba and got *shaktipat* from him, she never did anything to indicate that event had ever occurred.

For the last several years of her life, my mother lived in an assisted living facility. The aides and nurses where she lived were astonishing because they did not fight her. They allowed her to be "Anastasia," a princess. And so my mother was as rude and mean to each of them as she had always been to me. As for me, I had reached an acceptance of "not counting" in her world. I was her dutiful daughter who was not to be acknowledged. And yet I continued to care for her every day to the end.

Why? Because Baba taught me service.

I continued to care for my mother because she is me and I have lessons to learn. If I were to fight her, I would be her. So I used the principles of Tai Chi Chuan with her. I wanted to know that if our interactions were taped, I would be revealed as clean and clear. She did not understand or know how I live and for Whom I live. She scorned my life. If anything, I would rather have faced benign neglect than her derision for living a rather stupid life from her point of view. To her, I was boring and trivial, while she was alive and charismatic. I did not compete or even disagree. When I called her every day for the last ten years of her life, I let her have it her way, and that left me at peace and able to be in relation with her without her attacking me and erasing my line. She didn't know my line.

There was no love, care, or respect from her because she just never knew or wanted those things. I knew that, and so did not look to her for them. Sun Tzu says know yourself, know your terrain, and know whom you are playing with. I knew and was okay.

Many years ago in regard to another person, I was accused of enabling when I knew I was serving the situation. My strategy changed when serving the situation came to be more about speaking up. I wanted to serve the situation and still call things what they were.

I only hope some of the people who took care of my mother were doing just that. Unfortunately, some aspired to be like my mother, or at the very least looked up to her.

I am sorry for those people. Baba taught me to see the Truth and not be deceived. To speak the truth and act appropriately. To speak the truth and not get angry. So I loved her not for how she was but for who she was in Truth. I loved, in her, God's willingness to play such a part in order to teach us all. We just need not to forget who we truly are and walk down the street like Mohini looking for a man.

In this way, I loved, cared for, and respected my mother. She was a great teacher for me. Where is she now? Hopefully laughing at the part she just played. More likely all ready to return, and to learn the kindness that she unwittingly taught others. When I saw her body, it was clear that she was refusing to leave it even though it was dead. I kissed her on the forehead and told her, "Go now and learn kindness." She will learn. She has no choice. In the end, we all must learn to Love.

The greatest lesson I learned from my mother came in the form of the challenge she posed. Could I be kind and true around someone who was unkind, who didn't love, who had hurt me and would continue to be hurtful? Thanks to Baba, I was able to meet that challenge. Thanks to my mother, I learned that kindness comes from within.

Gratitude and Care….

Ian, David, a student, and I had just walked out of the house and were examining the student's amazing sculpture of a head. "This should be in parks and gardens all over the country," I said. "People of all ages will love this." Suddenly there was a loud crash. We turned our heads to see a tree falling in the road and a large car going over the tree. The car, a minivan, came to a stop in front of the driveway. We ran to see if the driver was all right. Then the student and Ian quickly moved the tree off the road and onto the grass. It was about 9am, so traffic was brisk in both directions. The car was still in the middle of its lane, so we began directing traffic around it. David went to call the police, because the driver, a woman, was still in her car, talking on the phone.

Another driver stopped by the damaged car, and the two women started talking. I said, "You have to move on; there are people behind." "Has this happened before?" she demanded as if she were in charge and the tree's fall was somehow my fault. I said that it was not my tree, and could she please move on. She continued, "It is scary."

Wow, I thought. Everyone has to make this about themselves.

The woman who had driven over the tree was of no help. She remained completely sealed off from everyone else. She was rude, and not at all willing to see that people were being impacted by her car. We told her to call AAA. Because she had never removed the sticker from the card, she called the wrong number. I took the card and scraped off the tape so she could call. She clearly felt entitled, and did not acknowledge what we were doing to keep the situation from becoming chaotic. Her demeanor was condescending at best; in her mind, we were just there to serve her. She had no responsibility toward others—either us or her fellow drivers. I offered her water, but she refused. We were not up to her level.

Her arrogant refusal to be part of a momentary community was fundamentally unsafe, for her and everyone else. Rather than be safe by engaging with us, she chose to insulate herself, which was hazardous.

Safe	Hazardous
Insulated	Engaged

We were thrilled when the police arrived. They quickly realized that talking to the driver was useless, so they spoke with us instead, and politely asked if they could roll the woman's car onto our grass. We agreed to it though we knew the car was leaking fluid. The police were nice, respectful, and efficient. Once the car had been moved off the road, they left to handle some other situation. The driver didn't speak to them, but we made sure to thank them.

A tow truck from AAA would take thirty minutes. Again, I asked the woman, who was standing by our mailbox still talking on her phone, if she wanted something to drink, knowing full well at this point she would just say no.

As I was walking away I very loudly said to her, "You're welcome."

The situation revealed this fourchotomy:

Grateful / sharing	Ungrateful / isolated
Obsequious / lost in others	Detached / own person

Here we were, four adults with work and lives, joining this mess to share in the humanity of it all. We did that only to find the recipient was completely ungrateful. She did not care. The police cared. We cared. Some of the drivers who followed our directions cared. But the driver who needed the help was arrogant and isolated. At one point I even said, "Can you help here? I left my work to help." Not even looking away from her phone, she spat, "Well, go do your work." There was no humanity, no connectedness, no sense of responsibility for the situation.

I have been in accidents, and have been so grateful for the help of people who happened to be nearby and acted with humanity and responsibility. I have helped out when others have had accidents. When I go out of my house and engage with the world, I am glad for the fact that we are All here together and share in our common Source. How sad it was that this moment, which could have been an occasion for all of us to come together, share, and help, was instead just another lesson in how people isolate, hate, and refuse to Love.

Thankful for the Jewel....

The Jewel is always here. It is the key to life. The answer. I am thankful for that Jewel. I am thankful that I know there is a Jewel. I am thankful for Baba, who embodied the Jewel. I am thankful I could see the Jewel in Baba—in everything he did, said, and didn't do or say. I am thankful for everyone who recognizes the Jewel, who longs for the Jewel, who knows that somehow we will all long for and find and merge with that Jewel.

Baba used to tell the story of the great Guru Nizamuddin and his great disciple Amir Khusro. When we hear it, we tend to pay little attention to the third man in the story, the man who went to Nizamuddin for help in getting a dowry for his daughter. Nizamuddin said to him, "I have nothing but what people bring to me. Stay here, and whatever people bring you can have." Now this poor man could not see what Nizamuddin did have: the prize beyond all worldly objects. As the story goes, the two men sat for three days and no one came. No one brought anything. For three days, this poor man sat with a great being and got nothing. Finally, he said that it was better at home because there at least he could get food.

How sad to have missed the opportunity. But this man did not have the eyes to see. He did not have the subtlety of intellect to actually fathom what he was in the presence of. As the man departed, Nizamuddin felt for him and gave him his only possession, a pair of sandals. The man left completely unaware of the treasure that had been given to him. The sandals of a Great Being hold and transmit that Great Being's energy.

Because Great Beings intuit the whole of any *lila*, Nizamuddin knew that Amir Khusro was on his way to him. The poor starving man and Khusro then met on the road. The man asked for some water. While obliging the man's request, Amir Khusro noticed the sandals and felt the energy in them.

"Where did you get these?" he asked.

The man replied, "Nizamuddin. I stayed with him for three days hoping he could help me afford my daughter's dowry, and no one came, so his sandals were all he had to give me."

"I have eight camels laden with treasure," said Amir Khusro. "I will give you seven of them for the sandals, taking only the one that holds my food and water."

The man was delighted, and left with the camels. Amir Khusro sat down under a tree and placed the sandals on his head. Immediately, he went into *samadhi* for a very long time. When he opened his eyes, he continued his journey to Nizamuddin's retreat. When Amir Khusro arrived, Nizamuddin looked at his own sandals in his visitor's hand and asked, "How much?"

Amir Khusro answered, "Seven camels laden with all my worldly wealth."

All Nizamuddin said was, "You got them cheap."

Amir Khusro remained a faithful disciple of Nizamuddin for the rest of his life, and both are revered as Great Beings.

Too many of us, I fear, are the man who sat for three days without seeing anything. I am thankful that I saw the Jewel within Baba and continue to cherish it. My wish for all of us is that we know there is a Jewel to long for, and that a Great Being like Muktananda reveals it to us.

Tending Our Garden....

When I was a child, my parents worked in our yard. We lived in Waban, Massachusetts. Lots of rock. We had rock walls and rock gardens, with a very hilly, up-and-down-and-up terrain. Behind us was an aqueduct, and on the other side of that a swamp. Woods were everywhere. So there was cultivated and wild land. I wasn't involved in the cultivating part of my world; I watched.

In 1976, when I first went to Ganeshpuri, I encountered an amazing garden: seventy-five acres of ashram with cultivated gardens amidst the jungle. As Kipling said, the jungle could come in so quickly. The world was teeming with life and needed to be disciplined. Baba walked the gardens most days. My first job was to maintain security, so I walked the ashram gardens daily. The perimeter was important. I always had to check for the influx of the jungle one way or another—not that it could be completely kept out. The jungle and the people had a working relationship.

Most ashramites worked in the garden as their *guruseva* (service). They learned to weed, dig, compost and plant. It meant steady, everyday effort. A dear friend, Mark, was in charge of the garden. Venkapa, whom I loved dearly, was in charge of the physical plant. Baba directed everything, even at one time directing Mark to plant roses. All this was for our benefit; we learned how to take care of the world.

In the 1990s, I lived in a church rectory on church grounds. My two sons were young, and my then husband was the priest. He had been in Ganeshpuri and had worked in the garden. He wanted a garden for the church, so he built a garden that had a Japanese flavor. There were many beautiful specimens and a pond made from rock. It was lovely. But no one worked in the garden. No one tended the garden. And the garden was rather rigid and formal. It was not very inviting, and the parishioners did not venture in unless something specific was happening there. No one volunteered to keep it up. Decay and weeds intermingled very quickly. From the beginning, my children and I were forced labor in this garden. It was never our garden.

Many years after we had left and the priest had been defrocked, we returned to find that, though the parish was still there, the jungle had moved in. No one had felt it was the church's garden. Now, English ivy had smothered the variety of plantings. No one would have known what had once been there.

When my sons and I moved to our present home seventeen years ago, the yard was without trees or even worms. Clay was the essential element of the property. Gradually, we planted a garden; I always kept Baba in mind, as well as the upper garden where I had walked both on my own and gratefully with Baba on his daily walks.

In 2005, we started our visits to Cambridge in the UK. There the gardens are tended with great care and love. They reminded me of Baba's ashram. We feel the welcoming and the expanse and the harmony. There is no struggle, no fight. Nature, though perfectly cultivated and controlled, is not tight, rigid and unwelcoming.

Over the years, I have directed our own garden's expansion, so that now there is very little grass left. We can walk on paths in the shade of the trees we planted years ago, and enjoy the different layers of growth. Like Baba's gardens, it is a place for quiet and reflection.

This weekend we will be working in the garden spreading mulch. We have done this every year since the garden began. Why should we go to this trouble? Why do this? In Baba's ashram, we worked every day, internally and externally. Both complemented each other. If we only work internally, we become self-absorbed and lost in our my-ness. If we only work outside, we become superficial and lost in the material plane without any understanding of its cause. But when we are with our experience, let whatever comes up come up from that vibration, and then function appropriately because we are now discerning from within, we are able to truly practice and weed out what is not true.

Many spiritual and literary traditions use tending a garden as a metaphor for the work of life. Here, the garden is truly a metaphor for *sadhana*. Our job is to work over a long time without interruption and with great devotion. The garden receives steady care, and the weeds disappear and remain, for the most part, gone. Love is the ground of the garden.

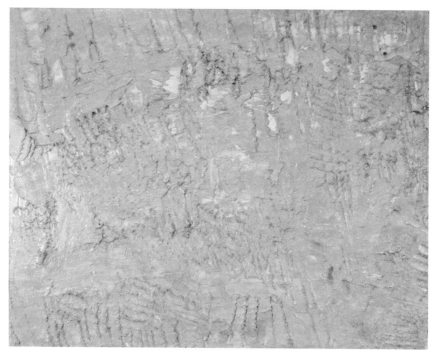

Botanica

covidiot....

like lady macbeth

       wash hands   again

again   to wash the sin   of ignorance

clean enough   think not   scrub   again

solving   solvents   not   resolving

clarity   of sun   light   missing   mark

to murder   virus   before   murdered   meeting out

musings of   delusion   deep within   breathing

with no   air   as if   hand   washing was enough

while hiding   behind masks   hoards   from

death

Gathering

hymn to Muktananda....

not the outfit
not the religion
not the ritual
All was the Self of All

not the education
not the money
not the pedigree
All was the Self of All

not the institution
not SYDA
not something else
All was the Self of All

not someone else
not the things
not the place
All was the Self of All

Swami Muktananda
knew the Self
lived the Self
worshiped the Self
was the Self

Swami Muktananda
loved the Self
taught the Self
shared the Self
was the Self

Swami Muktananda
meditated on the Self
honored the Self
exalted the Self

modeled the Self
was the Self

the Guru in the form of
Muktananda
revealed the Truth
revealed the light
revealed the darkness
revealed the Self

the Guru as Muktananda
showed the way
to satcitananda
the Self of All

o rohini do not stray
from the path he shines
do not distract yourself
with shadows

Muktananda is the Heart
Muktananda is Love

Muktananda is the Self
he is the only sacred place
meditate on him
go to him
find him in the Heart of All

Muktananda my Guru
is the manifestation of the Self
opens the gate that takes us
to the Absolute Self

Jai Gurudev

way to be....

so polite
     eats and never runs

  leaves a tip
every   time

   good manners
      knows how
         to be
   have

  respect for what
              is
    delicate with all
         picks the bag
 opens up
finds the course

       is never coarse but
  turns the lid
 to   a plate
the   appropriate
  napkin

no mess   efficient
         delicate
no waste
      receives the meal

with honor
   and   leaves

the bones as
       prasad

finally

       leaving
a tip

five and some ones
      a ten
never leaves
    without a

      thank you

the model
    raccoon

ode to the washbear....

the gentle   man
                        well
    mannered
                        never
    intrusive
                        quietly
    going
                doing
    his   business

            respectful

    until   this
            morning
    when   he
lay
                just by

        the   road

dead   unceremoniously
            left

                    discourteous   driver
well   mannered   raccoon

On the 35th Anniversary of Muktananda's Mahasamadhi....

Only because of Muktananda do I exist.

Baba left his physical body, but I will not let him leave me. I am a stubborn child who demands he stay with me. He may want me to be independent, but I hold onto his feet and won't let go. He must stay close so that I do not cause him any trouble. He must take care of me because he knows my weakness.

My love binds him. And out of his Love he stays and plays with me.

It so looks as though he is my slave, but I am his; willingly I have bound myself to his joy and Love. If I get close enough, I disappear and he is All once again. There is more of his play now, and less of mine.

And as I surrender to him, we are bound all the more, and there is no conflict as there is no difference between us.

I study and studied *bheda* to *bhedabheda* to *abheda*, but not until I gave up my differences could I see the world as it really is.

Baba, I wanted you to remain in your body and play with me. But out of Love for your disciples you left that physical body in order to push and encourage us to find you beyond the physical.

I pranam to my Guru, Swami Muktananda.

Sadgurunath Maharaj Ki Jay.

Concerned

Concerned	Careless
Worried	Carefree

CHAPTER SEVEN
OCCASIONAL PIECES

Mother's Day....

Today in the States, we celebrate Mother's Day. Baba was for me both my mother and father. He brought me up; he cleaned me up. My first mother and father were my first teachers. They continue to teach me my life lessons. I owe them much, since they introduced me to the part I am playing and helped reveal the "tools," so to speak, that I am using. From an early age, though, I knew there was more to life. But could not find it on my own, and surely could not figure out how to change on my own.

The great beings come in and free us from the repetitive soap opera, the boring drama where we repeat the same lines and never are free. Baba was willing to provide for each of us the framework that would free us from the tyranny and monotony of our shrunken self. I am most grateful for his parenting, because I was sick of my drama and wanted to grasp what rests under all this. Like any good parent, he used everything he needed to get through to me. Sometimes it looked ugly—not because of him but because of me. I required him to appear as the harsh parent in order to get through my stubborn ego.

As a teacher, I play a similar role, and I am not arbitrary. Baba modeled teaching each individual appropriately. Each of us has a different play, though our roles may intersect or appear similar. So I am listening for what is right for you. If I tell someone to do something, I mean it. If you want to know why I say what I say, then ask me then and there. Deciding not to do what I say and then sneaking around really does not work. Be straight with me and then we can move forward; deviousness undermines everything.

If you want to see me privately, you need to be practicing throughout the week. We cannot have the same class again and again and again. That is inappropriate. If you are working, we can grow; otherwise, we are wasting time. It is okay: I will still like you, I will love you, I just won't see you privately. There are plenty of ways to ask me questions, if you have them and are working.

I have written about the treasure hunt. The clues are everywhere; we have to see them and then discern appropriately. There is nothing that cannot be used as a lesson. When we see the world this way, everything becomes heightened and amazingly alive and vital. Every event with Baba, no matter how mundane, was a lesson to be pondered.

We tend to focus on the dramatic moments in life and look to them for teaching. Living with a great saint showed me in truth there are no such moments if I am awake. Since everything is God, all events are designed for each of us to learn. The simplest event around Baba could have the greatest import for those of us willing to learn something. Daily life with nothing for the shrunken self to grab onto was where the work really happened. The routine wore the ego down, so that then Baba could easily chop it off. Isn't that what a good parent does?

Running away from lessons never helps. We then find ourselves stuck and unable to free ourselves. Honest answers are the only way to unlock whatever is preventing us from moving forward. Running away allows us to continue sitting in the same mire. We are left to repeat the same dramas again and again. We can sit there and believe that we do not need to change, that everyone outside needs to.

Spiritual teachers remove our identification with the original part we play and bring us back to who we really are. We are then in right relationship with the universe. Just as a child must be taught that they are not the center of the household, we must be taught that we are not the center of the universe. A good parent or teacher will discipline us and provide the appropriate lessons and tools to establish ourselves in right relation. And then they send us out able to be free and not dependent on them. We should know that our teacher has our best interest at heart. We do not run; we respect the one that gave us life.

So today I acknowledge my mother for giving me life and being my first teacher. And I acknowledge and honor Swami Muktananda for giving me my life and showing me the way Home.

Happy Holidays....

At this time when we celebrate two important Jews—Judah Maccabee and Jesus, the Christ—let us receive what each of them offers the world. Though I prefer to think of him as Scottish, Judah Maccabee campaigned bravely and sagaciously to regain and restore the temple in Jerusalem. Jesus also came to restore, but for him the goal was to restore the temple of the Heart to its rightful place at the center of our lives.

In a completely different tradition, but with the same goal, Swami Muktananda lived his life. Baba called Jesus the Incarnation of Love, and in the ashram, we would celebrate his life and the lives of all great beings. So I wish each of you a Merry Christmas and a Happy Hanukah, with the awareness that God dwells within you as you.

With love and best wishes for the holidays and beyond,

Rohini

Redirecting Our Resolutions....

As we approach the New Year, our tendency is to look forward with hopeful, positive thoughts. We smooth out the past and move into the future with a smile and a raised glass. The world will be better, we will do better, we will care and love more. And every year we approach this time with this same ritual. There is nothing wrong with being hopeful or positive, except that we are then also setting up the opposite. We live in a world of dichotomies. If we are hopeful, then we are also disappointed. If we are positive, then we are also negative.

We may retort with "No, I am always positive." If that is the case, then we really do have a problem. Attachment to positive will throw us into a state of being out of touch and oblivious. The same goes for negative. If we are attached to being negative, we will occasionally find ourselves in the place of realistic and clear. So the seesaw is all we get, if we live on the surface of life. One man's positive will be another's negative. We are not universally in agreement.

Positive	Negative
Out of touch	Realistic

Spiritual Practice is not about reaching the point where everything is positive and sweet. Spiritual Practice is also not about being a cold renunciant. Spiritual Practice will take us to an acceptance of what is. When we have negative thoughts, people will tell us to be positive. And when we are a Pollyanna, people will tell us to open our eyes and wake up. Neither the negative nor the positive is the right spot. We need to redirect to the center.

Good	Bad
Burdened / suffering servant	Free / does what wants

Spiritual Practice is about redirecting our attention to the center of our soul. When we are focused on either positive or negative, good or bad, pure or impure, we are off center. We may believe we are centered on our authentic self but in fact, we are aligned not with our core at all. We are centered on an idea that will dissolve away as we delve into Spiritual Practice.

So as we move forward into the New Year let us align ourselves with Reality. Acceptance and surrender to the real Center, God, will bring us all to Love.

Merry Christmas and Happy Chanukah!....

We are all feeling the effects of a globally rough year. So much pain and misery through illness, natural disasters, war and conflict. As we approach the holidays, we need to look to how these observances began. The world was no more peaceful then than it is now, but God shone through the chaos of those times with great Love.

Why we celebrate the holidays has so often been lost. At their core, these holidays call us to remember God manifesting clearly on earth. They call us to surrender, so that we know how God informs our lives, and we live in that awareness. Great Beings like Baba have shown us how to answer that call.

Today is no different from back then. God shines through and suffuses all with Love. Our work is to live each day being connected to God in the Heart, and to participate in the great Game with the Love that is our birthright.

Peace,

Rohini

Thankfulness....

In America, we celebrate Thanksgiving. In this day and age, we may be finding it difficult to say and be Thankful. The world is having a rather rough go of it. We are being challenged everywhere we turn.

Thank you, God. Thank you, Baba for showing me that God is everywhere and God's action is always Love. Therefore, each test we are facing is for our good.

What good can come from this nightmare we are facing? We must ask that question over and over again. If we keep digging into the next answer that arises and not resting on the simplest and most superficial, we will find ourselves with an answer we never expected. The challenge is an opportunity, a tough opportunity, in which God and His Love are embedded in every fiber.

In my Saturday scripture class, we are presently reading the *Bhagavadgita*. The scripture tells of the dialogue between Arjuna and Krishna on the nature of Reality. This dialogue takes place on the battlefield just before a great battle is about to occur between Arjuna and his relatives. Forgetting his path and not understanding the Truth of Reality, Arjuna loses heart and wishes not to fight.

We are Arjuna. How many times have we decided we "knew better" so that we could avoid action, right action? How many times have we bemoaned our fate instead of thanking God for providing the opportunity to get closer to who we truly are? We should be so thankful, and yet we will deny God.

Perceiving that I was submerged in the flood of the great illusion, Thou, Hari, didst indeed plunge into it and rescue me.

There is none other beside Thee in the whole world; but see our fate, that we imagined ourselves existing [apart from Thee].

Filled with pride in my personality I thought that I was Arjuna in this world and said that the Kauravas were my relatives.

In addition to that, I had the evil dream that I would kill them and then what should I do? But the Lord wakened me from my sleep....

I, being no one, thought I was a person and called those my relatives who in reality did not exist. Thou hast saved me from this great madness. (Jnaneshvari 11.49-59)

We have all been through trials appropriate to our path. Most people do not know what each of us has been through. Hopefully, we do not advertise or wear on our sleeve what has occurred. Hopefully, we have learned so that we can be and are thankful for all that we have faced. And we have the clear vision to see that whatever God does, He does for good. Hopefully, we have learned that the nightmare was only a dream in which the individual, not who we truly are, acted its part.

O Śiva, you have produced a three-world drama which has in its interior Maya as the source of all the existents. You have presented the introductory portion of the drama. Where is the creative artist other than yourself who can bring about its conclusion? (Stavacintamani 59)

If we know that God is both the producer and the soul (haha) actor of the entire play, then we will be thankful all the time, like the man in Meister Eckhart's sermon who never had a bad day:

You wished me good day. I never had a bad day; for if I am hungry I praise God; if it freezes, hails, snows, rains, if the weather is fair or foul, still I praise God; am I wretched and despised, I praise God, and so I have never had an evil day. You wished that God would send me luck. But I never had ill luck, for I know how to live with God, and I know that what He does is best; and what God gives me or ordains for me, be it good or ill, I take it cheerfully from God as the best that can be, and so I have never had ill luck. You wished that God would make me happy. I was never unhappy; for my only desire is to live in God's will, and I have so entirely yielded my will to God's, that what God wills, I will. (qtd. in Underhill, Mysticism, 209)

Spiritual practice is about arriving at true Thankfulness at every moment of every day.

Joyous....

Joyous	Despairing
Intoxicated	Grounded

When reflecting on a fourchotomy to paint, I begin with the top left quality, knowing that each component of the fourchotomy must not be conflated with the other three. Every quality has its own vibration that arises from within, becoming less subtle and more material. As the vibration manifests, letters express it, and a word is formed that truly represents the vibration.

Ideas about joy, especially in this time of year, are lively, fun, and upbeat. But as I meditated, I felt the vibration of the joy within us all as a steady, underlying hum. Joy is more quiet than we tend to believe.

So my gift to each of you is the separation of each of the vibrations in the form of a painting. Let yourself feel the difference between joyous and intoxicated; between despairing and grounded. How many times have we thought people were deep and grounded when in fact they were despairing, or thought they were despairing when in fact they were nonattached and grounded?

How many times have we thought someone to be joyous when in fact they were intoxicated? Or discounted someone's joyousness because we decided they were intoxicated?

Know all of the vibrations as they really are. Know that each is within you. Learn and practice, so that you can choose to be both joyous and grounded, and live in the Love of God.

With Joy and Love and best wishes for the season,

Rohini

Happy Mother's Day....

A person tells me that they love me the way they loved their mother. Their mother didn't like it, but put up with it. I don't have to put up with it. This person is just superimposing on me what they brought to the table with their mother.

How often are you projecting, or being projected onto? I am not loving you based on your ideas. Thank God. Have you examined your ideas? Have you ever asked yourself some basic questions about your relationship with your mother?

Did you respect your mother?
Did you believe your mother?
Did you obey your mother?
Did you value and cherish your mother?
Did you compete with your mother?
Did you win with your mother?
Did you love or power your mother?
Did you model yourself after your mother?

What *did* you bring to the table around your mother? How was it received? Did it get you the love you wanted?

So much of Mother's Day is really about the child, not the mother. The mother we each had was a person, *and* an idea we projected on them, *and* an ideal/abstraction we also projected on them, *and* who they really were. We tend to conflate person, ideal, and projection, without ever seeing who our mother really is. As children, we loved our mother as best we knew. The question is always who is it that we loved. As adults, will we cling to our idealizing and the resulting deep disappointment, or can we see our mothers as our first teachers, who were unique for each of us?

As teachers they brought the lessons we were to learn from life. They presented these lessons in so many ways, and yet, true to where we were, most of us did not understand them. We misread and therefore took in or rebelled against the lesson, and so ended up in the center of a play where the scenes changed, the characters changed, and the lines and outcome remained the same. We were the stars of a boring drama.

Our mothers wanted us to be happy; the question is what that meant and what it now means.

So again:

Did you learn from your mother?

Was your mother happy?

Did she love?

Did she pleasure?

Did she power?

Did you imbibe the lessons she presented and become the spitting image?

Did you rebel and therefore ironically become the spitting image?

How much did you really look at what you brought to the table, or were you so lost in your mother that all you cared about was what she brought to the table?

What did she bring to the table?

What did you call what she brought to the table?

What did you call what you brought to the table?

Are we now ready to learn our lessons and free our mothers from the box we put them in? What a great Mother's Day it would be to free both our mothers and ourselves from the rigid misunderstanding of the words "mother" and "child."

To honor our mother means for us to grow up into who we each were meant to be, truly ourselves, and to manifest so we are true reflections of God. Isn't that really what God wants for us? Isn't that really why God gave us each the mother we needed to fulfill our true destiny? We can either remain small and trapped in our boring drama, or we can give up our smallness and play in the most magnificent theatre.

Merry Christmas!

When we think of the Christmas Story, we tend to think of Mary, Joseph, the three wise men, the shepherds who hear the angel Gabriel announce the birth of Christ, and Christ Himself. We rarely think about the innkeepers who turned away the couple.

When we read teaching stories we are to place ourselves in the story as one of the characters. As we grow, we move among the characters until finally we are ALL the characters.

The innkeepers who turned away the couple were not bad; they had no room at their inn. They were just functionaries moving the couple toward the place where Christ was to be born. And yet they did not recognize the Truth of the situation. They were blind to what was in front of them. They could have seen, and though there was no room, made room. They could have recognized Joseph and Mary for who they were, known there was no room, and left the inn to be with Mary and Joseph at the stable when Christ was born. The three wise men saw the Star of Bethlehem, knew inwardly what it meant, and followed, bringing gifts. Even when they had not physically seen the couple, they understood.

So who are the innkeepers? When is it that we are to identify with them? Always. Because until we are completely surrendered to God, there will be times when we are blind. If we refuse to acknowledge that blindness, we will never get to "see" Christ. We will never get to the stable. We will never encounter the other characters. We will never get to be ALL the characters.

So this holiday season, I wish that each of us surrenders our shrunken self so that we ALL are ALL the characters in this great play God is performing.

With Joy and Love and best wishes for the season,

Rohini

Happy New Year 2017….

Dickens could not have said it better in his opening to *A Tale of Two Cities*:

It was the best of times, it was the worst of times, it was the age of wisdom, it was the age of foolishness, it was the epoch of belief, it was the epoch of incredulity, it was the season of Light, it was the season of Darkness, it was the spring of hope, it was the winter of despair, we had everything before us, we had nothing before us, we were all going direct to Heaven, we were all going direct the other way—in short, the period was so far like the present period, that some of its noisiest authorities insisted on its being received, for good or for evil, in the superlative degree of comparison only.

Some people would say 2016 was a great year. Others would say they had suffered; that this had been a difficult year. Depending on our lessons and how well we learned them, the year was great or hard.

We can intellectually know our responsibility is to walk towards Love with brutal honesty within ourselves. That is why we are here: to go Home. But until we each do that, when even one of us is suffering, we are all suffering.

So as individuals we may have had a good or even "the best" year. But we in the truest sense did not. We in the understanding of Absolute Reality had a great year—never had a bad one. But until we each live in *abheda* (Unity) and manifest *bhedabheda*, seeing the unity in the diversity, there is a part of us that remains in *bheda* (multiplicity) and therefore suffers.

Amid all this suffering, without empathy and compassion we cannot move forward; otherwise all we will manifest is a smugness that contributes to the division and hate in this world.

Dickens was writing about a time of great upheaval. We are living in a time of global upheaval, a time when governments are serving the people less and less, and instead serving the pleasure of their leaders. They are self-serving; the representatives and associates of the government from top to bottom are its chief beneficiaries. And though the time that Dickens wrote about started out as hopeful, in the end everyone suffered. There was no winning side; just two sides of the same coin.

As we move into 2017, what is it we must contribute? My wish for each of us is to move towards truly living the Unity in the diversity. To experience this in our everyday lives so that we overcome the hate that has stained the very fiber of our lives.

We cannot just decide to do this. We have to have courage. The path is steep and dangerous, but we each have to climb. We can try it alone and see how far we go, or we can have a guide who has climbed the sheer side and knows how to help us. We can also share with community. But in not doing it alone we have to be willing to surrender the shrunken self that separates us from the guide and community.

In other words, we have to surrender the very thing that keeps us suffering. This seems easy enough, and of course we would want to do that. But we do not. And changing the vocabulary in our narrative to sound lofty does nothing but perpetuate our own pain and the pain of others. We are to surrender the individual that thinks. We tend to believe we need to get rid of the dysfunctional thinker and keep the "good" thinker. No: we have to surrender the thinker.

It is the best of times, it is the worst of times. For whom? In 2017, can we discern that there is only us? Can we at the very least refrain from contributing to hate and division?

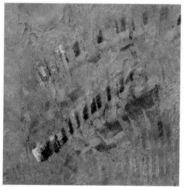 

Upheaval

Upheaval	*Steady*
Transformation	*Stagnant*

groundwater....

    connected   uses

                not

senses

    connected   sees

                all   we

  use   one

    connected   dissolves

                          i

    connected   manifests

                Love

    connected   vanquishes

         invisible   enemy

                    me   i

that   uses   mines

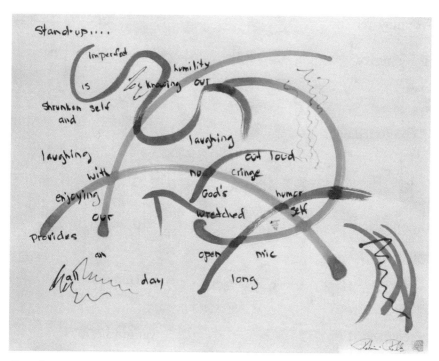

Stand-up

centric....

selfless
   they do not seek
      the center
    of attention

they seek
      the center
    of God
to the glory
      of One

all attention
   then
   is God
   to God

attention
   at attention
our will
    steady

as we look
   all ways
   one way
  Love

the selfless
   will
   their wills
    to all
no one neglected
   left
   behind

the selfless
   love the
      Self
        of
    All

ark of ascent....

whether miniscule
                or
monumental

the way home is
        the same

whether one by one
    two by two

    or All by All

we return by
    slowly or
        instantly

destroying ignorance
breaking bonds with
            temporary

and the emergence
    of the Real the
            Always

preserve the practice....

alive
always
alive
hidden maybe
still alive

wake up
wake
up
already

awake

see
veiled
see
unconscious
see
all
us
all

God

by being
with experience
let manifest into letters
act cleanly
discern
discriminate
from within
no thoughts
no vibrations
Love to manifestation

Preservation

Preservation	*Upheaval*
Congealed	*Renewal*

GLOSSARY

Abheda: the state of nondualism, in which all separateness has dissolved in the Absolute and there is only Unity

Absolute Reality: God, Love, the Ground of All by which All exists and which cannot not exist

Ananda: the Bliss that is, and emanates from, the Self

Ananda samadhi: the stage of *samadhi* in which the one-pointed consciousness experiences Bliss

Anava mala: in Kashmir Shaivism, the primal ignorance that allows shrunken Consciousness to believe it has a separate, limited existence apart from Shiva

Anavopaya: in Kashmir Shaivism, the term for the first level of spiritual practice, using the senses and sense objects as means of worship

Anu: "a point"; the shrunken self; the individual

Asmita: absorption; in the negative sense, it is the loss of Subject in object and one of the five miseries (kleshas) of the Yoga Sutras; in the positive sense, it is loss of all separateness and total absorption in the Divine

Asmita samadhi: the stage of *samadhi* in which the one-pointed consciousness is totally absorbed in the Self

Avadhoot: a realized being whose complete nonattachment places him beyond conventional behavior, and who may appear eccentric or crazy to ordinary people

Avidya: "different knowledge"; in the Yoga Sutras, the first and foundational misery (klesha), which is the primal ignorance of our true nature as the Self

Bheda: difference; the world experienced as a multiplicity of separate things, with no underlying unity

Bhedabheda: "Unity in difference"; the world experienced as Unity giving rise to a multiplicity of manifested beings

Buktimukti: "pleasure and liberation"; the tantric doctrine that, understood appropriately, pleasure and liberation are not mutually exclusive

Causal body: the vehicle of the Self that carries karma from life to life

Darshan: "seeing"; the Grace of being able to look upon the Guru; also, the word for the six dominant orthodox schools of Indic philosophy

Dharma: right action; what one is meant to do, or what is appropriate to do

Dualism: any worldview that posits a gap between the Being of God, the Self, Absolute Reality, and the existence of created beings, where the universe may be seen as illusory or created ex nihilo

Ego: the function of the intellect that identifies with decisions

Fourchotomy: a tool for spiritual practice devised by Rohini, designed to help us free ourselves from wrong identification; it is a grid showing both the positive and negative components of each quality in a dichotomy, so we can recognize, understand, and accept all four qualities within ourselves and free ourselves from identifying with any of them; the resulting freedom is called "being off the grid"

Ganesh: the elephant-headed son of Shiva and Parvati, who is both a gatekeeper and the remover of obstacles

Ganeshpuri: the location in Maharashtra, India, of Swami Muktananda's first ashram and the site of his tomb

Grace: the power by which God draws us back to Unity

Gunas: in Indic philosophies, the three fundamental constituents of the manifested universe: *tamas*, or inertia and darkness; *rajas*, or activity and agitation; and *sattva*, or calm, brightness, and clarity; the *gunas* combine much like the primary colors to create infinite things and states

Guru: both the Grace-bestowing power of God and the person through whom that Grace is passed to disciples

Guru Purnima: the Guru's moon; the full moon in June or July, which is dedicated to celebration of and devotion to the Guru

Guruseva: work of any kind performed as service to the Guru

Heart: the innermost ground of a person's being, where the relative existence of the individual meets the Absolute Reality of the Self; the cave deep within us where the Self resides and we connect with God

Intellect: the faculty of knowing; the subtlest vehicle, which tends to confuse its own activity with the true Subject, the Self

Ishvara pranidhana: as referred to in the Yoga Sutras, total surrender of one's entire existence to God

Jiva: the individuated self or embodied soul; in Kashmir Shaivism, the shrunken self

Kaivalya: in the Yoga Sutras, "aloneness," or the point at which the Witness, the Self, has realized its own nature and is liberated from having to engage with *prakrti*, or the manifested universe

Kanchukas: in Kashmir Shaivism, the five coverings by which Shiva conceals Himself in bodying forth the manifested universe; they are *kāla* (time), *vidyā* (shrunken knowledge), *rāga* (desire), *niyati* (cause and effect), and *kalā* (limited agency)

Karma mala: in Kashmir Shaivism, the form of ignorance that makes the individual appear to be the doer of good and bad deeds when, in Truth, only God is the Doer

Kashmir Shaivism: the conventional term for a closely knitted set of nondualist tantric traditions rooted in Kashmir, in which Absolute Reality is represented by the god Shiva, and his consort Shakti is the power by which he bodies forth the universe

Kleshas: the five miseries explained by Patanjali in the Yoga Sutras; they unfold in a sequence that binds us: ignorance of our true nature (*avidya*), loss of Subject in object (*asmita*), attraction (*raga*), aversion (*dvesha*), and clinging to the life of the shrunken self (*abhinivesha*)

Kundalini: the form of *shakti* that rests dormant in each human being until *shaktipat* ("the descent of power," or spiritual awakening and initiation), at which point it spurs the individual toward liberation; it is often represented by a snake coiled three and a half times around the base of the spine

Lila: "play" or "sport"; generally, the world as the play of Consciousness, and more specifically any game or dance played out on the stage of the world

Lokananda samadhi sukham: "the bliss of the world is the bliss of samadhi"; the nondualist truth that the entire manifested universe is pervaded with the Bliss of God, and that one can move through the world filled with that Bliss

Mahasamadhi: the great *samadhi*; the final dissolution of all separatness when a Great Being, a *jivanmukta*, leaves his or her body

Matrika shakti: "the power of the un-understood Mother"; in Kashmir Shaivism, the power of letters to constrict Consciousness, both shaping the manifested universe and binding the shrunken self to its limited existence

Maya: in Kashmir Shaivism, the power of Shiva to conceal himself in creation

Mayiya mala: in Kashmir Shaivism, the form of ignorance that leads us to believe we are imperfect rather than the perfection of Shiva, the Self of All

Nirbija samadhi: *samadhi* without seed; the advanced form of *samadhi* in which attention becomes absorbed in complete Subjectivity, without any need for an object on which to focus

Nirvikalpa samadhi: *samadhi* without any thought-forms

Niyamas: observances; in the *Yoga Sutras*, the practice of doing the right things, observing the right outward activities, as a foundational way to discipline the will and encourage stillness

Pashu: "a beast for sacrifice," in tantric traditions, the word for any person who is lost in ignorance of his or her true nature as Shiva

Pati: "a lord"; in tantric traditions, a person who has advanced on the spiritual path and become established in the knowledge that he or she is truly Shiva, the Self of All

Physical body: the coarsest of the vehicles in which the Self operates in the world

Prakrti: in the *Yoga Sutras*, the term for all that is not the purusha, the Witness, the Self

Pranam: an act of devotion in which one drops to one's knees and bows to the Guru or prostrates oneself completely

Psychic instrument: another term for the intellect

Puja: the altar where God and/or Guru is worshipped, and also the act of ritual worship

Purusha: in the *Yoga Sutras*, our true nature as the pure Subject, the Witness, the Self; in Kashmir Shaivism, the separate, shrunken individual self

Rāga: desire

Rajas: the guna of agitation, activity, desire

Relative reality: the manifested universe of difference, where our lives unfold

Sadgurunath Maharaj Ki Jay: "praise to the True Guru"; a saying used as a prayer or blessing, often at the beginning or end of an activity

Sadhaka: someone who commits to and sustains spiritual practice over a long time, without interruption, and with reverent devotion

Sadhana: spiritual practice, usually in the context of tantra; in some limited contexts, it can mean the pursuit through spiritual practice of powers rather than liberation

Sahaj samadhi: "walking bliss"; resting in the Bliss of the Heart while functioning appropriately in the world

Samadhi: "absorption"; a state of sustained, conscious, one-pointed focus where the meditator, process of meditation, and object of meditation become one; there are different kinds and stages of samadhi

Samskara: a latent impression on our vehicles left by past experience and action, often from past lives, that manifests as a predisposition or mental habit

Sat-chit-ananda: Absolute Truth (or Existence)-Absolute Consciousness-Absolute Bliss, the classic Vedantic formulation of the nature of the Self

Satguru: a True Guru, as opposed to a lesser teacher or false guru

Sattva: the *guna* of calm, brightness, and clarity

Self of All: our true nature, God, pure Subject without an object, *sat-chit-ananda*

Seva: service; work done in the spirit of devotion to God and Guru

Shakti: the Power by which Shiva, the Absolute Reality, becomes dynamic and issues forth the manifested universe; the Goddess

Shaktipat: "the descent of Power"; the awakening of the kundalini by a transfer of spiritual energy, normally from Guru to disciple

Shaktopaya: in Kashmir Shaivism, the term for the second level of spiritual practice, in which we use the mind to draw closer to God

Shambhavopaya: "the way of Shambhava (Shiva)"; in Kashmir Shaivism, the term for the third and deepest level of spiritual practice, in which one rests constantly in the Heart by a mere orientation of the will

Shiva: the Hindu god who destroys the universe at its appointed end; in Kashmir Shaivism, Shiva represents God, Absolute Reality, the Self of All

Shraddha: faith; the commitment to God and Guru necessary for realization

Shrunken self: the contracted consciousness and sense of self we have when we are not yet fully realized; the normal human self

Shunya: the void; that which exists beyond all difference, without any support (necessary), and therefore Absolute Reality

Spanda: in Kashmir Shaivism, the pulse or impulse of Bliss in the Absolute that brings the universe into existence, sustains it, and makes things happen within it

Subtle body: the vehicle of the Self that contains the mind and within which the kundalini shakti functions

Supracausal body: the Heart, the subtlest inner juncture between the relative and the Absolute, where the Self abides in each of us

Tamas: the *guna* of inertia, darkness, and ignorance

Tandra: the visionary state of consciousness on the threshold between waking and sleep

Tantra: roughly "weaving"; a term covering a wide range of spiritual traditions that operate outside and, by their own account, above and more efficaciously than the more conventional traditions of Hinduism (or Buddhism)

Tapasya: "cooking"; the use of ascetic or highly disciplined practices to grind down the ego and remove ignorance

Turiya: "the fourth"; the Divine Consciousness that underlies the three ordinary states of waking, dreaming, and deep sleep

Unidualist: someone who imposes a sentimental or intellectual idea of nonduality on relative reality, and believes they see the Unity of All everywhere when they are really refusing to be with their experience and face facts

Unmesha: "unveiling"; Shiva opening his eyes; the revelation from within of our true nature

Vedanta: "the end of the Vedas"; one of the six classical *darshans*; a closely related schools of spiritual practice; the most famed is the *advaita* (nondualist) school, but there are also schools of dualism and modified nondualism

Vehicles: a term for the manifested and layered forms used by the Self to operate in the world, from the intellect to the gross physical body

Vidyā: "knowledge"; in Kashmir Shaivism, limited knowledge, ignorant of the Self, and therefore the source of bondage

Vikalpa: a thought-form

Vitarka samadhi: a *samadhi* in which one enters a sustained one-pointed concentration on a physical object or activity

Witness: in the *Yoga Sutras*, the *purusha*, the Self, our true nature as a completely free, nonattached Subject

Yamas: prohibitions; the practice of avoiding things and activities that agitate consciousness and create or deepen attachments

ABOUT THE
AUTHOR

Rohini Ralby is the author of two previous books published with Bancroft Press: *Walking Home with Baba: The Heart of Spiritual Practice* (2012) and *Living the Practice, Volume One: The Way of Love* (2022).

Originally from the Boston area, Rohini completed her undergraduate studies at Washington University in St. Louis and earned a graduate degree at Mills College. After graduate school, she was encouraged by her Tai Chi Chuan teacher, T. R. Chung, to open her own school in Cambridge, Massachusetts. In 1974, she met her Guru, Swami Muktananda Paramahamsa, who gave her direct experience of the bottom line of existence. She studied one-on-one with Muktananda until his *mahasamadhi* in 1982, and has remained a devoted disciple.

Since 1990, Rohini has shared with people around the world the spiritual practice she learned from her Guru. Along the way, she has developed her own distinctive tools, which she has shared in her writings. She grounds all she undertakes in the Love she learned from Muktananda, including her work as Managing Director of a consulting firm that addresses global security issues, as Chair of the Board of a nonprofit that provides targeted solutions that promote harmony around the world, and as a painter in both oils and ink. She collaborates in this work with her husband and two grown sons.